Light-flooded paths

A journey from mourning to healing in Bali

"Look! The flowers are showing you:
Through the darkness they grow upwards, seeking the light.
There they open up to show their characteristic beauty."

Christiane P. Simon

Christiane P. Simon

Light-flooded paths

A journey from mourning to healing in Bali

Bibliographic information at the German National Library:
The German National Library lists this publication in the
German National bibliography; detailed bibliographic data can be
found on the internet under: http://dnb.de.

Dieses Buch ist auch in deutscher Sprache erschienen:

Lichtdurchflutete Wege – *Eine Geschichte über Liebe, Hoffnung, Glaube*

English translation: Heather Müller, B.A. (Dunelm)

Cover photo: Nana Artana, Bali – Artana_rs@yahoo.com

Coverdesign: Dirk Stegner, Coburg

Printed and published: BoD – Books on Demand, Norderstedt

ISBN: 987-3-7534-6296-7

Preface

Dear Readers,

to heal my grief and dismay over my husband's death, I faced many profound experiences. I want to take you along on my healing journey, which includes my visit to the beautiful island of Bali.

My husband Ray and I had a worry-free life, which we both enjoyed for many years. Up to that day, when we got his diagnosis of "you have cancer."All of a sudden, our life as we knew it was upside down. Within minutes of the diagnosis, our carefree life came to an end. Suddenly I was challenged with unfathomable challenges. For me, his perishing up to his death was very moving and profoundly life-changing.

I want to challenge the Reader to answer the following questions for themselves:

What should we do when our life gets out of control? When all of our future aspirations and dreams come to a halt. What's our initial reaction when we have to face an incurable disease? Additionally, when somebody we deeply love gets a death sentence or, worse, dies? I believe the first reaction for many is helplessness. Many of us fall into an emotional hole.

Do we ask ourselves how we should continue living our life? In my own experience and after the diagnosis's shock wore off, my reaction was to get moving and moving out of my helplessness. This active approach to deal with my grief reminds me of the story of the frogs.

As these two frogs did, when they fell into a bowl of milk. Having swum around a Bowl, they realized that the bowl's edge was too high and steep for them to get out unaided. The first frog, realizing that it was useless to waste his energy by continuing to swim since that would not get him out of the bowl, gave up swimming and drowned. The second frog persevered, refused to give in, and gradually the milk turned into butter until the frog could use it as a foothold to jump out of the bowl.

The moral of this inspiring little story? Those who don't give up and persevere may be in for a pleasant surprise!

In my book *"Light-flooded paths"* I recount the cancer diagnosis and its far-reaching consequences. Here is my story:

Quite unexpectedly, my husband Ray was diagnosed with malignant colon cancer. I was taken aback and shocked by the diagnosis. Yet, somehow our everyday life continued. Ray decided to follow the doctors' recommendations for his care. With that decision, he struggled through chemotherapy and many aggressive chasms, including many hospital stays.

Despite the procedures' brutality, we did our best to live everyday life. All we had left was hope, and the promise of a better result, even the audacity of full healing, crossed our mind.

We started to go on long nature walks, meditated, and used relaxation exercises. We changed our diet dramatically. First, we consumed less meat and followed a wholesome nutritional diet with plenty of fresh vegetables and fruit. We both opted for dietary supplements and mustered up the sheer will to stay positive.

We were grateful for every additional day we received. Moreover, we fulfilled our dreams, travel goals and enjoyed life with family and friends. Despite the exhausting therapies, we relished the years we had left as a couple. Until death would cast the shadow, our primary goal was to live the way Ray wanted.

A few weeks after Ray's death, when I understood his death's finality, I fell into a bottomless pit and had no idea how my future would shape up. During my emotional despair, I listened to my inner voice. I suddenly saw a path of light at the end of a tunnel in front of my inner eye. During a deep mediation, my inner voice spoke clearly to me, telling me to escape to Bali.

At that very moment, I knew that Bali, Rays, and my preferred vacation spot, where we spent so much time together, called me to return.

First, I took some time getting away from the grief and shock. It took some courage to do the first step, but once I made up my mind, I was on my way to Bali.

During my time away from civilization, I learned many things about my life and myself.

I like to share some of these experiences with you. I hope they will come as close to your heart as it did to mine.

In Bali, I kept to myself and lived a very peaceful life. Every morning I went hiking through the beautiful nature of the tropics.

"Again and again, I rested to enjoy the view of the rice fields. Whenever I stood before the light- green colored rice fields which were glistening in the morning sun, my heart jumped for joy. I would take deep breaths and felt how my body filled with happiness."

The Balinese culture centers on spirituality, ceremonies revered, and rituals to connect us to an unseen world. Balinese practice is to receive, send out, and hold in, symbolized by incense and fire, water flowers, and rice. Its believed that the art of gratitude purifies and reconnects us to the divine world.

My mourning, disappointment, and even anger toward God expressed themselves creatively. Something inside of me changed. Although I had gone away from it all, many friends around me supported me. My experience in coming to terms with my mourning sums up in two basic statements:

Every darkness is flooded with light. The inner potential of each human being contributes to the healing.

Each person and their way through life are different. The ways others have gone cannot be copied or replicated. They serve as impulses, as inspiration for one's way. I captured the essence of my experiences in my book.

Each person is unique. Each of us experiences joy and pain very intimately. Each of our lives life paths differs from others. Coping with the loss of someone we love is one of life's most significant challenges. Whatever your loss, it is personal to you. Whatever the cause of your grief, though, there are healthy ways to cope with the pain that, in time, can ease your sadness, and you come to terms with your loss. You find new meaning and eventually move on with your life. Grieving is a highly individual experience.

There is no right or wrong way to grieve, and it depends on your coping style, life experience, faith, and how significant your loss was to you. There are no one concepts that fits all. There is no comfortable road map or instruction manual through coping.

Throughout my grief and experience searching out a path toward the light, I learned this:

It is well worth taking responsibility for your life. Develop your potential. It's worth it.

Ask to confer with the doctors and medical personnel. Become part of the conversation and trust your intuition.

Live purposefully and mindfully. Take care of your body, your spirit and soul. Fulfill your dreams, even during dark times.

Love yourself and others. Ask for forgiveness and forgive others.

Grief is your way and spirit. Believe and trust in the process even though doubts. Know that God holds you and carries you. God is with you.

Dreams!

Growing old hand in hand

"Hey, that tickles!"

My hand wiped the blade of grass away from my nose. I had nodded off to sleep. In my husband's arms. At any rate I heard his voice just by my ear."

Do you know what I'm hungry for, my dear?" No, I had not been expecting this question. I blinked hard, sat up and looked at him enquiringly.

"*Gulai Kambing.*"

I ignored his culinary excursion and tried to distract him. "What? Here on our comfortable wooden bench you are dreaming about food? How unromantic!"

Like a cat, I cuddled up to him and began to purr gently. He did not seem to be enthusiastic about that. My dear husband simply could not stop thinking about *Gulai Kambing.* There was nothing I could do about it.

This somewhat warm spring afternoon had the effect of driving us out of our flat into the open air. Wanting to absorb the first rays of sun, we strolled hand in hand through the castle's extensive park, looking in amazement at the first rhododendron flowers following their circular paths, the small yellow and white flowers pushing their way out of the cool earth towards the light and the fresh light green leaves of the sturdy deciduous trees.

From the top part of the castle's park, we surveyed the vast lawn, with a slight downward slant, dominated by the ancient oak tree with its deeply scarred bark and projecting branches. We lay relaxed on wooden benches, which were just wide enough for two. For people who liked each other, as we did. Ray had pushed his arm under my head. We looked up to the sky and contemplated the small stratocumulus clouds on the gentle blue sky, which the mild wind of spring seemed to be blowing about.

"The bench is just tailor-made for us", I could just hear myself saying, yet in the course of gazing at the clouds drifting by I must have nodded off to sleep. Until the blade of grass that Ray was using to emphasise his unusual request was tickling me on the nose.

"What makes you think of *Gulai Kambing*?" I asked, certain that I could not divert him from this subject. "We only eat that when we're on the island of Bali."

"Yes, I drifted over there with the clouds," my husband said with a smile, looking up to the sky dreamily. "I'm simply longing for it just now, you know. I can taste the small, juicy pieces of soft meat that have been cooked in coconut milk on my tongue and smell the different varieties of spices."

"Are you serious about that?" I was not sure as to whether he was just pretending and started to provoke him a little.

"Why don't we go home so you can cook it for us? We must buy the meat, possibly lamb instead of goat. Then we'd need some lemon grass. The other ingredients we've got at home." Indeed, Ray thought it was a good idea.

"Oh, that is practical," he said and went through the list of ingredients."We already have coconut milk, chilies, garlic, ginger, cardamom, cumin, fresh curcuma and cloves at home. I wasn't at all aware of that."

Amazed, I turned my head and looked into his face.

"Apparently, you haven't stood in the kitchen for rather a long time."

Ray's thoughts had gone even further. They were on our favourite island, in the Kopi Bali Restaurant. With his mind's eye he could see the steaming *Gulai Kambing* on the table in front of him. "This food, Chris, is just heavenly. Delicately soft, the spices surrounding my tongue and the after-taste of a fresh lime."

I sat up, slightly tilting my head to the side and mistrustfully observed the expression on his face. Ray smiled dreamily, his face gazing into the vast expanse of the sky. His mouth seemed to be chewing something tasty. Obviously, my husband was in another world.

We usually went to our favourite restaurant, Kopi Bali, with our friend Suryani and her family. She had six sons and over twenty grandchildren she was very proud of. Yes, she even wanted more grandchildren.

I remember one of these meals at the restaurant exactly. Suryani and her son both ordered *Gulai Kambing*. As this dish was not familiar to me, I asked what it was. She looked at me significantly, rolling her eyes.

"*Enak*," she said, "try it."

"Delicious," I repeated, turning to Ray, who had been listening attentively, "if Suryani thinks we should try it, then I'm going to order it, too." Ray nodded and did the same.

"Mm," our enthusiasm knew no end. The small, mildly spiced pieces of meat almost melted on the tongue with an indescribable, intense taste.

From this time on we always ordered the same: *Gulai Kambing*. We made no secret of our enthusiasm for this excellent dish. That seemed to spread over to the others at our table, who, after Ray's order simply added "*Sama*", "the same". Sooner or later, we were known as "the Gulai Kambing family."

My memory of this stimulated my organs of smell and taste. Now I was also smelling the many kinds of spices in the liquid the lamb was slowly cooked in. I gave Ray a light push.

"Your enthusiasm is spreading over to me, too. Just as we're lying here and enjoying the view of our dreams."

My husband was unimpressed by my demands and continued dreaming, gazing into the endless scenery before him.

"Wouldn't it be wonderful, my darling, to lie in a hammock beneath Bali's sun? Under coconut palms and luscious green tropical plants?"

This drew me into his dreamland. With a deep, dreamy sigh, I answered: "That would be fantastic. And then, in the evening, in a circle of friends, we have our *Gulai Kambing* in front of us smelling delicious."

I cuddled up to his side, gave him a light kiss on the lobe of his ear. Ray turned round towards me and murmured temptingly:

"Maybe we should go back there soon?"

"Would be nice!" I nodded to him expectantly. "Then our dreams would come true." I laughed out loud.

To my surprise, the scenes of an impressive cleansing ceremony came to me again.

"Ray, do you remember the cleansing ceremony Suryani invited us to?"

"Oh yes," Ray smiled to himself. Not knowing anything about it, we had accepted. Ray laughed again.

On that occasion, we arrived almost punctually at Suryani's house. That was unusual because you do not have to be punctual on Bali. It is all right for any appointment to be postponed for anything up to two hours. They are so flexible. For this reason, we were surprised to find Suryani's husband, Cok Alit, waiting for us.

"The others have already set off for the High Priest's residence." He pointed at our Sunday western clothes, which apparently were not suitable for the occasion. Ray

16

and I looked at each other in surprise. Indeed, we had not thought about temple clothing at all.

Cok Alit asked the house servants to dress us in the right clothes und in a few moments we were standing on the terrace in our underwear, like dummies in a shop window, waiting for temple clothing.

We did not arrive at the Priest's residence punctually. But although we were somewhat stressed, we sensed on entering that something special was certainly happening in the temple in the High Priest's house.

"The *Pedanda* is descended from the highest Hindu caste, the Brahmin caste," Cok Alit explained to us while we were driving there.

Indeed, we were immediately deeply impressed by this High Priest. He was radiant in a way we had never experienced before. Round his waist, he had a white cloth with gold threads in it, as a sign of purity. On his head he wore a tall hat like a turban with golden embroidery. I was filled with awe at this holy person sitting in the lotus position, completely absorbed in himself, despite being awake and concentrating. In one hand, he held a gold-coloured bronze ladle, which he used to draw water from a golden bowl. With his other hand, he held a golden bell, which he rang constantly to send his words from the old Indian Vedas and the Upanishads up to heaven.

Ray and I did not venture to go any further and followed the cleansing ceremony from a distance. After a short time, they signalled that we should come forward. Yaya stood next to us. He translated the Priest's words. We took our cue from him for the whole cleansing ceremony. We rather helplessly followed the ritual somehow.

Later on, while talking about our experience, we both said we had been fascinated in a way we had never experienced before. It was difficult for us to explain this.

"Perhaps it was the mist from the incense or the constant sprinkling with holy water or the constant penetrating sounds from his golden hand bell?

"Yes, I can't explain our enthusiasm any more today. But when I look at the photo on the shelf at home, we seem to be staring absently into the camera."

An American psychologist took the photo, who was also at a cleansing ceremony for the first time, because Suryani had apparently invited various friends to come to it. Straight after the ceremony, he had come up to us and asked if he could photograph us. Probably he thought we were rather amusing.

"That was certainly one of our most impressive moments on Bali," Ray kissed me gently on the tip of my nose, "perhaps there will be more of them on our next trip there."

I nodded agreement, cuddled up to him again, took a deep breath and knew at this moment how our common experiences united us. I was drawn out of my thoughts by a few drops of rain on my face.

"Hey, it's raining!"

"These few drops won't do us any harm." Ray had also been startled by the raindrops, but they did not seem to impress him particularly. He was quite right there, as the rain cloud moved on quickly and left behind it cumulus clouds, white as snow with the sun shining on them.

"I think the idea the town council had of putting a wooden bench for two in the upper part of the park was splendid," my husband reflected on our comfortable place and put his arm under my head again. I enjoyed the closeness and could feel the spring season deep inside me. Ray must have felt that way, too, for he whispered into my ear softly:

"I would like to grow old with you, going on together hand in hand, and," he added after a short pause, "go on a lot of journeys together."

His words sounded honest. They fluttered right into my heart and left there the wonderful feeling of a deep relationship. I showed my unconditional agreement by squeezing his hand.Encompassed by a cloud of well-being, we remained silent.

My thoughts turned to Ray. I experienced him as an honest, reliable, credible and respectful person, whom I trusted implicitly. He had the talent of always looking at the person he was talking to and adapting to that one person. Others valued this quality of his, too, and Ray had a lot of friends. In comparison, I was not able to listen as patiently as he was. I was temperamental, with a big portion of the joy of life, was talented in different areas, creative, and was able to stimulate others sometimes. But as I got older, I had developed more peace and inner balance. Ray and I supplemented each other well with our different characters. He kept me in balance and I stimulated him.

"My darling, I am looking forward to travelling with you for many years of our lives." Looking into the sky, I saw cloud formations that I interpreted as being for us.

"Do you see the cumulus clouds? I see two figures in them that seem to be going in the same direction with each other. Just as we are."

Ray watched me with a smile. My creative interpretations were just starting.

"And look, there is a third figure ahead of us. Perhaps it's Noe." Ray burst out laughing. I sensed that my imagination was making him cheerful.

Ray's daughter from a previous relationship had inherited certain good qualities from her father. She was just as likeable, open and friendly to everyone, could keep her distance or equally well express her opinion. Experiencing both of them together was great fun. Unfortunately, these occasions had become rarer after Noe had passed her Abitur (A-Levels), as she loved travelling, too, and went out with friends in her spare time.

"You are right, it really does look as though three figures were flying in the same direction. Look, the wind has already changed our figures. What a pity!"

With these words, my husband sat up and looked as though he now realised where he was.

In front of us, there was a slightly downward sloping, extensive lawn with some old trees on it. The sun was shining on the first succulent, light green leaves. A wonderful sight! Like a picture book. In front of the whitewashed red sandstone castle, there were wild-looking, dark green bushes, forming a strong contrast in colour.

"The Lebanon cedar is peeping over the castle wall. Do you see it?"

"The biggest Lebanon cedar in Germany," Ray added.

"Come!" I took his hand, pulled him up and started to run downhill, over to the cedar with its spreading branches.

"How mighty!" he called, his arms around the trunk, "certainly six metres!"

"As I stand in front of this tree, I am conscious of the mightiness of nature. How small we are and how short-lived."

I tried to imagine what stories this tree could tell from the course of its long life.

"Noe has phoned to say she's coming for the weekend.

"Oh, how nice!"

The days up to the weekend flew past. We were glad when she arrived by train. I had prepared the meal. Chatting, we sat round the dining-room table.

"Just imagine, Noe, Dad is dreaming of the *Gulai Kambing* in the 'Bali Café'. I think it's time to plan our next trip!"

"Have you got any definite plans? I would so much like to travel with you. When do you want to set off? This year?" Noe's love of travel was stimulated.

"I would love to pack my travel bag today. Unfortunately, I can't do that now in the middle of the semester. There are still a few exams coming up."

She paused and pouted at her father. He raised his shoulders. "Another time, Noe." Our daughter seemed to be comforted. Her mood changed.

"I can well remember your first trip to Bali. It was in the summer when I was going to Ijssel Sea with our teenagers' group. Can you remember? You were anxious about the long flight to Indonesia and hesitated to book it."

"Yes, that's right. We were simply afraid of the unknown. On the one hand, the huge land of Indonesia was enticing us, on the other hand we were afraid of the long flight. As a precaution, we decided to the tourist island of Bali first, before continuing to Java and Sumatra."

"Among the tourists of Bali, we wanted to get acclimatised and to get used to the foreign culture." Ray added.

"That's true. After that decision, the journey into a completely unknown land was easier for me."

"And on your return, you hardly said anything about your experiences on Java or Sumatra. You just enthused about Bali." Noe grinned to herself. In my thoughts, I was on my first trip to Bali.

"Yes, it was amazing. This island fascinated us from the first moment. The really special Hindu tradition, the way they lived their religious lives quite openly, quite different from the other two islands that are more under the influence of Islam."

"I thought the Balinese were unusually friendly and open. Do you remember, Chris? People kept on talking to us, asking us our names, where we came from and where we were going. At some time or other, we started asking them. In this way we learnt a lot of interesting things about the life of the people on Bali with their particular Bali-Hinduism."

"Don't forget that we sought to stay with families so that we could participate in their everyday lives and tradition."

"That's right. Now I can remember that. We had settled down in the residence of a Balinese family, were sitting on the terrace in front of our room and watching their family life. And because life in Bali happens almost entirely outdoors, we observed a lot."

"Then it was all new to us," I said, turning to Noe, "I felt enchanted by the everyday life and the religious life. Everything was so new. The smells and sounds, too. In the evenings, the rhythms of the gamelan orchestras hovered over the island."

"That must be a super experience, when you are sitting outside and there is music coming from all directions."

"Imagine, Noe, the Balinese play without any sheet music. Isn't that fascinating?" added her father enthusiastically, "They learn what they play by heart and pass on the sequence of notes to the next generation. The fathers let their sons sit on their laps while they are playing in the orchestra. And so, they learn the rhythms and tunes from childhood on." Ray's enthusiasm was obvious.

"You should have done that with me, Dad. Then I might have become more musical." She laughed somewhat provocatively because her father was not all that musical. But I had something else I wanted to say.

"Do you know what also fascinates me on Bali? The sweet perfumes all over the place. No, not just from the numerous blossoms and flowers, but from the sacrifices that they place on joss sticks. The smoke carries their prayers to heaven. Several times a day, the Balinese put small sacrificial gifts on palm leaves in front of their houses and on temple steles. Noe, when you walk along the street, the smell of all this goes through your nose and lifts you up onto a cloud."

We were wallowing in our memories. It just spurted out of us. "Yes, the Balinese live out their religious traditions in public, their temples are open on all sides, the processions are on the street. Everyone is invited to celebrate with them, all the tourists, too. That's fantastic!"

"Is it because of the warm climate?" wondered Noe, making a connection with our Christian culture. "Our services are behind closed doors. Hardly anything finds its way outside. I think that is rather a pity. I also think that the entire spirituality is now absent from our Christian faith. I miss that. Our services are so dry and serious." She took a deep breath before continuing. "Among the millions of tourists who are enthusiastic about Bali's temple festivals, are there not countless Christians, who like the colourfulness, the creativity shown in dances and masquerades? I would like that, too. Did that give you ideas, too?" Now Noe was inspiring us.

"You could be right, Noe. But what we love about Bali is the combination of spirituality lived out in public, lovable people who include us in their lives, the warm weather and the tropical nature."

"I understand. It's the combination. Not just the living faith. What a pity that I can't be with you on your next trip because of my approaching exams. Isn't it simply unfair that they're in the vacation?" She looked up accusingly, but seemed to reconcile herself with her fate quickly, as she nodded to us: "It's OK for you to go on your trip!" And so she put an end to the subject of Bali.

"Oh dear, with all the talking we've forgotten about our meal!" We had planned as a celebration meal Frankfurt green sauce made with eight different herbs, hard-boiled eggs, yoghurt and sour cream. Our substitute for *Gulai Kambing*.

"That tastes as good as it always does," Ray praised the meal and helped himself to another ladle full. Noe and I nodded in confirmation, our mouths being full, and continued to enjoy the meal.

"Frankfurt green sauce with peeled jacket potatoes seems to be our favourite meal," I said while clearing up the empty pots and pans.

"What about a games evening?" suggested Noe, while I was putting the crockery into the dishwasher. I turned round and saw Ray standing there, simply beaming. He was as fond of table games as his daughter was. I did not like them so much.

"I would play Scrabble with you," I suggested.

"I'll start," answered Noe promptly. She fetched the game out of the living-room drawer and distributed the letters. "School. I'll enter eleven points. It counts double!" she joyfully proclaimed with a smile and a look that showed she was feeling certain to win.

"That's not bad for a start. You seem to have good memories of school," I laughed. It took a moment for her to realise my remark was intended to be a joke.

"Dad, it's your turn." It took time for Ray to find a suitable word. "Countries. Noe, write sixteen points down, it counts double." He turned to me: "And which word will you find?"

"Countries, people, adventure – what can I find that fits?" With my letters, I managed to find a short word:

"Turn. Only twelve points, but it also counts double."

Our game was long and drawn out. After almost two hours, we declared Noe to be the winner.

"The way you do that is really admirable. You have a talent that nobody can beat, Noe," was our opinion and Noe beamed with joy all over her face.

Live like you're bringing heaven to earth!

Suddenly everything is different

"Life is just beautiful," said Ray, beaming with joy, contemplating his breakfast plate, which had a fresh buttered pretzel on it, with a slice of boiled ham and a tomato, fresh from the garden, cut into four.

He was perfectly right. It was Saturday. The day that we liked to organise to be a pleasant one. Usually, we cycled into town after spoiling ourselves with breakfast. We strolled around the market, bought bread and vegetables from the farmers, and finally indulged in a cappuccino at our favourite coffee shop. Usually, our friends joined us.

"What more can we want?" I thought repeatedly as we sat together chatting.

At the breakfast table at home, we played soft classical music as a background. I had a good look at my husband as he was enjoying his breakfast and repeatedly looking into the daily newspaper beside him.

"There's a certain charm about getting older," I thought, looking at him lovingly from the side. Ray was good-looking. Especially now, with a fashionable haircut from his recent session at the hairdresser's. The slightly mixed shades of grey showed he was aging. Both of us felt vital and young, but occasionally I noticed we were getting slower with everyday things. This made everything more comfortable, but it gave me the impression that we were getting older. Time and again we talked about our approaching retirement. We agreed that we would put in for retirement at the earliest possible time, because we wanted to travel to make our dreams reality.

"What will it be like when we're no longer working and can decide without any restrictions how we will spend our time?"

"Then we won't just go on short bicycle trips, but on long ones as well," Ray laughed and got absorbed in his paper again. But I did not drop the subject.

"I really can't imagine what it would be like having all the time in the world. Not thinking about going to work the next day and preparing for it, just living for work. Instead of this, planning our own time as we like, travelling without any time limits. Then we will be able to meet friends and relatives at any time, not just at weekends. We'll be guided by our own inclinations. We'll go to the theatre, to the ballet or to the opera. No, not just near here. My darling, we could go to Stuttgart, to Munich, Berlin or Hamburg." And I added with the wave of the hand: "Oh, we'll certainly think of various other things, too."

Ray was only listening with half an ear. But on hearing the word "travelling" he looked up from the paper. "Yes, what I'm looking forward to most of all is travelling together, no matter where. Not only in Germany or to South Asia. I'd like to get to know the African continent, too."

I was not so keen on travelling to Africa but did not say so. Instead, I suggested: "It would be best to plan more distant journeys first. We're getting older every day. Who knows how long we will still want or be able to travel?"

"Well, we haven't reached retirement age yet."

We kept on talking again and again about our retirement when we would be spending time without end together and living out our dreams.

In January Ray went skiing with his friends he regularly played cards with. Just before that he had had his "annual check-up", as he put it.

"And how did it go?" I asked curiously when he came home.

"The doctor recommended that I should have my liver examined more thoroughly. He saw some white spots." Noticing my inquisitive look, he added: "That's certainly nothing to be worried about, my love."

As my husband drank truly little alcohol and did not seem to be at all worried, I trusted his statement and gave it no further thought.

Every evening Ray telephoned me and told me about the fantastic snow conditions for skiing, a good atmosphere in the group and his lack of luck in the evening card games.

And a week later all four members of the skiing party stood in front of our house, waving. I had cooked a strongly spiced goulash soup to help to build them up, which they praised above all else. During the meal they gave humorous reports of their experiences, each trying to be funnier than the others.

Before we went to bed, I asked my husband: "Have you told your friends about your appointment at the doctor's?"

"No, there was no reason to say anything." Ray still seemed to be optimistic and not at all concerned. Not even when further examinations were necessary because there was still no clear diagnosis. In due course, there were results. Ray was given an appointment for consultation in the nearest big town, where he had had his most recent examinations.

"Will you come with me?"

Not expecting anything in particular, I agreed to go with him. Ray was still expecting positive results. But when I noticed that we had been summoned to a department with a surgeon as its Lead Consultant, I was overcome with a most uncomfortable feeling, which increased when the secretary said:

"Please take a seat. The Lead Consultant will soon have time for you."

"What does that mean?" Irritated, I looked at my husband, who seemed to be asking himself the same question. In the meantime, we were talking in subdued tones. Each of us grabbed one of the magazines from the table in front of us to while away the time spent waiting for the Lead Consultant.

At last! The consultant came along with a swing, carrying a pile of folders under his arm. After a friendly greeting, he ushered us into his consulting room, pointing at two comfortable chairs in front of his desk.

"Please be seated." He introduced himself as a reliable expert in this field, with many years' practical experience at a well-known university teaching hospital. That only served to increase my worries, because I was afraid, we would be hearing something unpleasant.

"Why does he have to give us this prelude?" went through my head. I was feeling increasingly uncomfortable. In an attempt to calm down, I felt for my husband's hand. It was rather clammy. He looked attentively at the man in white who was about to give us the result of the examination.

"In your intestines there is a tumour." Then, to soften the blow, he added: "That is not really bad. That often happens."

My body became rigid. Only one word stuck in my head: "Tumour!" Ray had cancer! Two sweating hands came together.

The doctor went into further detail and we hung onto every word he spoke.

"Unfortunately, your tumour has already spread and formed metastases in your liver. But there are not many, and they are only very small." He paused for breath.

I held my breath and felt dizzy. "Go through with it!" an inner voice called to me. Yes, I would do that. Stand at the side of my dear husband. His arm touched mine. I felt the pleasant warmth of his body. Yet, at the same time, we sat rigidly on our chairs.

"Your metastases are distributed over the whole of your liver. That is not advantageous. One larger metastasis would be easier to remove."

The surgeon noticed how rigid we were and was trying to speak in a softer voice while explaining the medical facts. "The liver has the unusual capacity of regenerating of its own accord after an operation. It can grow back to its original size. That is why it is an advantage if the metastases are only in a small area, which, unfortunately, is not so in your case. But, as the metastases are so small there, is the possibility of using other methods to get the better of them."

So, there was hope! But was it real? Was it a light on the dark horizon suddenly appearing to us? Ray's diagnosis was cancer of the intestine with multiple metastases of the liver. Now we were informed. But it had not registered, not even in our heads. I felt that I was looking at the wrong film. We could not accept this diagnosis. I still held firmly on to Ray's hand. I had probably pressed a dent into it. Silently, I turned my head towards him.

"How can I help him?" This question went round and round my head. "If only I could cancel this verdict."

I desperately asked the doctor questions. I cannot remember what questions they were any more, but they were full of hope that these dire results could be improved on. Ray also seemed to be going along with this, for I do remember bombarding the surgeon with questions. Unfortunately, we did not manage to change the results of the tests.

"Your cancer of the intestine is not the problem. It is in the rectum and operable. We can also operate on the liver. But before that, I would like to recommend that you go to our chemotherapy specialist. Find out what he recommends. He is most competent, with decades of practical experience, and familiar with the latest research from all the further training he has had at an international level. Ideally, chemotherapy could have the effect of completely removing all your metastases."

With this, he gave me the motto: "We will get the better of the cancer." At first, I just thought that, then I said it quietly to my husband. This hymn of hope inside me made me more relaxed. I squeezed Ray's hand and gave him an encouraging look. And indeed: he nodded back encouragingly. We were ready for the fight.

"Together we'll succeed." I took a deep breath, which everyone heard. The chief consultant responded to our positive impulse and finished the consultation with words of encouragement:

"So, maybe the diagnosis sounds terrible in the first moment. Yet we will bring things in order. You are still fit; you have the appearance of being strong. Something like that is always an advantage."

"We are starting the fight against the cancer. We will win it!" was our battle cry in the following days. That made us strong and welded us together. Indeed, it encouraged us. Externally at least when we were together. Yet deep down inside, things were rumbling, especially when I was alone, I felt an inner unrest, I was afraid. My thoughts turned back to the time when the surgeon had given us the news about the cancer, and I had stared at him dumbfounded.

I did not tell Ray about my anxious thoughts; instead, I cheered him up when he seemed to be gloomy, talking about our victory over the cancer.

One evening I was overcome with thoughts of doubt. I was suddenly no longer sure we would win the fight. I remembered the time when my brother had been diagnosed with cancer. That was when we were living in the same house. One day I was very much aware of the way he was walking with slow steps when I saw him coming up the short path to our house. He kept on stopping for a rest. I went out to meet him and asked if everything was all right.

"Chris, I'm on my way back from the doctor's. I've got lung cancer." In his words there was deep mourning combined with a dismal hopelessness. I heard these words in my ears as though they had been spoken the day before. But since then, more than a decade had elapsed. Then I had suspected that something bad would happen. I knew that my brother needed my support. Also, because his life partner had died a few years previously. He was still suffering from the loneliness. I then researched on the internet for more information about lung cancer and found out that the average survival time was two years with this kind of cancer. And that was the way it went, too. The two years that he was still alive were punctuated with doctors' appointments, tests, and chemotherapy at a special clinic fifty kilometres away. My brother followed implicitly all the doctors' directions, always hoping this would lengthen his life.

Ray's cancer diagnosis aroused in me the memory of my brother's cancer, the illness, and his early death. And also, the memory of my sister's husband's early death from a cardiac infarct.

"And now? Is it my husband's turn? May Heaven help!" But Heaven did not seem to be helping. I prayed, I begged God: "Why, God, why must my husband have this terrible diagnosis? Let this cup pass us by! Please, heal him!" I did not want to give the appearance of having doubts when I was with my husband. He needed the strong side of me, speaking words of hope and healing. His behaviour changed with the diagnosis. He was more reflective, frequently tired, even exhausted, often sitting in an armchair absorbed in the newspaper or a book.

Our slogan "We'll get the better of the cancer!" remained. That was a help. It united us. Partially. The other side of the situation, however, the sadness, the despair, each of us carried alone, inwardly. I became increasingly uncomfortable when I thought about the diagnosis.

"Perhaps we ought to talk to each other, perhaps I ought to admit to my mixed feelings and not always show myself as the strong one who is always in a good mood."

On one of the following afternoons, I ventured to start an honest conversation.

"You know," I began hesitantly, "your cancer diagnosis has made me feel rather insecure, it's really floored me. Somehow, I'm in a condition of shock, afraid of the future." So, I had blurted it out. I grabbed Ray's hand, not wanting to look into his eyes. When I did look up to him, I noticed tears in his eyes, which had their effect on me, so that tears were dropping onto my jeans, leaving dark blue stains as they dried. In a few minutes, I regained my courage. "We'll keep at it, man!"

Relieved, Ray followed the thread of my words. "We'll succeed, my dear. Now I feel healthy and full of energy. Besides," he paused and said with a grin: "Besides, we want to grow old together."

That was our start signal. I jumped up and called: "Come, let's cycle into town and drink a coffee."

My love followed me. "How delicious, with a Havanna cake."

Quickly we got ready to cycle enthusiastically to our favourite cafe.

Noe informed us that she would be coming for the next weekend. She was not yet in the picture. Her father had simply told her about various examinations. He was planning to tell her about the diagnosis himself.

"I'm driving to the station to fetch Noe." Father and daughter appeared at the kitchen door. I could see how happy they were to see each other again after some weeks.

"He's not said anything to her yet," was my impression and went up to Noe to give her a hug.

"How was the journey?"

"All went wonderfully well. The trains were punctual."

"Well, the supper is already on the table."

"It's always good to eat," she said, picking up the ladle and sniffing at the pumpkin soup.

"I added freshly squeezed oranges and a little coconut milk."

"Delicious, it smells so fruity."

"Well, I love it when you enjoy it, Noe. It's nice to have dinner together."

The sad news came, as it were, with the dessert. Ray told her about his examinations, emphasising the doctor's encouraging words. "We'll bring that in order." Noe reacted somewhat calmly, seeming not yet to have grasped the extent of her father's cancer.

"And why should she?" I thought to myself. At the same time, it became clear to me that I wanted to talk to her alone, because I sensed that the therapy in the near future would make it necessary for us all to stand together. After Ray had adjourned into the next room for a rest, I sat down next to her.

"Noe, Dad has told you about his diagnosis. This kind of cancer can become a difficult process. We should be prepared for that. Dad may well need our special support quite soon."

Noe was silent. Looking into her eyes, I wondered whether my words had meant anything to her, as she had not had any experience with cancer. It was different with me: I had accompanied my father throughout his cancer of the pancreas as well as my brother with his lung cancer. Yet I still did not know what we would be going through, as each illness has its own course, and it is not possible to know in advance exactly how things will go with each one. My father and my brother had both died of their different sorts of cancer, although both had had great hopes of recovering and living for a long time afterwards. They relied on the doctors who encouraged them and wanted to overcome the cancer with chemotherapy and an operation.

After all these unwholesome thoughts, I took a deep breath. I did want to betray my doubts and scepticism to Noe. Instead of that, I said comfortingly:

"Noe, we'll hope for the best for Dad. We'll fight it out with him, won't we? It may be that we have a stony way before us. Let us go on it together."

"Of course. We'll do that," she said, showing her willingness to stand at her father's side. I was relieved to hear her agreement in this way.

"Well, that's the end of the difficult part. Would you like to drink a glass of wine with us?" I fetched a bottle of bio red wine from the cellar, took a packet of unsalted peanuts out of the cupboard and sat on the couch next to my daughter. We had a lot to tell each other. Until I started yawning. Noe, who thrived in the night hours, was still feeling lively. While I was saying "Good night", she was getting out her university papers ready to work on them for her next exam.

"That was a really wonderful weekend again," Ray seemed to be deeply satisfied after he had driven Noe to the station. We hugged each other and each held the other firmly in their arms. "It feels so good to have our small family together."

In the next days and weeks, Ray and I did not only talk about our hopes; we occasionally spoke about our fears. Sometimes we sat together in front of the computer, researching on the internet on cancer of the bowel with metastases on the liver, prognoses, chances of recovery, forms of therapy. Ray was especially interested in the reports of fellow sufferers, which they had given in the internet.

Whenever we told friends and acquaintances about Ray's illness they opened and told us about their own illnesses or those of their close relatives. We were comforted to know that Ray was not the only one with this fate, as we had thought just after hearing the diagnosis. Gradually we gained the courage to talk about it and in doing so, the fellow-sufferers gave us further information which they had. The illness was still in the early stages and we had a lot of questions. We gathered information, especially from specialists we went to see together to ask about the chances of recovery. Our hope was great.

The great variety of information that had come our way appeased my emotions, bringing things down onto the level of mere information. In this phase of his illness, I was increasingly able to keep things at a distance, which sometimes went so far that I considered it abstractly, as though someone else had the bowel cancer and not my husband.

"Will you come with me to the appointment I've made with the Lead Consultant for oncology?" Ray asked me one day. "The experts in all of the fields involved have considered my case in the meantime. In what they call a 'tumour conference'. They talk about all their cases, in order to develop the ideal therapy for each patient, and to come to an agreement with each other. My specialist has asked me to come so he can tell me the result of this consultation. I would be pleased if you would come with me."

"Yes, of course, we'll go together."

The day clinic was in a separate part of the hospital. After a short wait, we were ushered into the chemotherapy specialist's consulting room. In the meantime, he had become the spokesperson of the group. We were agreeably surprised at his personality and his competence. He spoke quietly and confidently.

"We would like to recommend a chemotherapy as a start. As your metastases are partly very small, there is a good chance of removing them."

"What an edifying sentence!" I remarked very quietly and touched Ray's arm lightly. The next sentences, too, sounded positive: "It would be a mild form of chemotherapy. Your hair will not fall out. Please think about it. You don't have to decide today. Telephone me in the next few days when you have decided."

"Thank you for the suggestion. I would like to think about it."

"Have you got our telephone number?" Ray nodded. While we were still in the hospital corridor, I asked Ray how he would decide.

"I have a good feeling about this doctor. I think he can be successful."

"What do you mean by that?"

"Well, I hope that the chemotherapy will remove the metastases in the liver, before the original cancer in the intestine is tackled."

"Sounds OK."

On the way home, we were happy, as we had not been for ages. This mood of hopefulness lasted a few more days, but gradually the doubts found their way back to us and made us feel increasingly insecure.

"Did Ray decide for the right procedure?" I asked a girlfriend of mine who lived in Berlin during a telephone conversation. I trusted Hanna implicitly. And I had also found her to be a competent advisor and a sensitive comforter. Conversations with Hanna were edifying, I always phoned her when I needed her advice.

"What can your husband do other than go this way? He will get no alternative."

"But chemotherapy is a highly poisonous substance, which also attacks healthy tissue. It weakens the entire immune system. Can Ray afford to be weakened in this way? He needs his inner powers to resist the cancer cells."

"Were you given any possible alternatives?"

"No, the doctor mentioned only the use of cytostatic drugs. At our first appointment at the hospital the surgeon talked about the possibility of an operation."

"Hm." Hanna paused for thought. "You know, going against the doctors' standard treatments costs a lot of strength. And where would you get support? It is hard to find someone with competence and experience in the field of alternative medicine. The money available is spent on standard medicine. I think one should take on the role of the specialist oneself." She seemed to be rather helpless. "Enquire about possible alternatives."

"That would certainly not be a bad idea. Ray has already decided for chemotherapy. I have my doubts, but his decision is what counts."

Ray discussed his decision with Noe, too, and with his sister who lived in the USA. Both believed there was no effective alternative to chemotherapy.

The appointment for the first stages of the treatment was drawing nearer. First of all, a line was set near his collarbone to lead the medicine directly into the bloodstream.

"Poor man!" I thought secretly when he came home with the small plastic tube under his skin. A few days later, my dear husband was fetched by a taxi and driven to the day clinic for his first treatment. From then on, he was fetched regularly to have the infusions given to him for a whole morning or a whole afternoon. At the beginning they did not seem to be weakening him in any way. He lived his everyday life, continuing his work in spite of the infusion bottle. It all seemed to be simpler than we had feared. Ray gave me the impression that he was coping with the therapy without any effort at all. At least, that was what I was thinking. Until the evening when we were sitting together comfortably on the sofa and he started to talk about his illness.

"I admire the way you are coping with your illness," I said. Ray's mood changed. He seemed to be sad.

"You know, one word, one sign of hope, that I would like to hear above all else, no doctor has spoken in all our consultations." I looked at him enquiringly. "Nobody has talked about healing. They only talk about life-lengthening measures. But I would like to be healed, Chris." I could fully understand his words. That is what I would also have wished. "Of course. You would like to be healed and be a healthy man again." I gave a big sigh of sadness. Then came silence. I slid up to him and took him gently in my arms, stroked his back. Ray was visibly enjoying the closeness and the stroking.

Before going to sleep, I whispered into his ear: "We'll manage that, Ray!"

Making the most of every day!

Living with the cancer

"Germany has really wonderful landscapes and towns. And the cycle path alongside the river Elbe has been enticing me for a long time," said Ray, showing his interest on going on a cycling tour. He was already looking for suitable accommodation for the overnight stops. Beside him on the dining-room table, there was a brand-new cycling map. Now, in the long break before the continuation of the chemotherapy, he felt his physical powers returning. And with them his love of adventure!

"I would like to ride on the Elbe Cycle Path," he emphasised once again. "On the way, we could have a look at some beautiful towns. What about Dresden and Meissen?"

In this case, there was nothing to question, as far as I was concerned. Ray's wishes and needs were to be fulfilled. He knew what was good for him.

"OK. Let's do that. It's a good idea."

Soon his plans became reality. Ray found in Radebeul accommodation which seemed promising, on a vine-growing estate with a restaurant.

"We'll spoil ourselves with that," was his opinion. On this point, he was also right. At least, that was what I thought. This statement of his influenced our actions, the choice of our journeys and accommodation, more and more. We would spoil ourselves with tasty meals, pleasant and beautiful things, comfort and culture. We spoilt ourselves with whatever made Ray's heart joyful. And mine, too. In the background was the unspoken thought that our time together would be limited. For how long? We did not know.

My beloved husband still had some strength. We were still sporty. Moderately, but at regular intervals. And it was like that on the Elbe Cycle Path: cycling along comfortably with the most beautiful sunshine and pleasant temperatures. That was just what we wanted. We had allowed five days for it. The day before, after our arrival in Radebeul, we had launched into the Karl May Festival, which Ray had been most enthusiastic about.

In the evening, we had strolled through the small and cosy town centre looking for somewhere to eat. We had discovered an idyllically situated restaurant in the pedestrian zone and ordered cheese soup.

"This is something we simply must try," I said, having read through the menu and had looked at the neighbours' plates.

"Well, let's order it, then," said Ray, easily convinced. "After a mixed salad as hors d'oeuvre."

"I'm looking forward to Dresden," was my comment on going to bed, already thinking about the next day.

We parked our bikes and explored Dresden's historic city centre.

"The Renaissance and the baroque buildings remind me of Florence. You, too?" I asked my husband, while we were wandering through the old part of the town centre, devoutly contemplating the historic facades. He squeezed my hand in agreement but steered me back in the direction of our bikes.

"Yes, just like Florence. But let us leave the Church of Our Lady, the Opera House or the Old Masters in the Museum till tomorrow or the day after. Today I would like to cycle as far as the Elbe Sandstone Mountains."

During the cycling tour, Ray showed no signs of tiredness. While we were cycling, he pointed out the various impressive rock formations along the Elbe. He was also enthusiastic about the small, traditional villages we rode through.

"They have not yet been taken over by the big concerns or spoilt by advertising boards. That is interesting." Ray showed his interest in contemporary history, he tried to find out more about the development of the villages in this area, stopping people along the road to ask them questions. This east German landscape interested him a great deal. This helped us to suppress our thoughts about the cancer.

"All good things come to an end," Ray murmured to himself while fastening his bike onto the cycle stand.

"What remains for us, is to carry the memories in our hearts," I reassured him. And that was the way it was. After returning home, we gave anyone who was willing to listen glowing reports of our experiences on our super Elbe cycling tour.

To our regret, Ray's next series of chemotherapy treatments was due to start right after our return home. The dark–coloured taxi was waiting in front of our house. Ray, tall and slim, walked upright up to the vehicle and got into it with a faint smile. Strangely enough, he was wearing black clothes on this day: black trousers with a fashionable anorak and carrying a black briefcase. It seemed to me that everybody would be thinking he was being driven to work in the taxi! Both my husband and the taxi driver gave me the impression that they had been looking forward to meeting again. Before setting off in the Mercedes they were talking to each other with a smile on their lips.

"It's amazing, this mixture of tension and relaxation whenever he is driven to the day clinic." On his return, Ray was somewhat changed. The cytostatic substances were clearly showing their effects. His movements were slower, his face was paler, and his skin felt icy cold.

"My poor husband," was the thought that ran through my head each time, and I felt pain in my heart at the very sight of him. I felt deeply sorry for him. More and more often, I felt great sadness and despair in my heart. I could not show him that it was like this, no, I smiled at my husband. He did his best to smile back, even with his face as white as chalk.

"Have a rest, my darling," was my welcome at the front door. He was glad to accept this offer, took off his shoes and jacket, made for the living-room sofa and was almost asleep while I was covering him up with a blanket.

While he was sleeping, I prepared the meal he had requested before leaving in the morning. Now that he was ill, we were even more careful to avoid food with pesticides and other poisons. We bought food mainly from the bio-farmers in our region, freshly harvested and with short transport distances. We grew certain things ourselves. Our garden was not noticeably big, but big enough for fruit and vegetables in small quantities.

"It always tastes better when it's from our own garden," Ray remarked. "I am happy when the berries ripen, and we harvest fresh strawberries and raspberries." He said stroking his tummy. "Our fruit and vegetables are freshly harvested. We don't have to harvest them when they're still green and don't need any planes or freight ships to bring them to us. We are much more ecological."

With great pleasure, I took a bite into a cucumber and enjoyed its intensive aroma. When shopping, I often followed my nose and smelled the food yet again before deciding to place it in my basket. Arguments from friends who said bio-food was too expensive, I countered with: "We rarely go into restaurants, don't smoke, drink only occasionally, don't eat excessively and are discriminating with our shopping. We are thrifty, and so we can enjoy the privilege of buying healthy food. Just work out how much you spend on unhealthy food. That is certainly more than we spend in the bio-shop or the farmers' stalls at the market. We just love healthy food. It has an intensive taste and smell. Just smell a tomato and taste a carrot which have been mass-produced and compare them with biologically cultivated fruit and vegetables. Then you will also want to change to health foods!"

That usually brought our critics to silence, or they just shrugged their shoulders. They also hardly ever told us if they had made the test and noticed a difference.

"The saying that stinginess is luxurious is simply not true," murmured Ray after yet another of these conversations and turned away.

"We have the feeling that we are doing what is right for us," I comforted him. "We really think about what we eat." I increasingly listened to my inner voice and allowed myself to be guided in that way. With Ray, it was almost the same. We had a greater awareness of life.

We were interested in the different foods, their components, their effects on the human organism, especially in the case of cancer patients. Books on that subject were now on our shelves.

Ray had requested spaghetti with wild garlic pesto. There was a lot of garlic in our garden; it got in your way everywhere. I had no idea how it had got there. I made use of it for salads and pesto and put it on bread and butter. As hors d'oeuvre I prepared a beetroot salad, cut an apple into it and spiced it with caraway seeds and fennel so it would be easier on the stomach.

After his sleep and the healthy food, Ray seemed to have recovered. "The pesto is nice and hot."

"The hot taste kills the bad cells in you," I replied promptly. For me, the wild garlic had a rather spicy taste, as I had added pine nuts and Parmesan cheese.

"Probably the chemotherapy has already brought about changes on my taste buds."

"Yes, that may well be so." I reflected. "What do you think? Ought we to think about strengthening your body? The chemo attacks both the sick and the healthy cells in your body. That weakens your constitution." Ray turned his head on one side, as though he were thinking about it. He was silent, which for me was a good enough reason for continuing to promote my idea.

"There are ways and means of reducing the effects of the chemical treatment. And it is never wrong to strengthen body, mind and spirit."

"It would not be a bad idea to strengthen my immune system."

"We could concentrate on doing that."

"Well, why don't you give me advice on this? You're the one who knows all about holistic health."

"Oh, now you've taken me by surprise!" I laughed out loud, because I had not reckoned with the fact that my husband might consider me as an expert on the strength of studies which were getting forgotten in the course of time. "Actually, I was meaning we could think it out together."

Again, Ray turned his eyes away. This time I decided it meant he was tired. I cleared the table and continued to think about the subject of our conversation. Basically, my husband was right. It was a field I was interested in. Right up to then. Even though my intensive studies had been twenty years ago. During the time of my studies at college and university I had with great interest researched everything that had anything to do with a holistic view of health. Later on, it was the factors that keep people healthy that interested me. I was passionate about both things. Right up to the present. Because of my profession, which gave me truly little space for this field of interest, I had rather lost sight of it. Perhaps the time had come to continue with this subject. My application for pre-retirement had gone through, so the end was within sight. So, what was there to stop me from taking up my former interests in this field again?

"I'll deal with it," was my unspoken decision, which led me into our workroom while Ray was already asleep. There I got out my notes from my student days and soon had my final dissertations in my hands. One of them was about how to promote holistic health in the course of school lessons. The other one compared the behaviour of young people from different cultures when confronted with the problems of everyday life.

I had developed these questions during my time on Bali. The young people there seemed to be more free, friendly and stable than the young people in Germany, whom I had often found to be sullener. I turned the

51

pages of the dissertations, this time recalling, my questions, my studies.

"It's a long time ago," I thought, laying the dissertations aside, as they did not seem relevant to our intentions at this point. The next heap of papers contained scripts on the subject of "health". Back in the 1980s it meant little more than prescriptions for medicines for reducing pain or maybe an operation for removing pain from the body. After that, if fortunate, one was healthy again. But was one really healthy again? What did it mean to have been declared healthy, but not feeling healthy and still feeling pain? Could a sick person also have the feeling of being healthy?

Finally, I learned in lectures a further concept of "health", whereby body, mind and spirit were co-operating within the body. The term "feeling well" appeared. That corresponded with my feeling, my concept. I thought that with both the diagnosis and the treatment the person as a whole must be considered. Their thinking, their everyday life, their feelings, their place in society. It is, indeed, the whole person, who wants to become and be healthy. I was not satisfied with this concept of illness, either and thought: "If someone would like to become healthy, they look to health for orientation. That disturbs everything that concentrates on illness. Houses of health would be ideal; there would be more joy in them. In the word itself and in the atmosphere found when living there. And a good atmosphere is healthy."

The concept of *Salutogenese* (Aaron Antonovsky 1979: Health, Stress and Coping) completely convinced me. Here the question for research concentrated on health.

What keeps a person healthy? What factors influence a recovery? What is there about people who go through a time of great worry, and even benefit from it? And why do others suffer endlessly from the same conditions?

It became clear to me that even after the passing of these twenty years, I was still convinced of the holistic approach in the health field. Indeed, *the holistic approach* had become part of me.

I switched the desk light off. "That's enough for today," and said to myself: "I guess, my bed is calling me." Because I suspected that my thoughts would not come to rest so easily, I decided to meditate. Sitting peacefully and concentrating on my breathing, I soon fell asleep.

On the following evening, I devoted myself to the work I had done in my studies so long ago and discovered research results on the question: "What keeps human beings healthy?" In the field of personality structure, researchers had found out that people who felt well and were at least satisfied with themselves and the world would have good chances of remaining healthy. The same applied to people who had a firm place in a circle of people who were intricately connected, or in a network of good relationships. Some results described the healing effect of a deep faith in God.

"Strange," I thought, "these factors certainly hit the nail on the head, but there must be some more factors." I kept on looking and found some international research that tested fruit and vegetables and made detailed lists of the results as to how their components had a positive influence on health. In addition, results that showed that sport in moderation and movement in nature keep one healthy.

"It's interesting, to keep moving in spite, of being ill. This thesis is not represented by all doctors." I wanted to discuss the research results on nutrition and movement with Ray. I put them in a place where I would not forget about it and, as I was putting the rest of the papers back into the cupboard, I noticed some lecture notes on a seminar about *subjective theories*.

"Oh yes, the *subjective theories*! This university lecture had really fascinated me at the time!" Within the health sciences, there was indeed a trend for researching how successful healing is when the patient makes contributions to his healing with his positive behaviour, his attitude to life, his nutrition and more. "That is the naked fact, but is it taken into account in the doctor's surgery? Definitely not!" First, my thoughts seemed to be quite crazy. I gave a lot of thought to the doctor-patient relationship. Addressing somebody as "Doctor" puts him or her in an inaccessible, elevated position. He or she lays down what the healing process should be. The patient follows what is being said, more or less.

And there were female researchers who had formed a thesis: "Each person basically knows for him- or herself what does him or her good and what helps him or her personally." This thesis was confirmed after being examined scientifically.

"Wow!" That was like a flash of lightening. Now I realised why that seminar had fascinated me so much. It confirmed my inmost feelings. I suspected that each human being had deep down an intuitive feeling telling him or her what was right and necessary for him or her. This knowledge is significant and points the way to recovery.

"Ideally, there should be two people in a doctor's consulting room, who talk to each other about what each of them knows." No doctor really knows the patient, his or her thoughts, feelings, emotions, soul- and spirit experiences as well as the patient him- or herself does. The doctor, on the other hand, as a medical expert, knows what can be done by way of intervention. Together they find the best way for the patient. "If both work together," was my opinion at that time, "the complaints are perceived holistically; individual, tailor-made ways in the direction of healing are embarked on. I'm sure that a wider spectrum of medical possibilities will be developed."

The subjective theories involved the patient in the healing process. They demanded the patient's own responsibility and initiative. Not exactly comfortable for the type of person who prefers to lean back and let others decide for him or her. But in this way the chances of becoming healthy again or having a pleasanter life for a time are greater, because what has been decided together fits the needs of the individual.

I had thought like this in the nineties and I can remember that quite clearly. "Basically, I am still of this opinion. But times have changed and progressed in the direction I had wished." Quite a few doctors involve patients in forming a concept for treatment. Supporting measures are suggested, for instance in the case of a chemotherapy.

"Go for walks in the fresh air," doctors like to recommend, or "Indulge in sport in moderation. Give up smoking. Eat more healthily." These recommendations are often very superficial. The reason might be that doctors are being allocated less time for each patient. There is often not enough time for a detailed conversation or an exchange of information. Other doctors have not been trained as to how to give thorough information.

"But a human being consists of body, mind and spirit. A purely medical therapy comes too short." Obviously, a *holistic* approach cannot guarantee better chances of survival. No such guarantee exists. With some illnesses, there are factors related to a genetic disposition.

"We must admit that there are always uncertainties reasons for explaining why one person leading a disciplined life dies early, whereby another with a most unhealthy way of life lives to a ripe old age."

Sitting on the sofa in our workroom, fully absorbed in my thoughts, I spoke my statement aloud, as if somebody else had been in the room with me. When I became aware of this, I smiled to myself.

It was a good feeling to be devoting myself again to my student's notes and my thoughts from so long ago. Fortunately, I had not thrown the papers away. They made it possible for me to work out ideal accompanying measures for Ray's medical therapy.

"In the coming days," I resolved, "I will inform Ray in detail about my research and we will together think out an alternative concept fitting for his requirements."

Then I remembered that up to now I had been excluding my own cancer. About ten years after graduating, I had had cancer of the breast. I had worked out my own programme, as there were hardly any alternatives to the usual three treatments: operation, chemotherapy, radiation. The hospital where I had had the operation had a little to offer in this direction. Straight after the operation, an art therapist came to see me.

Under her fine-feeling directions, I first expressed my present feelings in colours and shapes, and then we talked about what I had created. What I found very pleasant there was a comfortably furnished common room available to us who had had the breast cancer operation and to women who were about to give birth. That was remarkably interesting for me. Especially when I saw somebody, I had got to know a few hours previously coming back into the room with her baby on the breast. And so, we talked about the new life, which did us breast cancer patients the world of good. In this common room, there was always a most inviting plate of fruit. And there was a big assortment of tea.

In the clinic that I was in next, where I was to have the strong chemotherapy, there were extremely friendly doctors and nurses, who also spoilt us with a dish of fresh fruit. In the first consultation I was given a folder with explanations about chemotherapy, pointing out what we could do alongside the treatment, all decorated with short texts to encourage us. The doctor responsible for my treatment prescribed me vitamins, selenium, and zinc to help reduce the side effects. He told me about a doctor near where I lived who had specialised in cancer patients and included alternative methods in his offer. I went to him for consultations. He took plenty of time for each conversation, informed me about further possibilities for giving me more strength and discussed the possible effects with me in detail. He encouraged me to gather more information in books and on the internet. Finally, we developed a tailor-made programme. I took good care of myself, my body. Mentally I strengthened myself with confidence, the joy of life and intimate relationships, especially, as I remember, with God. I was convinced by his positive attitude and good will. In this time of chemotherapy, my body needed a lot of peace and quiet, which I granted it. Yet the daily half-hour's movement in the fresh air was compulsory. I asked a yoga instructress I knew to come and visit me on the day after my chemotherapy, which she was pleased to do. With her, I practised gentle yoga, which was exactly right for my condition. I used to make special preparations for the strong chemotherapy, which was quickly causing me to lose all my long hair: once I went on the day before with friends into the mountains to do some skiing. It was a fantastic day with lots of sun and fun. I also ate special food, such as onions, garlic, and wild garlic, too, in large quantities, often with a tomato salad.

The therapy was extremely strenuous as it neared its end, but even today, I am convinced that I got through it well in this way. The radiation therapy, which I had after a short break for recovery, did not give me any major problems either. Perhaps it was because of my positive attitude, my confidence, my deep faith in God. Or perhaps because I got into the habit of treating myself to a good portion of chocolate ice cream with cream after each of the daily radiation treatments. My joyful heart made this difficult time easier for me, I was sure about that. On the other hand, my patience in following the standardised medical treatments began to ebb in the course of time. Something in me resisted the daily medication I had been told to take over many years. I was suffering from side-effects and long-term after-effects, which showed themselves in the form of physical exhaustion which went on for years, and further unpleasant side-effects.

My brother, too, on my advice, was careful to take exercise in the fresh air every day and gave up all indulgence in alcohol and tobacco. But in his heart, he was not so positive to it all. And for his healthy food he relied on invitations from me. I rose to the occasion and gave him plenty of healthy foods. Sitting and chatting at the table with friends or relatives was the nicest thing imaginable.

"How will things go with Ray?" I asked myself, taking a deep breath at this deep question, and answered it myself with my next breath: "We'll see."

On one of the next evenings, we took time to talk about things in detail. "Ray, you are the centre of attention. Your interest, your opinion, your feeling, your inner voice," I began.

Ray nodded. He wanted to know what I had found out in my research in the past nights. I gave him a report on the test results from my student days, what I thought about them and my experiences over the years.

"And now it's your turn, my dear husband. What about some meditation and relaxation to make you calm? It would help you to experience breathing in depth, your feelings, and your awareness. What about us walking on a set route in the fresh air every day? We can take our sticks with us. What about being careful to avoid sugar, and unnecessary fats and carbohydrates?"

Ray was quiet for some time, not exactly pleased. "I am well aware that my present condition and my immediate future demand my initiative. There are hardly any alternatives." He added after a short pause: "Chris, I'll do that," but not looking particularly happy at the prospect of it.

"My dear, we won't lose our joy of life! No matter what happens!"

"Nor our confidence," he added, as I was taking him into the living room with me. I switched on the music and soon we were turning round in circles, laughing and singing the songs we heard.

"We are celebrating our life, every day of it!" I sang out loud, as we were turning round. Never mind whether both of us believed it or not.

"I'll do it with you, Ray," I gave him the confirmation again before we went to bed. "If you want it that way, I'll be with you in all the measures accompanying the treatments. You know that we're stronger when we're together!"

From then on, our exercise in nature was a part of our daily routine. Mostly we walked directly from our house across the fields, using our walking sticks. Once a week we met up with two friends at a car park by the woods, to go hiking. The subjects of conversation never ran out on these occasions. We briskly walked through the woods, the walking sticks clicking, telling each other about what had happened in the past week. Sometimes we stopped when certain details on trees, flowers or other things fascinated us, or when we heard interesting cries from birds. Then we were amazed and found words of admiration for the beauty of nature. Full of all this and rather tired from the exercise, we got back home and rested.

In the evenings, we practised the meditations we had learnt from our friend, Professor Suryani. To do this, we concentrated on sitting upright and following our breath as it went through our bodies. That was very pleasant and brought our whole bodies to rest. Ray occasionally withdrew for progressive muscle relaxation. The subject of nutrition was constantly with us.

"What components should foods have for reducing side-effects of a chemotherapy?"

"Such specific questions are hard to answer."

"I'll research it." It was usually Ray who looked for information on the components of foods and their effects in books or on the internet. "Look, here it says that certain components of foods can actually destroy cancer cells."

"Oh, which components?" I became curious.

"So-called secondary herbal contents can prevent the growth of the cells."

"All right, but which ones and what should one eat?" I was more interested in the practical side. Ray named some foods with components that prevented the development of cancer.

"The antioxidants, which are frequently found in fruit and vegetables, in avocados, broccoli, cabbage, carrots and garlic in larger quantity, which you already know about."

"I always thought the dark coloured foods like raspberries, blackberries, bilberries and beetroot were so healthy."

"Yes, that's true. Basically, fruit and berries are always healthy. Especially grapefruit, figs, oranges, lemons, but you already know that." We became more purposeful in our shopping and cooking. Our shopping lists changed to include foods with a high omega-3 fat content, such as linseed oil, hemp oil, freshly caught cold-water fish, unsalted nuts. Herbs like parsley, basil, sage, peppermint, rosemary, thyme, and estragon we harvested from our garden. Coriander, ginger roots and curcuma, pepper, and cinnamon we always had in the house. When Ray was feeling well, he cooked, or else we would stand in the kitchen together to conjure up something tasty and healthy.

"I really love to eat. And if it is healthy, it fits perfectly."

"By the way: How about walking? Or rather have a time of rest?"

Mostly, we did our round of walking. On some days, we preferred to have an afternoon rest first.

"Today I can't manage anything but lying down and sleeping," Ray said briefly on coming back exhausted from several chemo infusions. On days like this, he could not bring up any enthusiasm for healthy meals. I just waited and, after a long sleep, he was mostly willing to eat something healthy. After that, I could ask him if he felt able to have a short walk round the block.

"Your body will recover from all the strain and stress more quickly."

"I can give it a try," he usually answered. Indeed, after a healthy meal and some exercise Ray seemed stronger and in a better mood.

Of course, we were not living picture-book lives all the time. On some days, we simply stretched a point. Ray loved having a cup of coffee in the afternoon with a substantial piece of German cake. Knowing about the fact that sugar is a necessary factor for the growth of cancer cells was no help at all. The inner urge for a piece of delicious cake was greater.

"That is how to enjoy life!" was his self-satisfied comment.

"Oh, raspberry cake today?" We were sitting in our favourite cafe. Ray happily pushed a pastry fork full of the dark red raspberries into his mouth. "Do you know that cancer cells don't like raspberries? I read that yesterday evening in our new book of eating tips for cancer patients."

"OK, that just fits the bill," I said, smiling to myself.

"Oh, concerning the evening," I remembered to say, "Phil just phoned. He wanted to know if we would like to have a game-evening together. He would bring his newest games with him."

Ray was enjoying his raspberry cake, spearing each raspberry with his pastry fork, looking at it lovingly, before pushing it into his mouth with great pleasure. "Good idea! What about this evening?"

"Why not? Let's call him back and ask." I dialled his number and finished the conversation laughing.

"Phil suspected that we wouldn't have any beer at home, so he's going to bring some chilled beer with him."

The evenings we used to spend playing games together were great fun. Each time, Phil took games that were new to us out of his basket and explained them to us very patiently. While we were playing, we would talk together. Mostly about politics or history. Sometimes our conversations were so interesting that we had heated debates and forgot about the game.

"Chris, you're cheating!"

I enjoyed testing my husband, to see if he would notice and correct my mistakes, which he did with a loud laugh.

"Yes, you can laugh! Some time I'll catch you cheating. Laughing keeps you healthy!"

"I've always enjoyed laughing, for as long as I can remember."

Involuntarily I started remembering incidents from my past, which I wanted to tell him about. "During adolescence, when the subject of certain school lessons was dry and uninteresting, I used to start giggling, knowing quite well that the girl sitting next to me would also start. I puffed out my cheeks, blew gently at first and pressed my lips together until my tummy was full of air. Sooner or later the air would force its way out. Putting my hand in front of my mouth, I wanted to prevent myself from producing indecent sounds, but exactly the opposite happened. The poor teachers! Some got annoyed and thought I was laughing at them. Then I got an attack of the giggles. Up to the present day I have kept my joy in laughing."

"And don't let your laughing be taken from you," Phil said, bringing me back from my memories of youth. There was something about Phil's carefully chosen theological-philosophical comment. I think he was meaning:

"You will be experiencing enough of the hard side of life. Don't lose your positive view."

It was easy to keep our positive view in times when Ray was not having chemotherapy or any other medical treatment. Then life was easy, and we felt free, laughed a lot, danced and sang. We pretended everything was going well and suppressed the negative side of it. Yet there were other times. In these times, pain and sadness, combined with fear for the future, were more in the foreground. My view of the future was dark. It made me feel miserable. One evening, when sad thoughts and feelings were overcoming me, I lay down on the sofa and daydreamed about Bali. My inner eye saw friendly, smiling Balinese people, who brightened up my sad mood.

I remembered our first journey to Bali. My first impression of the island was: "Here everybody laughs." I thankfully smiled back and noticed how my mood was brightening up and a good feeling was developing. "Why is it like this?" I asked myself and soon found an answer.

"That is certainly because smiling, friendliness and happiness in social contacts go together with the Balinese and have a way of integrating me into this unknown culture."

"That's strange, as I'm used to being with people who rush past me with a stiff expression on their faces. Even though we in the West are materially better off." I did not give myself satisfied with my first attempts at an explanation, as I soon had further questions: "What about the problems the Balinese might have? Why can't I see their problems written on their faces, as I do with people at home?"

That was during the time when I was studying pedagogy at university. My studies were focused on the factors that cause stress and those that reduce stress. In the first instance, I reviewed the influence of people's social environment. My observations on our first trip to Bali came into my mind and I was increasingly confronted with the question of how far social factors influence behaviour when under stress. I wanted to investigate these questions in research.

"What is behind the Balinese people's enchanting smile? Do they cope with their problems differently from the way we do in the West?" I resolved to come back soon and to prepare for the next journey. That involved learning the Indonesian language, reading books about Bali's cultural life, about their special Hindu faith, about their family life and the village community. Using a detailed questionnaire, I intended to research in more detail their handling of stress situations.

On my next trip to the island, I asked both young and some adult Balinese people about their behavior in certain stressful situations and was surprised at their answers. Both their awareness of problems and their behaviour in problems were different from everything I had known before. They gave a relaxed impression as they told me about their worries and fears, and even smiled. Even illness they seemed to take more calmly than I was accustomed to. "They have their emotions under control," was my first explanation, which I then wanted to pursue. "What is behind this?"

Gradually I had a picture of it: The Balinese are firmly integrated into their religious fellowship, which, like any other religion, has a code of behaviour. This is under the control of the family, which relates to the village community or the community of the part of the town they live in. I learnt that the Balinese do live out their emotions. They live them out one at a time. Within the framework of their religion, in the temple feasts and ceremonies, in which everyone – old and young – must participate. In the most artistic of ceremonies, the emotions are drawn out intensively. An orchestra starts to play. The sounds of its metal instruments penetrate bones and marrow. There is dancing as if in a trance. Also, the theatrical acts and masked dancing, presented with unusual precision and intensity, often end in a trance. In this trance, there is no sense of pain. People walk over broken glass, on glowing coals. With a circle of bent sabres, the opponent is pierced in the chest without any blood falling. Nearly always there is a presentation of the battle between good and evil.

When visiting the most different temple ceremonies I felt emotions in an intensity I had hardly known before. Gradually I became aware of the significant differences in culture that could explain the different behaviour in the face of problems.

"But why do the Balinese smile so enchantingly, why do they appear to be so friendly, calm and relaxed? Or am I just imagining it?" A sixteen-year-old boy, who indeed seemed to have introverted laughter, answered my question about what made him so relaxed and how he and his friends cope with their problems with the pithy sentence:

"Most of all, we like to laugh our problems away."

"What! You can laugh problems away? How am I to understand that? Do the Balinese smile to prevent a problem from coming into existence?" Until now I had known it was possible to suppress problems or to express them with aggressive behaviour or talking about them. Conversations with Balinese were like tiny mosaic stones for a picture I was gradually forming. One of my conversations was with a university professor, a woman, who was researching a similar question to the one I had formed. This encounter was the start of a most interesting exchange of thoughts and experiences about our two differing cultures. We told each other about our various experiences, about education and religion, reflecting on forms of behaviour that develop from both cultures and their religions. I came to understand that Bali's culture and religion lead to a relaxed treatment of problems and thereby to the smiling that had so impressed me.

Slowly I got to know the university professor - it was Dr. Suryani – better as a person. She told me about her meditation that she had carried out daily since the time when she was a young girl. "I taught all my six sons this meditation. Would you like to learn it, too?"

Ray had been with me on my most recent journeys. We decided to make use of Suryani's offer. She gave us her books with instructions and background information, which we read and took with us to various meetings in which she was teaching meditation. Gradually we got into it und noticed a change in ourselves: peace, relaxation and calmness found their place in us.

That evening on the sofa, I decided to concentrate on the meditation more, as a way of working against the fears that sometimes overcame me. Before going to bed, I meditated.

"The doctor said I could have a few weeks break from the chemo, so my body can recuperate," Ray burst out on one of the next days, when he had hardly come into the house from a consultation. His enthusiasm was infectious.

"Hurray! We will have time for doing things together, for living out our dreams!" In breaks like this one, we were enterprising and active. It almost seemed that we were in a great hurry. We quickly forgot the strenuous weeks of cancer therapy and steered our lives in the direction of the blue sky. Nobody talked about the strain of the past weeks. Instead, I shouted out the happiness I was feeling. That encouraged my husband. And so, we went around with beaming faces, enjoying life.

"I think people notice our thankfulness for every day we can spend together," Ray cuddled me firmly, kissed me and then whispered: "Your happiness is greatest when you share it," kissing me again. We were radiant. Yes, we shared our happiness. Not only with each other. We laughed it out of us like the people on Bali. And indeed, people laughed back!

On the following days, we thought about plans for possible projects, which we could usually do without any difficulty.

"What about a short cycling tour? Maybe to Munich? I'd rather like to cycle along the River Isar again."

"That's not a bad idea. Let's call Noe and ask if she can come, too. Perhaps she can organise some free time for herself."

"A wonderful idea!" I looked at the calendar "It might just be possible, with a long weekend, at least."

Our cycling tour together with our daughter got well planed, the weather was also just right. We cycled at an easy speed along the river Isar, with its turquoise colour and gentle splashing on that day. We went round the sights on our bikes, enjoyed the English Garden, the Victuals Market and, of course, went into the idyllically situated beer gardens.

"That was simply lovely," was Noe's short but pithy comment when we were bidding her farewell at the station.

In breaks like that, we built up our power again for the everyday life of a man suffering from cancer, like Ray.

It was time for the next doctors' appointments. And as Ray had decided to follow the doctors' advice, we were wondering what the next thing in the plan would be.

"We can congratulate you on a success. Your metastases in the liver have got smaller from the chemotherapy.We recommend that you have an operation, as now is a good time for it. If we do this, we can remove the remaining metastases."

Surprised by this suggestion, we looked at each other. It sounded good, but Ray decided to sleep on it for one night. After another consultation with the doctor, when he was given further explanations, he decided to have the operation. His hope of recovery was in the background of this decision.

That was, indeed, hopeful news! Loudly, we proclaimed it to Noe, Ordi, to Ray's sister and our good friends. We believed the surgeon who had promised to remove the tiny metastases completely.

"That would be terrific!" With these words, I hung onto my husband's neck. "Just imagine how it would be to have all the metastases out of the way!"

"And we could grow old together and live out our dreams." Ray, too, was beaming with joy and pressing me close to him.

Strangely, I got somewhat nervous. The nearer the operation day drew, the more restless I became, with no idea why this should be so. It was a feeling. I quickly decided to phone Noe.

"Noe, I'm a bit worried. Do you think you could come here in the days that your father is away for the operation?"

"I'll see what can be done. I think I could be away from here for a few days." I was relieved that Noe was willing to be here during the critical days, even if only because of the major operation the specialist had told us about. It was obvious to me that he had chosen his words well in order to allude to the risk involved.

Noe's prompt arrival was welcome. It was good that she could be available for her father, but she was also available for me, as my anxieties built up at the approach of the operation day. I told Ray nothing about my apprehension. Noe and I would be thinking of him for the duration of the operation. My aim was to be a strong support for Ray. Noe's pragmatic manner that she had inherited from her father was supportive. Together with her, I had more success in developing solutions, which I would never have thought of alone. Maybe quick decisions would be necessary.

Ray was visibly happy to know he would have both of his dear ones around him. It was good in principle, and particularly now in the precarious situation, when no one could say how things would go.

On the day of his operation, Noe and I each travelled from a different direction to the hospital. We had arranged to meet in the reception area. Noe was also tense, as I sensed when we hugged each other. Because I had been the first to arrive, I had had time to get informed about the present situation.

"The operation is still going on dear. Dad will be transferred to intensive care two hours later than expected. I hope that doesn't mean anything bad!" I nodded anxiously.

"And what shall we do in the meantime?"

"Waiting in the hospital for two hours would only make us nervous. Let us drive into the town, walk around there and go for a coffee."

Noe was beaming, which I interpreted as assent. In a short time, we were wandering through the lanes of the old part of the town. With a knowing smile, I steered her into a cafe that looked comfortable, from which we could observe what was going on in the pedestrian zone.

"Two cappuccinos, please," I ordered and turned to Noe. "A piece of cake to go with it?" Here, too, Noe was like her father. She ordered a piece of redcurrant cake topped with meringue.

"For strengthening body and soul," I said with a laugh, as she pushed the cake into her mouth with the pastry fork. She nodded agreement with her mouth full.

The nearer we got to the hospital, the more uneasy my stomach was feeling. We hurried along the endless corridors to the intensive care ward.

Ray was still in the operating room! The ward sister comforted us with the thought that we would soon be able to see him. Our nervousness was now obvious for all to see. We hardly talked, instead turned the pages of the magazines, and looked up, relieved, when the door was opened for us. When we were allowed to go to him, he was still asleep from the anaesthetic, lying in a sterile room, with thick dressings around his chest and abdomen, from which draining tubes filled with blood and secretion came out. In a reflex action, I put my hands together and prayed to God that He would have mercy on my husband and stand by him.

"Dad! We're here. We're with you." Noe spoke gently to her father, who still did not react to anything. I also spoke softly and quietly to Ray, holding his cool hand and massaging his arms in the direction of his heart. Noe helped to activate Ray's circulation with a light massage. We looked at each other. It was a worried look because Ray was not reacting at all.

The nurse on the intensive care ward obviously noticed our distress and gave us some hope. "Tomorrow afternoon you will find your husband and your father livelier."

At that point, I could hardly imagine that it would be so. We spent some hours of anxiety beside his bed before deciding to drive home just before midnight.

The next day Ray was still lying without any strength in his sterile room. He spoke to us with slow and quiet words. I felt so sorry for my husband.

"I hope that all his torture has been worthwhile," I thought to myself. For in the following days Ray could hardly stand on his two feet. In the meantime, he had returned to his room. He needed our help to get to the toilet, we washed him and supported him so he could sit up. The scar from the operation, which went right across the top part of his abdomen, made every movement difficult. It was obviously very painful.

We drove to the hospital every day, to stand by his side, to cheer him up and to practise the first steps with him. Slowly he started to recover and in a week's time, Ray walked slowly and purposefully, without any help, to the toilet.

"Look!" He was proud of himself and seemed more confident and stronger. We applauded enthusiastically.

"Take it easy, Dad, snails also get where they want to," Noe called out to him and advised caution.

After Ray's condition had become more stable, Noe went back to Frankfurt. Our dear patient was discharged from the hospital a few days later.

We quickly noticed that it was not the same as a hospital room. Ray went up the stairs slowly and with difficulty and found other things hard, too. The wound right over his chest presented problems with lying and walking. I was deeply sorry for him, but as Ray put on a calm appearance, I did not show him my true feelings. I was also surprised at the way he played down the strenuous operation when talking to friends and did not mention the hard days afterwards.

"I would rather be honest and mention my pains, and my miserable condition. Perhaps I would exaggerate a bit." Then I had to laugh at my remark. "But my dear husband acts as though the operation had been child's play. That bothers me. I also experienced his torture firsthand."

I poured out my heart to my girlfriend in Berlin on the phone. She was understanding about my reaction, my worries in the past days and my efforts at standing alongside him with his pain. He pointed out that he might be coping with his pains in a different way.

"Perhaps your husband is protecting himself by remaining friendly in the difficult situation."

"You may be right, Hanna. It does me good to talk it over with someone else and hear their opinion. Thank you!"

When someone looked at my problems from the outside, it meant a lot to me, especially in times when I was burdened with worry about my husband. My thoughts went round in circles. I felt I was in a hamster's wheel that I could not get out of. In such situations, it did me good to talk to familiar people. After a conversation like that I always felt relieved. And also when I meditated, I managed to find my way out of the hamster's wheel and found inner peace.

At the end of the second week after Ray's liver operation, we got a phone call from the surgeon's secretary, asking us to go for a consultation to review it all.

"Well, of course we'll come." Ray sounded confident and gave me a triumphant look as he hung up the receiver. I encouraged him immediately.

"If we go by your big wound, it can only have been successful."

Feeling courageous, we strutted arm in arm through the hospital's endlessly long corridor, as it seemed to us. But it was not as we had imagined. This time, the chief surgeon pushed us right into the icy cold water.

"I'm sorry to have to tell you that your tiny metastases have spread through the whole of your liver and were therefore inoperable. I had to put an end to the operation."

We were out of breath. We looked at each other. Found no words. The doctor reacted by giving us a ray of hope.

"Fortunately, the metastases seemed to be crystallised. That could be a seen as a good sign. They have probably been killed off by the chemotherapy."

I could not make sense of either of the statements. I was simply disappointed, incapable of any reaction. Instead, I thought: "Now the doctor is trying to take a few coals out of the fire, by talking about crystallised metastases." I felt for Ray's hand. Again, he seemed to be less depressed than I was.

The surgeon quickly concluded the consultation. He wished my dear husband a good recovery and shook hands with us. Speechless and unable to look around properly, we trotted through the long corridor.

"An operation all for nothing! Can you imagine anything like that?" I burst out when we were back in the car. "All that trouble, the torture of it!" I was really fed up and let it all out. Ray was silent.

"Aren't you of the same opinion?" I asked and sensed immediately that my outburst had been a mistake. It did not help Ray to get well again. Yet, my disappointment was still not over. Hanna had to hear about it. Although an experienced person, she listened to the account of my frustrations. That did me good. Then she navigated me into calmer waters with her comment that there was nothing I could do to change the result. And, in addition, it would indeed be of little help to Ray.

"Yes, I've already experienced that."

After a sleepless night, tossing and turning, I found peace again. I reproached myself and resolved that Ray's well-being should be in the foreground. Being annoyed would not help him to get well again.

"Today, I'll spoil my husband," I planned early in the morning. "He was the victim of this operation, after all. I will bring him his breakfast in bed. Love goes through the stomach." I quickly threw the duvet away from me and addressed him in delicate tones:

"Good morning, my love. May I give you breakfast in bed?"

My dear husband seemed to be still rather sleepy, but he blinked with his eyes and looked at me in surprise. Then he understood what I was offering him, blew a kiss to me and smilingly ordered scrambled eggs with ham and a piece of bread and butter.

"The bread, baked in the wood oven from the bio farmer, please." I immediately made my way into the kitchen.

"And will you bring me the newspaper, too?"

"Ye-es!" I laughed to myself, because I knew Ray's weakness for reading the paper at the breakfast table. I rather opposed this habit whenever we had breakfast together. I wanted to serve the breakfast as in a hotel. I carried it all into the bedroom on a white tray, adding a white, cotton serviette.

"Mm! It looks delicious. Thank you." Ray looked radiantly happy. I kissed him softly on the tip of his nose and withdrew quietly. He already had his newspaper just next to him. Today, it would be his breakfast companion.

"Enjoy your breakfast!" I called, before slinking away. I finished getting ready in the bathroom and thought about what a suitable start to the morning might be. My wish was to walk barefoot through the grass and feel the morning dew on the blades of grass. I did that. The light warmth of the morning felt fresh on my skin, my bare feet made their way through the still moistened grass. That felt wonderfully refreshing.

"Lovely!" I shouted out loud, without any consideration for the neighbours. "Yeah, this is just lovely!" I picked fresh peppermint leaves for the breakfast tea and for my smoothie fresh spinach and dandelion leaves. I had brought a large sieve with me. I put some of our first vegetables, beans, paprika, tomatoes together with some parsley from the herb garden for a vegetable soup, which I wanted to flavour with curry and caraway seeds – that was my feeling. It that time I let my feelings guide me as to what spices I would use.

When I got back to the house, Ray praised me:

"You've done well today, my dear. Your food is enchanting! I'm feeling really well today!"

He beamed over to me and raised his mouth ready for a kiss. I felt flattered, kissed him tenderly and forgot about the time with the doctor the day before.

"What about a short walk?" Today, it was my husband who was asking me to walk with him. He knew quite well that I would answer in the positive!

Shortly after lunch, we strolled hand in hand towards the botanic gardens. The sponsor of a firm had donated this dream of a garden to the town. Ray used to call it "my garden", not only because of the many different flowers, bushes and trees growing there, but also because there were enough benches put there to rest on and admire the splendour. Now, just after the operation, they were welcome places of rest.

Whenever Ray was feeling stronger, we picked up our walking sticks and walked further. The sticks helped to carry our weight when we were walking faster and strengthened our arm muscles. The regular rhythm made by the sticks' noises speeded our steps.

"It was a good idea to buy the walking sticks," Ray remarked again and again.

We made good use of the time when Ray's condition allowed sporting activities: we went away for several days, spent time at a wellness hotel, went on cycling tours or hikes, visited friends or relatives.

After the major liver operation, my husband was offered the opportunity of a time of convalescence, which he was pleased to accept. He was impressed by the offers for strengthening, reflection and creativity, as he told me in his evening phone calls. I visited him at the clinic for a long weekend. We rented bicycles and cycled through the nature within easy reach of the clinic: through woods and past small lakes. Ray seemed so strong and joyful. I was amazed at his quick recovery - you could not see any sign of the previous, strenuous weeks on him.

"How quickly a human being can recover! A few weeks ago he was lying wrapped up in bandages, could hardly move, and now we're cycling through the woods!"

Yet, he was hardly back home, when the cancer was the focus of attention. Reality caught up with us. The doctors recommended, as a preventive measure, a further series of chemotherapy treatments. Ray accepted it. I personally was rather sceptical. My inner voice said: "Yet again this weakened body is expected to go through the next chemo. And my husband just takes it without any objections.

Wouldn't it be better to strengthen his body as a whole? During his times of rehabilitation, he is much better, he becomes stronger in body, mind and spirit. That is a great help. That does more to resist the spreading of the cancer. Do the doctors really think that chemical means are the general cure for cancer?" Such thoughts whirled round my head. Ray, however, had to decide on his way for himself. After all, it was his body, his life. For that reason, I did not talk about my doubts to him.

What remained were the measures we had thought out to accompany the treatment. Basically, we continued to practise the things that had helped hitherto. We went out into the beauty of nature, ate various cereals, fruit and yogurt for breakfast, did not eat meat, but cooked more vegetable dishes. We meditated and Ray did muscle relaxation and visualisation exercises.

"Life is to be enjoyed. Every day of it!"

"Quite right, Ray. I thank God for each day I spend with you."

Meanwhile, I had been given the opportunity of working reduced hours, in pre-retirement, which I was pleased to accept. That meant my time was not as limited as it had been before and I could be at Ray's side whenever he needed me.

"That is a blessing! From now on, we have unlimited time together!" Ray called out in my first free week, to add emphasis that he approved of the idea. "What about a short cycling trip before my next chemotherapy starts?"

At first I was not so sure. "Do you really think you can manage another cycling trip?"

"Why not? I feel well."

"OK, if you think so. Let's follow my mother's motto: ' A person's will is his heaven', and go on a cycling trip."

"I'll phone Noe and ask if she has the time and the inclination to go with us," said my husband, reaching for the receiver.

"Dad, you make a suggestion. Where would you like to cycle?" I heard Noe saying on the phone. Spontaneously, which was unusual for him, he replied:

"Southern Bavaria? The bavarian freshwater lake, named Chiemsee?" he turned to me, to see my reaction. At first, I just shrugged my shoulders slightly, then nodded in agreement.

"Noe is coming," said Ray after they had planned the journey on the phone. "We have agreed that she will come here next Thursday evening and we'll start on Friday morning."

"Fine. There are not so many people by Chiemsee in the latter part of the summer. I'm looking forward to it, my darling, going away for a few days with our daughter."

A few days later, we fastened three bicycles to our car's luggage rack and set off for Chiemsee. With the most beautiful late summer weather we cycled comfortably in short stretches along the lake. We stopped to admire wonderful views and enticing smells. In a beer garden and enjoyed a freshly fried fish. Later we stopped by a wooden pier that was hidden behind reeds. Noe jumped into the water right away and swam out into the lake.

"It's not at all cold. Come on in. From here there's a much better view of the mountains further south," she called to encourage us.

"Let us test the water first." I put my big toe into the water before going down from the pier. Ray did the same. It took a while for us to get used to the temperature of the water.

"Look! The mountains look both mighty and gentle at the same time!" I called, pointing at the Karwendel Mountains and swimming firmly with my other arm so as not to go down.

"And we're swimming in the clear water of wonderful lake. Isn't that fantastic?" Noe added. Ray swam more carefully, but you could hardly notice his serious illness.

"That was really a super cycling tour, Dad, that we two planned together," were Noe's words of praise while we were eating a whitefish in a fish restaurant. "What shall we do for our next excursion? A trip to a town? I'd so much like to revisit Hamburg." That idea was like a bull's eye for Ray.

"That would be just possible if we plan the journey straight away." He was thinking about his approaching chemotherapy.

"You know what! In the next few days, I'll look for a suitable train. We might get a cheap offer. Then we can talk about the cultural programme. Do you agree?"

Noe had really caught the travelling bug. Ray agreed with her. The two of them discussed the trip in the next days. I noticed how they were looking forward to it. They came back from this weekend trip together beaming with joy. Over supper, they told me about all they had experienced. Both of them had filled themselves up with energy.

"Incredible, what a human body can endure," I thought to myself. "Ray looks so refreshed. He recovers from everything when he's on the way somewhere." Also, when we were invited to meals or celebrations by friends he appeared so vital, that I kept observing him from the corner of my eye and was surprised at how fresh he seemed to be, as he conversed with his friends interestedly and got absorbed in his favourite subjects of conversation: history and politics.

"You don't notice anything at all about Ray. I can't believe that he's so ill. How is he really? What is the doctor's prognosis?" more than one friend asked me with his hand in front of his mouth. They did not want to ask their friend questions like these.

"Ray has had some bad times. But he is recovering quickly, as you can see," I often replied. What else could I say? It was too hard for me to attempt any prognosis on the progress of Ray's illness. My dear husband was still like a jack-in-the-box. I lived with an ambivalence of hope and doubt, which had become a part of my life in the meantime. Whenever we were having enjoyable experiences, when we were celebrating with friends and relatives, dancing, singing, going to concerts and exhibitions or simply enjoying being together as a twosome, then we did not ask these questions. We lived each moment, which was full of happiness. Yet doubts remained.

"When we're both well, Ray, I can't imagine at all that you are so seriously ill. Is it like that with you, too?"

My husband answered with a slight nod of the head. Not more. That told me that he did not want to talk about it. Not even when I asked him in quiet moments: "How are you, Ray?" he simply answered "I'm well," each time, and it sounded genuine.

"He's probably ignoring the danger of his illness," I then thought. But I listened carefully when he told me how much good the talks with the oncological psychologist had done him. They had certainly talked about his incurable cancer and maybe about death. He also talked about his illness when he was alone with his best friend. Be that as it may, the friend always told me that Ray had talked to him completely honestly.

Ray was at least so convinced of the wisdom of the therapies the doctors advised him to have, that he accepted their offers. In the meantime, it had become a circular process of chemotherapy, radiation, operations and convalescence in a special clinic.

At the conclusion of each unit, he was invited to a consultation to review the situation. When the result was positive, that the metastases had come back, they recommended further chemotherapy or an operation.

For me, it became more and more difficult to endure it all. I sensed that it was all the result of a feeling of helplessness, which they were countering with chemo or an operation. But together we concentrated on the positive part of the consultation. Yes, we even celebrated the result.

"Yoo-hoo! The metastases are on the decrease! Let's go out for a meal on the way home. What about the Hotel Post?"

Soon after the quick decision, we had places overlooking the river that was flowing into the old part of the town. With a glass of champagne in his hand, Ray said to me: "I will succeed. And I won't give up hope, my darling."

An elevated feeling, once again. Pleasant time as a twosome, once again. We smiled at each other as a couple in love, stroked each other gently on the back of the hand. Ray had wonderful, delicate fingers. Evenings like this one, when we just forgot the negative side of the illness, helped to build us up. They gave us strength for the next round for which we would need more of the powers of life. In the meantime, Ray's body had been subjected to the medical cycle for two years. Gradually, I could observe that he was losing powers of resistance and his body was changing. He lost weight, the surface of his abdomen had clearly swollen and gained a different shape because of the operation scar across the upper part of his abdomen. The doctors, too, observed his weakening and advised him to go to a convalescence clinic again. As my husband had hitherto had good experiences in convalescence, he gladly followed the recommendation. In our evening phone calls, he gave me enthusiastic reports on the treatments that strengthened him and the positive advisory conversations. He always found like-minded people quickly, to play cards with or do something musical together. In one of the phone calls, he reported:

"Just imagine! I enrolled for a course on healthy nutrition yesterday morning. We learnt a lot of new things about the components of our food and their effects on our health."

"How nice! Then you will soon be our nutrition expert and cook more meals." I said, laughingly and secretly looked forward to having more support with the cooking. "And what did you cook?"

"Oh, a whole menu, with carrot soup, semolina slices turned in sesame with fennel as the vegetable, and for the dessert fried pears with honey and nuts. It tasted super. I'll cook it again when I'm back home."

My husband gained more interest in healthy nutrition, looked around in bookshops for literature that was concerned with his questions as to any food that killed off cancer cells, and if so, which ones. Whatever he cooked, it tasted delicious.

"Let food be your medicine and medicine your food," he quoted Hippocrates and delved further into the knowledge about healthy food for an illness of the intestines.

"Do you know that secondary herbal materials can indeed intervene and put a stop to cancer cells? I believe that and I'd like to test it, darling."

"Why not, if it does no harm? I'm in favour!"

Of course, I supported each of his attempts to put an end to the cancer cells. Why not through the nutrition? From then onwards, our shopping lists did not have certain things on them any more: no more fatty and salted meat, sausage of any kind, certain kinds of cheese and particular sorts of saltwater fish. Instead, we looked out for fresh vegetables with a high beta-carotene content and flavonoids: sprats, lettuce, fruits, berries, spices like curcuma, ginger, cinnamon and chili, nuts, fermented foods and much more.

"We'll never learn about everything. We knew about some of these things and ate accordingly, but now we know more."

I willingly added the new information to my repertoire and listened to Ray with interest when he told me about his new knowledge about the components of the different kinds of food. Ray did not abstain from anything he really enjoyed. He just loved to have his afternoon coffee with something sweet to go with it, occasionally.

"Now I'm eating only dark chocolate because of the high percentage of antioxidants," he said surprisingly one day, as he was putting some pieces of the said chocolate into his mouth to go with a cup of espresso.

Supported by the right kind of food, Ray prepared for his next round of chemotherapy and felt strengthened for the following day. He ordered the taxi driver who usually drove him to the clinic, and he stood at the front door the next day, with his black taxi. Ray had been looking forward to seeing him, as he liked him and they were absorbed in conversation when the taxi drove off.

"During the drive, we engage in interesting conversations about our lives, our philosophies of life, about politics and current events. I get the feeling that I'm talking to a friend," he told me once concerning this unusual relationship. I admired that. Two men who conversed so intimately on their way to a day clinic. May be it's not just that they like each other, but the element of anonymity, as they only see each other on these occasions. I told Hanna about it.

"It could be that the taxi driver learns more about your husband's apprehensions, which he dare not express in your presence," was her opinion, "I have often heard that people confide in a taxi driver about certain things. They never see them again, or hardly ever."

That gave me food for thought. I particularly found my husband's relationship to the taxi driver who drove him to his chemotherapy remarkable. Phone calls with Hanna shed light on some of the thoughts I told her about.

"You know, with his briefcase under his arm, Ray looks as if he were going to work. The serious purpose of the drive is not at all evident externally. I admire the way he seems to be accepting his destiny with his head raised up high. Recently, we resolved to strengthen his immune system with healthy food more intensively. With, of course, daily exercise in the fresh air and relaxation. But just think: despite all these good things, his body is getting weaker and weaker. He doesn't talk about it, rather pretends that everything is all right."

"Your husband is really a special person. What I admire about him is the way he just carries on, despite the illness. On our last visit, I could see: Ray doesn't let anyone notice his severe illness."

Many people who knew him expressed their honour and respect concerning Ray and the way he just carried on despite the illness. However, inside me, there were fears about the future and they needed to be talked about. "With all those positive thoughts about him, I can't deny the fear that overcomes me, particularly when he comes home from chemotherapy looking rigid and as pale as chalk."

"I understand that. I think I would be no different in your position. But your fear doesn't help you any further. You can't look into the future and don't know what the outcome of this illness will be. It's better to live in the present moment and enjoy it as far as you can."

After the last infusion, we were hoping for a phase of relaxation. And there was one, too. A few weeks before Christmas, Ray came back joyfully from a doctor's appointment and told me about a fairly long break he had been recommended to take. And, at the same time, he was overcome with travel fever.

"You know what? We could make use of the time for paying Noe a visit." In the meantime, our daughter had started to study in New York for a semester abroad. "Wouldn't that be fantastic? What do you think?"

Hardly waiting to hear my answer, he continued enthusiastically: "I'll phone Noe and tell her about my idea."

What could I have against all this? We had the time. And Ray knew what would do him good. His ideas went even further.

"All three of us could travel further on, to spend Christmas with your sister. Ordi would certainly be pleased if we did that."

"That's for sure. She loves having visitors for Christmas. But that would mean that we would be travelling for a month. What about your physical condition? Wouldn't it be too much for you? What I mean is: can you really recover with a programme like that?"

Ray was always optimistic and answered accordingly. In his head, he was planning a lengthy trip to the States. Noe was the first person he phoned. She shouted jubilantly over the phone.

"Super, Dad! I'll show you what New York is like in the time before Christmas!"

My sister, too, was endlessly pleased at the idea of celebrating Christmas together. It was a time when she felt lonely, as her husband had died a few years previously. They had been shopping on a Saturday afternoon, when said he would like to lie down and rest. My sister first sorted out the shopping. When she went into the bedroom a bit later, she found her husband dead. It was very hard for my sister to overcome this shock. And as they hadn't had any children, she was only happy to have visitors each year.

Now my husband had succeeded in making Noe, my sister and me happy all in one go. I was pleased to be there when his travelling desires went into fulfilment. We would celebrate Christmas and New Year all together. I was specially looking forward to that. We were fortunate to be served by an excellent woman at our travel agency, who did our bookings and all the formalities in record time. Ray had about two weeks left to recover from the last chemotherapy before our flight over the Big Pond.

Noe also made preparations. She rented a small room for us near her students' hostel. She was waiting for us in front of this house, as our taxi drove up in the early evening. She was shivering from the cold, but the joy of seeing us again was great. We spent a long time in each other's arms. Our faces were radiant! We were more than happy to be together again.

We quickly settled in our room and then hurried out with Noe, to experience New York by night. It was just before Christmas. There was newly fallen snow on the streets, adding a romantic note to this town of millions of inhabitants.

The three of us laughed together and were so joyful that our happiness at being together could be seen and heard by all. Our daughter led us through a suburb with very small houses that looked nice and comfortable, built with red bricks. The window frames and the doors seemed to have been painted white just recently. Each of them was decorated in its own way for Christmas with lights, which made the sugary snow on the trees and bushes in their gardens sparkle. On a small square with bushes, plants and benches to rest on, a choir was singing Christmas carols, and we spontaneously hummed along with them.

"Isn't it lovely here?"

"Enchanting! Just look at that. I would not have expected to find so much nature and romance in New York."

We repeatedly stopped to admire something, embraced each other or enthusiastically pointed out imaginative details on the houses, their gardens and the streets in this part of the city. Ray was in his best form again.

"It's all so unreal! The week before last you were lying in the day clinic and now you are standing in front of the biggest Christmas tree in New York, holding your wife and daughter in your arms."

We held firmly on to each other and our faces beamed as much as the lights on the Christmas tree. The days in New York passed quickly and it was though we were on Cloud X. Noe showed us her favourite places, the university where she was studying, her students' hostel, her favourite cafe and her favourite restaurant. On the following day, we strolled through Central Park, which she just loved, and enjoyed the fresh snow, which gave the trees and paths a layer of sugar. Of course, we did not forget to visit the Statue of Liberty, Brooklyn Bridge and Wall Street. We never got tired.

On our last day, a Sunday morning, Noe took us out to a typical American restaurant for breakfast with pancakes, butter, ham and syrup. "You must experience this," she said. Ray loved sweet things and ordered a second portion of pancakes.

"Noe, these three days in New York with you were splendid," said her father proudly. "We'll being seeing each other again during the next days." Ray and I flew to Cleveland, to my sister. Noe wanted to come by bus and join us there just before Christmas. She had events to go to at the university, and did not want to miss them.

My sister fetched us from the airport in her car. We did not see her at first. It was not until I noticed a huge poster fastened to the inside of her windscreen with "Welcome" on it that I ran up to her. We embraced each other heartily.

"Cheers! Welcome!" he had brought cool champagne and champagne glasses with her.

"To beautiful days together! Thank you for the invitation."

When her car turned into her driveway, there was a surprise for us. Her house, surrounded by an enormous garden, was decorated for Christmas. The fresh snow and the lights glittered together.

"This is the first time I have decorated my house since Will died," she told us with tears in her eyes. Amazed, we went into the rooms that were decorated with fir twigs, red candles and red Christmas tree balls. Ray had laid his arm round my sister.

"You can have my bedroom and bathroom. Noe and I will use the two rooms upstairs."

"How nice of her to give us the most special rooms," Ray said to me before going to sleep.

"She is simply a caring, older sister," I replied.

In my sister's house, Ray felt more and more at peace. Again and again, he retired to the bedroom and slept.

"He's suffering from intestinal pains," I explained to my sister, who was surprised that Ray withdrew so often. She spoiled him with Christmas cookies, which she got out time and again. Ray grabbed them. He also loved Ordi's cooking and had a big appetite. We were also hungry and also indulged in second helpings.

"It's good for him to eat so much. No matter what. It builds him up. He looks rather weakened." We talked together while he was asleep. "You mustn't say that to him, because he doesn't like hearing it. Ray keeps quiet about anything that is unpleasant." My sister gave me an understanding look and nodded.

On the appointed day, we were joined by Noe. My sister fetched her from the bus station.

"Now we're all here. Wonderful!" With these words, I invited people to come and eat. We had mashed potatoes with broccoli and steamed salmon. Anyone could see how we were enjoying sitting round the table together, our faces radiant. That did not happen so often, as we lived in different continents.

"What about going for a hike tomorrow through the woods with the winter snow!"

Ray gave me a look of surprise, as if he had wanted to do something more comfortable. But Ordi and Noe voted in favour, so Ray was outvoted.

About a quarter of an hour's drive away from my sister's house there was a wide belt of woodland, a nature reserve with a lot of possible walks, going right round the town. In the days before, according to my sister, it had snowed uninterruptedly with large flakes, which formed a white layer on the meadows and paths. That was reason enough to make snowballs out of the powdery snow and to start a snowball match. Noe and I started. Ray and Ordi could do nothing else but defend themselves by running after us. We fell down in the snow and laughed.

Powered out and with wet coats, we reached the house and decided to have a hike every day. Well wrapped up, we walked each morning through the dream woods with their deep snow. Sometimes the snow was blown up like a cloud of flour while we were walking. We were not always as lively as on the first day. Sometimes we enjoyed the silence of the snow landscape, which prepared us for Christmas.

"Winter can be so beautiful!"

"Yes,"answered my sister with conviction. "You don't expect to find so much untouched nature surrounding a big town."

"You are not only surrounded by this wonderful nature. You can also make use of all the cultural offers to be found in a big town. The art gallery with splendid works by international artists, the Rock and Roll Hall of Fame with its super exhibitions on aspects of the pop culture, gigantic sports stadiums with spectacular events, the Natural History Museum with life-sized dinosaurs and the Botanic Garden with its tropical garden." Our daughter loved big towns above all else.

"There is even a Hofbraeuhouse here!" laughed Ray.

Christmas was getting nearer. On the afternoon of Christmas Eve we all worked together in the kitchen to prepare our Christmas menu. My sister had bought lobster, and would put her efforts mainly into the main course. Ray and I would prepare a creamy sweet chestnut soup, flavoured with winter spices like cardamom, cinnamon and cloves. Noe would prepare the sauce for the salad and cut the vegetables for the salad. While she was snipping at the salad ingredients, she kept looking expectantly into the living room, where the fire was flickering and the presents were waiting under the Christmas tree. We assumed that she could not wait for the presents to be opened and joked about it.

The sweet chestnut soup tasted fantastic, Ordi removed the lobster from the shell like an expert and put the delicate, white meat on the plate. It went well with the salad.

"A delightful Christmas meal," we all agreed. Then we cautiously walked into the living-room that was full of light. The candles on the Christmas tree made the presents beneath them glitter. They were all wrapped in red and gold or blue and silver paper. My sister's place had the most presents on it.

"Off we go! Don't you want to know what's in your parcels?" She challenged us. Of course, we were curious and opened the presents.

"Thank you," Ray whispered enthusiastically, as he unpacked a scarf his daughter had knitted herself and proudly wrapped it round his neck.

"It really suits you," I praised it immediately.

Noe was joyfully holding a coloured bracelet with matching earrings from her aunt in her hands. We had given her different cosmetics made from natural materials.

The biggest present of all was for my sister. A painting of the market place, our favourite café and the chapel we were married in, painted by our town's special artist.

"What a wonderful reminder of my original home!" she said after she had unpacked the picture and held it up.

"Now the only present left is mine for you," she observed, and pointed to an envelope. Noe quickly took it and opened it. As she read it, her eyes widened!

"Come on, read it to us!" I could hardly wait. "What does it say?"

"Invitation to our trip to Sarasota, Florida, to a cottage by the sea, all of us together"

Noe jumped for joy. "Yeahhh! But you can't be serious."

"I'm speechless!" Ray went up to my sister and embraced her. "That is a wonderful idea!" he said, smiling at her. "My dear sister-in-law, it seems you're not interested in counting the cost. Thank you very, very much."

Ordi blushed a little, just as she used to in adolescence when someone had paid her a compliment. "That's OK; I'm also doing it for myself. I like to feel warm. And I've hardly been on holiday for the last few years."

A few days later, we packed our cases, drove at a temperature well below zero and through thick snow to the airport, which was covered with snow. We made our way through the fresh layer of snow to the terminal. The flight was delayed, as the plane was not ready because it had to have ice removed from it.

"The weather can only get better," was my sister's opinion. She was right, as in two hours we got out of the plane beneath a clear, blue sky. I stood on the runway, stretching my arms high up to the sky. "Thank you, God, for this present!"

"The snow in Cleveland was lovely, but the warmth here is cosier than powdery snow," Ray observed.

At the Sarasota Airport, we rented a car, as our cottage was a bit outside the town, by the beach. And we also wanted to see something of the town and its surroundings. After we had reached our cottage by the beach, we just left our cases there and hurried out.

"What a pleasant feeling on the soles of my feet!" I shouted, turning my feet round in the warm sand. "You try it out!"

It must have looked most unusual, as we stood next to each other barefoot, just radiant with happiness, looking towards the blue sea. The sky had turned orange and red in the meantime, with delicate clouds passing through the evening sky.

"This natural theatre competes with what goes on inside a theatrical building. And we can watch it barefoot, warming our feet in the sand."

"It tickles in such a pleasant way," Ray laughed, burying his feet deeper in the sand.

The first days of our holiday passed quickly. We went for walks on the beach, went swimming in the pool, lazed around on the beach with its fine sand, looking over the calm sea into the endless distance and dreaming. Ray sat apart from us in a deck chair, reading a book. We fully understood that he needed peace and quiet.

Late in the afternoons, we strolled around in the town, looking for a suitable restaurant for our evening meal, then strolling past an endless number of shops, or resting on the benches in the parks with their many brightly coloured flowers. On one cloudy afternoon, we went to a world-famous circus museum, which presented original turns from the circus world of the last century. Noe ran on ahead and squeezed her way into a miniature car.

"Quick! Take a photo," Ordi laughed and Ray obliged, all of us laughing.

On another day, when it was raining, we went to a research station for marine animals. It was super to watch sea horses, sharks, rays and saltwater terrapins so closely.

Before the sun went down Ray and I walked to the beach to enjoy the sunset as an intimate twosome.

"Looking into the vastness, without a care, and watching the sun go down is a very special experience," Ray said to me. This sentence touched me, it shook my ominous sadness. As a reflex action, I took a deep breath and felt better straight away.

"Please don't let the sun go down on both of us, God," my inner voice pleaded, as my head lay on Ray's shoulder, our breathing and bodily movements coming into the same rhythm, as if we were one. I felt a deep love for him and especially enjoyed moments like this. "It's just wonderful to sit here with you, Ray."

Ray turned his head towards me, kissed me and stroked my face gently. I felt surrounded by happiness.

"Come, let's enjoy a glass of red wine together," a voice called from behind. Ordi rushed over to us with a bottle of red wine and four glasses. Noe, too, who had been watching the sunset from a deck chair nearby, came over the sand to us at the sight of the bottle of red wine.

"Yes, of course!" was her answer, grinning and holding her hand out to her aunt. With the bottle in the middle, we sat next to each other in the sand, commenting on the colourful spectacle on the horizon. The sun had almost set, we were absorbed in our conversation, hardly noticing that it was getting dark. I kept on observing Ray. I was surprised at his vitality. He looked really well. The last glowing rays of the evening sun made his face look reddish brown. Involuntarily, I started to think about Bali, our evening walks in the north part of the island. Then we just lived according to what each day had to offer, as we both felt healthy. We ended each day with a walk and from the sand, observing the last rays of sun behind the sea. And after that, we strolled back to the village, looking out for a cosy restaurant. On one of these evenings, we discovered a restaurant where a small band was playing romantic songs. It inspired us to sing the songs we knew quietly with them.

My sister suddenly asked: "Which of you will come with me for an early morning walk on the beach?" This brought me back to Sarasota's beach.

"What! An early morning walk on the beach?" I asked in surprise, as Noe was declining the offer, as she liked to sleep in.

"I'll do the same as my daughter," answered Ray, so it was up to me.

"OK, then I'll walk with you. Knock on the door of our room when you're ready to go." I had no difficulty in getting up, as I usually wake up with the sun, as I had been used to from childhood onwards. We had a tradition of getting up early even on Sundays for a hike in the woods.

Once, when I asked my father why we started our hikes in the morning, he gave the reason that the air was fresh in the mornings, the birds singing at their best and it was easier to observe the animals in the woods. And I believed him.

My sister and I set off just after sunrise. The sea was calm in the early hours of morning, shimmering in a tone of blue. The early morning sun made the white sand look orange.

Apart from us, there was hardly anyone walking along the water's edge at that time. We did not get very far, as every few yards we found interesting shells which had been brought up by the sea during the night. We picked up the best ones to take with us.

As though he were waiting for us, Ray was sitting on the terrace when we returned. "Good morning, both of you," he said, smiling, and admiring our treasures. My sister proudly laid them all out on the top of the wooden fence on the terrace.

"And what shall we do with them when we leave here?" he asked.

"We'll leave them here for the next people to enjoy,"was my sister's idea. I shook my head disapprovingly.

"No, Ray, I'll take the best ones home and put them into the glass bowl with the fine white sand in it, as a souvenir of our wonderful holiday here."

My husband suspected he would not get this idea out of my head, so put on a friendly smile. As an act of reconciliation, I went up to him and kissed him on the lips. "Good morning, my dear. Have you slept well?"

He stood up, took me by the hand and led me back to the white, sandy beach, quickly at first, then more slowly.

"I'd like to grow old together with you, my love."

I looked at him tenderly. I felt my heart melting. With these same words he had proposed to me some years previously. But this time, I felt a big lump of sadness coming up inside me. "God, give us many more years together. Please!" I prayed secretly while my husband gently pressed me to him. I lay my head on his chest, feeling the beating of his heart. We started to breathe in the same rhythm while we were so close together.

"Does the sand under your feet give you a prickly feeling?" I asked, turning in a slightly different direction.

"Yes, it does tickle." I felt uneasy; the lump of sadness was getting active. I turned back to my husband and asked: "How are you?" hoping for an honest answer.

"I'm in the best form, my dear. I love you."

"And I love you, too. Very much."

We looked into each other's eyes, stroking each other gently. I felt a rumbling deep inside me. I just had to talk to somebody about my feeling.

In the afternoon, there was an opportunity to talk to my sister about my fears and anxieties, on another walk on the beach.

"I really can't understand why Ray, despite his serious illness, appears to be so light-hearted and stable, and even looks hopefully into the future. What is your impression? Do you think he has changed? With people you see every day, you don't notice changes so much." There was a fairly long pause, my sister then stopped walking and took a deep breath.

"You know that I wish him better health with all my heart, and many further years together for both of you. But, if I'm honest, I'm worried about him. He has lost weight, needs a lot more rests and I have the strong impression that he's suppressing his pains."

There was another pause, in which I took a deep breath.

"Yes, you could be right that he's getting slower and is having more rests. That is my impression, too."

"Just think: more than two years have passed since the diagnosis. The chemo destroys the cancer cells, but also healthy cells. And then there are the operations. How many has he already had? Each operation makes him weaker. The body must regenerate, because the next chemotherapy is due, which brings him back to square one."

I was aware that my sister felt close to Ray, despite the many miles between us.

"You're right. The next chemo is due as soon as we get back. I'm wondering how I can support him to help him to get his normal strength back again. We do think about our daily food, our daily exercise in fresh air, a good mood, laughter, relaxation exercises every morning and evening. But one thing bothers me: that Ray follows the doctors' advice. Yes, I do know that he must independently make the final decisions on everything concerning his body."

106

"Yes. That's obvious. Nobody knows better what's right for him than his own body."

After a pause, she advised me: "I can only tell you both: Enjoy your lives. Make the most of your time together, do your best and don't lose your optimism."

"It isn't always easy to do that, as I'm sure you know, too. I'm just so sorry for Ray."

"Yes, he is a wonderful person!"

"I've married a wonderful person!"

We both laughed out loud at the compliments, deciding to move away from the serious subject. We ran up to calf level into the water and splashed each other.

On the way back, I was overcome with the urge to thank my sister once again for her generous Christmas present.

"The days here are doing us all the world of good, and that is mostly because of you. I'm sure I'm speaking for Ray and Noe, too."

My sister ignored the praise, as she usually did. But I was sure that she was secretly pleased about it. She quickly changed the subject: "Can you believe that a few days ago we were making our way through deep snow, well wrapped up to keep out the cold? And our noses were frozen. Isn't it super to be here, where it's warm? I'm glad that you came with me. Without you, I'd have stayed at home.

The days beneath Florida's sun passed on like the clouds over the sea. It was sad to have to say "Good-bye".

Back in the cold north of the United States, we felt the felt the extreme cold. But just the same, we went for daily walks through the snow of the wintry forest and were pleased to warm up afterwards by the wood stove. But that did not last long.

"Beautiful days also come to an end," Ray started his farewell speech. It was not easy to say "Good-bye" to each other. We made it sweeter with a glass of champagne, with which we toasted my sister and thanked her repeatedly. I felt our holiday together had been a more intensive experience we had been more grateful for, and thought it was probably because of Ray's illness.

The first days at home were hard for us. We missed Ordi and Noe very much. Our daughter was staying in New York for another two months. However, everyday life inevitably started again. Ray had to have a blood test and then an appointment to find out the results.As usual, Ray was told: "You can be satisfied with the results. Just the same, we recommend you to have the next chemotherapy.

That did not seem to bother Ray much, but I was not happy about it. This time, there was an extra complication with his rectum. The doctors suggested an operation. I could have groaned audibly:

"Isn't that ever going to stop?" However, I did not dare to ask that, so, instead, I enquired about what this would mean.

"They will remove a part of the lower intestine. Then they started to talk about a temporary enteric stoma."

"About what?"

"About an artificial anus."

"Oh," I audibly took a deep breath. "Will you give me more of the details?"

After supper, my poor husband informed me of all the details, sounding rather nervous about it all. "I'm sorry about that, Ray. But you'll get through it all right. I'll stand by your side." I was trying to sound convincing and added: "Let us continue to look confidently into the future. Life is too valuable to be spent worrying."

Ray accepted the next available appointment for the operation. I was restless all day until a phone call came with a short message to say that everything had gone well. I drove off immediately to stand at his side and was relieved to see him smiling, when he saw me.

"Noe has already phoned," he said joyfully. I held his hand and stroked his heated cheeks.

"Soon everything will be all right."

Ray changed the subject. "Tomorrow a lady specialist is coming to help me to practise using the stoma. Would you come, too, please?"

"Yes, of course!" Despite agreeing instinctively, I had a strange feeling. I had no idea of what I would be having to do. An artificial anus was not exactly a pleasant thought. Ray mentioned that the hospital staff had assured him that it was clean. I laughed because I felt I had been caught in the act.

Our nervousness was noticeable before the lady came into the room. She seemed to notice it und very sensitively and patiently told us all about stomas, before calmly practising each movement with us. Then it was our turn. The first few times I was rather helpless, as Ray also was. But the next time I was in the clinic, the artificial anus had become part of our lives.

"I must give you special praise for your achievement, my darling." To confirm what I had said, I kissed him on the cheek. Indeed, I admired his patience and endurance with which he was going through with his cancer and all its consequences.

"The examinations showed that the operation was a success. In order to regenerate, they are granting me a few weeks without chemotherapy." He sounded relieved about that, when he told me this news after an appointment with the doctor. We embraced each other joyfully. Unfortunately, it was not yet possible to dance.

To celebrate the news, I cooked a tasty meal. Ray had asked for boiled beef with horseradish sauce and cranberries. We drank with it a bottle of our good bio-wine from the Palatinate.

"And what shall we do on the days without chemotherapy?" I asked him, as we were sitting on the sofa together before going to bed. "What do you fancy doing?"

"Resting a lot, going for a walk now and again, some relaxation and, of course, a good meal."

We spent the next days as he had wished. It was obvious that Ray had recovered from this operation. He quickly gained weight; his complexion looked fresher and slightly brown from our daily walks. The pains were soon forgotten and he started to look hopefully into the future.

Spring had come, and with it new energy. Noe had returned from her semester in New York and we enjoyed our happiness at being together again, spending days and evenings together.

"What do you think about having a big celebration this summer?" My words surprised them both. "Today I phoned my sister in the USA. This year, she will be seventy. And we, darling, will be sixty this year! Isn't that a good reason for celebrating?"

I could see by their grins that father and daughter were both in favour.

"I see, you approve of the idea. Let's collect our different ideas in the next days."

That gave us an aim that we could be enthusiastic about and work for. We soon found out that Ray would not be having chemotherapy in the month of July. We could use this free time for this purpose. We quickly agreed that we could invite good friends and relatives to a brunch. Then they could all sleep in on the Sunday and have enough time to get back home in the evening. Someone or other gave us the idea of having it on a bio- farm in a small village not far away. "They serve good quality food, some of it they grow themselves according to Demeter standards. And they cook and bake everything themselves."

Ray and I thought that was a very good idea. Noe also knew the farm and her opinion was: "I like the spacious terrace, the stables and meadows with their hares, goats and cows. Can you remember that?"

We nodded. We had cycled there from time to time. We decided to do that again. On a weekend when we were all free, we cycled on country roads to the farm and ordered something to eat. After the first bite, we agreed that we would ask if they would reserve the date in July for our celebration. That was successful. The next time we were there, we talked about the drinks, the buffet and the programme.

Noe said she would make an invitation card on her computer with a photo of us on it. After a brief consultation with Ordi, we agreed on the text, which would have in it: the reason for the celebration, the venue, time and some further information: "We would be pleased for you to make a contribution to our celebration. Rather than presents, please give us donations for a children's hospice near here."

The nearer the month of the celebration came, the greater was our anticipation of it. Nearly all the guests had accepted the invitation and some had offered to contribute to the programme.

A week before the time, my sister arrived from the USA.

"This will be our first celebration together," she said. "I'm really looking forward to seeing all our cousins and old friends."

"This Sunday is being true to its name," Noe announced on the morning of the celebration, as the sun was shining with its full, smiling face. The flowerbeds around the farm glowed in the light, against the contrast from the beige sunshades. We rushed around to welcome our guests as they gradually came in and drank to our celebration day with a glass of champagne. In the background, a friend of ours was playing French chansons on his accordion.

"Sunshine, street music and happy guests, that is a wonderful start to our day," my sister whispered into my ear. And indeed, the day was fantastic. Everyone who came contributed to the success of the day with their good humour and creative points on the programme. The delicious and delightfully served buffet was enjoyed by all.

I observed Ray, who was feeling very much at home in the midst of his relatives and friends and yet again enjoyed being the centre of attention. And that, even though his body was showing signs of weakness. At that point of time, he had lost weight considerably. His cheeks were not as bulging as usual. Yet my dear husband was enjoying being the secret star of the birthday celebration, not because of the musical, documentary and sung contributions that were to his honour, but also because his relatives and friends were admiring the sovereign way he was coping with his illness.

"Thank God we didn't have to clear it all up," said Ray on the way home. He was happy, but very tired, which was why we had decided to conclude the day on our terrace in deck chairs.

"My journey here has been worthwhile, if only for our birthday celebration. It did me the world of good to meet the relatives and friends again." Ordi's smile also showed she was thinking about the good company and experiences. We nodded our agreement.

Unfortunately, our daughter had to leave the next day to go back to her university. My sister stayed for another week, which we spent mostly quietly at home. We went on short excursions and were sometimes invited to friends' houses. We drove her to the airport together. "Yet another farewell," she sighed, near to tears.

For us, everyday life started again. Ray's appointments had not started again. One morning he surprised me at breakfast time with the news that he felt like going on an easy cycle tour.

"Are you serious about that?"

Apparently, my dear husband had already thought of something specific. "Yes. Why not? I'd like to cycle along the River Werra. I've been interested in this area for a long time, because there are a few places of old historical interest -there. You needn't worry about my health. We'll take it slowly, and then it will be all right. I'm sure about that."

I already had the impression that nothing would induce my husband to give up this intention. There would also be no point in that, I thought secretly, so my answer was: "OK, if you think so."

A few days later, we packed our cycling bags, put the bikes onto the cycle trailer and drove by car to the eastern part of Germany. The day before we had booked a room in a small, recently renovated castle, situated on a hill with a wide view of the landscape around the Werra. It also had a restaurant, which served products from their own bio- farm.

Short time after we got there, we already were sitting in the castle's restaurant enjoying a fantastic meal from the organic farm that was a part of this property. We were excited about this wonderful place we had discovered by chance.

"What about riding in the steps of Martin Luther tomorrow?" I was yet again amazed at my husband's ideas and just nodded.

Straight after breakfast, we cycled through delightful landscapes to the city of Eisenach. We went up the steep hill to the Wartburg slowly, on foot. We had plenty of stops to enjoy the view.

Each evening, we planned a new tour and made sure it was something we could easily manage. My sick husband coped with each day's programme very well. Only once we went back by train, as it might have been too much for him. For the last day of our short holiday, we chose an interesting route, where there was a small church that had been important in the struggles of the Reformation. An old schoolmaster, who was in charge of the key, unexpectedly gave us a most interesting guided tour, telling us all about the history. He told us about a pulpit that we would be passing. It was hewn into a rock face. It was said that Thomas Muentzer had preached there. Full of enthusiasm, we cycled back.

While Ray seemed to be perfectly all right, my thoughts kept on returning to his intestinal illness. I could see the sword of Damocles hovering over us, and then got annoyed at allowing myself to be distracted.

"Why can't I succeed in being content with the songs of the birds, the insects and wayside flowers? Why do my eyes see Ray's physical complaints and observe him so fearfully? That helps neither of us."

The result was that I tried to concentrate on the countless beautiful moments and to be happy about them. I also resolved to start meditating regularly, which we had been neglecting lately.

"What about starting to meditate regularly again?" Ray thought that would be a good idea. We took time for it in the mornings and the evenings. After each meditation, I prayed to God, thanking Him for all good things we were experiencing and asking for His blessing. That was a relief for me, giving me strength and peace, both of which were necessary, as Ray was already starting with the medical processes: chemotherapy, a break, the next blood test, consultation, the next treatment. The result was a weak physical condition.

I had my doubts about this mechanical rhythm, but did not want to tell Ray so. Because he was enduring the torture stoically, although he was needing increasingly longer breaks from the therapies and was sometimes so weak on his legs during a treatment phase, that he occasionally took a walking stick with him just for a walk round the block.

My support consisted of providing a good mood and good nutrition, and making sure he had fresh air and exercise. Ray contributed to the good mood, as he refused to let all the treatments get him down.

Surprisingly, he quickly recovered from these physically stressful times, wanting to do something special in the breaks. Each time, he had a new suggestion: "Do you know where I'd like to go to in the autumn?" He waited for my reaction. "To Morocco."

My eyes turned. "Are you quite sure?"

"Yes, I always wanted to go to the oriental market in Marrakech, the desert towns and the sand dunes."

"And do you feel strong enough to carry out this plan?" I was not so sure, although Ray had not taken on too much with this trip. For it was always Ray, who said what he wanted to do each time. He discussed his plan with his doctor, who thought that if he had recovered from the chemotherapy, and his blood tests were in order, then nothing would speak against this journey.

Ray reached his goal. He used the time spent recovering to plan the journey. He decided for a two-week, organised trip, the first week being a guided bus tour through the mountains of Morocco, starting from Marrakech to the sand dunes, which he wanted to walk over. For the second part of the holiday, we booked a wonderful hotel by the beach.

The flight to Agadir was pleasant. We soon occupied our room by the beach, with a view over the sea. We walked leisurely, arm in arm, along the promenade in the evening, taking a small meal and going to bed early, as the bus trip would be starting on the following morning.

The first stop, an overnight one, was at Marrakech. First, we followed the guide through the sights of the town. In the early evening, we had free time on the famous town square. Gradually, lights were switched on which enveloped the square – and us - in a mystical light, which transported us into the world of storytellers, artists and musicians, flute-playing snake charmers and stalls selling the country's culinary specialities. We absorbed all of it, stayed for a long time, observing the different way of life with great interest. The many different earth-coloured spice stalls and the many different sorts of fruit were fascinating. We were continually amazed. Ray was feeling very well! Later on, we were immersed in the interesting world of Souks with a thousand tradesmen begging for our favour. The lanes were becoming narrower. We were beginning to think we had lost our way. But we found our way back to the central square, just the same.

The next morning, Ray enticed me back to the Souks. This time, we followed our German-speaking guide who bargained good prices for the little souvenirs we wanted to buy.

Ray was getting what he wanted. He showed himself at his best. The week's bus trip in a small bus with a lot of room and pleasant travelling companions was something he could cope with very well. Nobody in the group noticed anything about his precarious health condition, and we found no reason for talking about it. But I kept my eagle eye on my husband and supported him. I was amazed at the way he went out of himself. He seemed to be relaxed all the time, was brown and as radiant as the sun.

While we were riding in the bus, we sat together holding hands like two people who had just fallen in love, watching the fascinating scenery passing by the big windows of the bus. Everything was just fantastic: the viewpoints, the palaces, the desert towns, the food in the beautifully situated restaurants on our way, the small hotels we spent the nights in. At the end of the journey, he walked slowly up the dunes, enjoying every step of the way, proud at having reached his goal. He sat on a sand dune and admired the sunset he had been dreaming about.

In the second week of our holiday in Morocco, we enjoyed the peace and quiet in the small beach hotel. It was perfect for us. We felt very much at home there. Ray loved taking a coffee in one of the niches in the big hotel garden, proudly wearing his new, bright red t-shirt with "Morocco" written on it.

"I simply must take a photo of you, Ray. Your t-shirt suits you so well," I called, pressing the button. We laughed at the photo of the Morocco fan smiling and sipping his coffee.

This journey through Morocco is something I will ever forget, particularly because I was able to share such significant experiences with Ray. Perhaps this was so important to me because I sensed that that might have been our last long journey together. It was no longer possible to overlook his illness that was at an advanced stage. In the background, the sword of Damocles was still hovering over us.

Enjoy being together!

We defy the illness and celebrate life

Our tradition was to celebrate the resurrection of Christ on Easter Sunday with friends. Our friend of many years' standing, Phil, and his wife, Ria, were our hosts. Over the years, we had all got to know each other well and often got together for a meal.

The centre of our Easter celebration was a sumptuous breakfast with all sorts of tasty things, from homemade German sweet bread, jam made from fruits out of the garden, the usual eggs, ham, cheese, to the Easter champagne with which we started the Easter breakfast. In the centre of the round table by the big window with a view over a vast landscape, there was always a bunch of daffodils. We sang songs together, read suitable texts to each other and talked about God and the world.

In the midst of such an intensive conversation, my husband raised his voice and said: "I would like to give you all an advance invitation to celebrate my seventieth birthday."

I looked up in surprise, and the others were surprised, too. Our conversations came to an end. And on our faces could be read: "But we celebrated your sixtieth birthday only last year."

Nobody dared say that aloud. We just gave puzzled looks. For Ray's body did not look at all good. He had visibly lost weight, his upper abdomen was puffed up, his complexion was grey, and his cheeks hollow, with the cheekbones protruding.

When we were greeting our friends on arrival, I noticed them looking anxiously at him. But now, he was radiant with a confidence that banished all questions.

I felt the same way. I did not have the courage to talk to my husband about his physical changes because I was afraid I would be told something that would be painful for me.

Ray mentioned that the doctors were talking about bone metastases, but this statement was somewhat vague. He also mentioned that he was going to go to a clinic where the growth of his tumour cells could be stopped with a hypothermic therapy.

"With what?"

"They explained to me that with a hypothermic therapy on a part of the body the whole abdominal area is overheated. If I'm fortunate, all the cancer cells die off, also the bone metastases."

"That sounds promising," I said, relieved to know that there was a further chance of surviving it all. And as my husband seemed to be so sure of himself, we did not ask any more questions. But deep down inside, I did have further questions:

"What does it look like inside him?" kept buzzing through my head. Ray was not prone to complaining, was never discontented, always seemed to be looking on the bright side, and I went along with this. We continued to enjoy the happy moments. And so, for Valentine's Day we had booked a "dinner for two" at a beautiful hotel and looked forward to the day. We had dressed in elegant clothes and walked proudly, arm in arm, across the market place to our dinner. That evening, we had celebrated our love, even though it seemed rather corny, but we smiled.

"My darling, I love you!" Our glasses had jingled in tune to the soft background music. We felt as though we had just fallen in love and enjoyed being together as a twosome in the midst of other couples.

And now, just a few weeks after that Valentine's Day, in the presence of our friends, Ray blurted out his invitation to his seventieth birthday. I was rather irritated, held my breath, and wondered what Ray was alluding to. Was it an indirect reference to his death?

But he was talking about life, about a celebration that would take place much later on. The silence at the table continued. Most probably, Ray had noticed the surprised faces around him, for he added to his sentence:

"Well, of course, I'll also be celebrating my sixty-fifth birthday."

We looked relieved as Ray told us about further plans: "In two months' time there will be another celebration: my only niece is getting married. I'm specially looking forward to that."

Our faces then relaxed and we all smiled at Ray. I involuntarily made use of the situation to move my chair as unobtrusively as possible so I would not be in Ray's field of vision, as I knew he would be looking at me. He was certainly expecting to see happy agreement on my face, but I was not feeling that way, I felt more like crying. His birthday invitation had aroused all the signals inside me. Suddenly, I became aware of his impending death. I was seized with a panic and thoughts came, like: "I cannot imagine life without him! How can my life go on? We spend days and nights together, share joy and suffering. We belong together." In order to deflect these questions, I involuntarily grabbed a piece of the freshly baked sweet bread from the middle of the table, emphatically praising the woman who had made it so early in the morning.

"It's wonderful, the way you have made the dough so light, and the almond slices on top! My deepest respect!"

The others continued in the same way. "Phil, have you been to the farmers' shop again and selected the cheese and ham so tastefully?" He nodded benevolently, stood up and fetched the bottle of champagne from the fridge. "I'm afraid I forgot that we hadn't toasted to start the meal!" Our champagne glasses jingled as if to remind us it was spring.

"Your health! To this Easter morning and our time together. May we spend many more Easter mornings together!" That changed the mood. It became merrier. Phil and Ria read Easter texts and spring poems aloud to us. Eric sat at the piano and accompanied our Easter songs that we sang in harmony.

Ray was in good form when the conversation concerned current political topics. He forgot everything else around him, reported different things and lectured on them.

It was 2.00 pm when I started feeling tired. "We could go on a circular tour round the fields," said Ray. I was amazed at his energy.

"Well, that's a good idea," Phil said in confirmation.

A short time later, we were strolling along the paths between the fields towards the next village, still talking together. I turned round to have a look at my husband who was absorbed in talking politics with Phil, as I was worried about him. "Shouldn't we start to go back?" I asked him.

"My dear, we can just continue walking," he said, removing my concerns.

"It's amazing how fit Ray is today," I told the women I was walking with.

"That's because he enjoys talking to his friends so much."

Freshened by the spring breeze, we got back to the place we had started from, embraced each other by way of farewell, wishing each other all the best. "Another happy day together!" was our unanimous opinion.

In the evening, before going to sleep, my thoughts went through the events of the day. I was feeling refreshed in every way. But in one small corner of my feelings I was aware of the lump coming from mourning and an omen that cast a shadow on it all.

Close together until death!

We are active and encourage others to be active with us

Easter Monday morning was a lovely day with blue sky and sunshine. Ray and I had already got up early. I went to the window and pointed at the delicate tones of light red and yellow that were driving the dark of night away.

"Look at this wonderful morning sky, Ray, fitting for an Easter Monday morning!"

"Yes, it seems it will be a nice day."

Together, we gazed at the morning sky, then packed our bags for our short holiday in the Black Forest. Just as we did every year, we had booked a few days in a hotel at the edge of the forest, near Lake Titisee. We loved this hotel with its different kinds of baths, saunas and the opportunity of early-morning yoga. Here, too, we set off each morning to hike through the pinewoods.

"I will drive. So you can relax, my dear."

My husband was pleased to agree; he looked tired. I suspected it was after-effects from the day before, because he went to sleep as soon as I had driven off. As could be expected, it was a very pleasant drive. Just before our journey's end, I stopped by a fresh, light green meadow, which was typical of the Black Forest.

"Come, let us throw our Easter eggs on this meadow," I said, waking my husband with a laugh. I loved this Easter custom from my childhood days: happily throwing the Easter eggs we had found on our Easter walk onto the fresh, spring meadows, continuing until they were broken. The winner was the person whose egg remained unbroken the longest. Ray had got used to this custom.

We got out of the car, smelt the fresh, warm spring air. I ran over the meadow and threw my egg as high as I could over the grass.

"Yoo-hoo! Success! A good throw!" was my comment on my throw. My egg, that had been coloured bright red, came down from the blue sky and landed undamaged on the meadow. Ray stood beside it and observed me.

"Come on, Ray, it's your turn!" I called to him, getting ready for a second throw. Ray's egg went straight up into the sky, fell down and broke into a hundred pieces. I laughed out loud, while Ray looked disappointed.

"It doesn't matter! You can have my egg, and we'll take turns to throw it up."

As we were throwing our Easter eggs, I noticed Ray's slow movements, but because I was feeling so well myself, I did not give it any further thought. Full of the joys of childhood, I drove the rest of the way to the hotel.

"Oh, how lovely that is!", I said, beaming, on arrival, in my mind already stretching in the hotel's wellness oasis. "Let's move into our room quickly, put on our dressing gowns, and then off we go to the swimming bath and the saunas."

I was so absorbed in my anticipation that I was late in noticing the silence surrounding Ray. "Why aren't you sharing my joy over our safe arrival, the pleasant journey and all the sunshine?" I asked Ray, disappointed because he was showing no outward signs of joy. Something or other was not in order.

"I'm rather tired, Chris. Everything is fine. I'm also pleased to be here."

I registered his unusual behaviour only subconsciously. At that point of time I could not make anything of it.

"You go on ahead, I'll join you later," he suggested while I was putting my dressing gown on.

"All right. I'll wait for you down in the rest area." I rushed out of the room, swam several rounds in the outdoor pool, relaxed in the steam grotto and then nodded off to sleep in the deck chair.

"He hasn't come yet."

I sat up anxiously, hurried back to our room and found Ray in a deep sleep. I noticed how hollow his cheeks were. I was seized with fear and felt helpless, wondering if Ray would give me an honest answer. Most probably, he would say that everything was all right, but it definitely was not all right. I decided to sit beside him and read a book while waiting for him to wake up. When he woke up, my husband beamed at me. Yet his smile seemed tired and weak. I came closer to him and stroked his face.

"How are you, my dear? Would you like to take your time getting dressed, and then we could go to dinner together."

Ray got up with a certain amount of difficulty. Holding hands, we slowly walked to the restaurant.

"Would you like an aperitif?" The waiter looked at us. Ray ordered two glasses of champagne. I was expecting him to join me in toasting, with his usual, sweet smile. But this time he did not manage that. His smile seemed laboured and I was deeply shocked, as it seemed that I was looking into the face of a dying man.

"Oh, God, help!" I cried out inside myself. I hoped that I would manage to smile and not show any sign of shock on my face. One thing I knew, that my husband's life was at stake. But how should I cope with this situation? Talk to Ray about it? I still did not have the courage to do that. I felt extremely helpless. Yet a firm resolution was taking shape in me: "From now on I just want to focus on him."

On that first evening of our short holiday, I did not manage to enjoy the fantastic food. My thoughts were wandering, my emotions boiling over inside me, my concentration was clear and confused, both together. At the same time, I was taking the trouble not to let him notice anything of it.

Ray could not eat anything. He was not hungry.

"Would you like to go upstairs?"

We slowly walked to the foyer, sat down on comfortable armchairs and listened to soft piano music, which helped us to relax, before my husband went to lie down and felt asleep again. So I went for a short walk in the forest.

"Look here!" he said when I came back. He pointed at his legs, which were badly swollen from the groins to the toes. I was overcome with fear, not sure whether I could do the right thing in this situation. I could remember from my first aid course that someone with swollen legs should put their feet up.

"Come, I'll make you something for you, to put your feet up on. Perhaps that will reduce the swelling."

Indeed, it did reduce the swelling to some extent. But he could not expect any peaceful sleep that night. Both of us woke up again and again, restless and not knowing how to cope with the situation. The next morning I suggested going to breakfast together, but Ray was against the idea.

"I'm not hungry," he said and stayed in bed.

At the reception, I involved the owner of the hotel about Rays health problems and asked for advice. He recommended his doctor to us, whose doctors's office was right near the hotel. He immediately booked an appointment for us. The doctor took one look at my husband and steered us past all the other patients, right into a consulting room. After we had given a short account of his medical history and he had examined him briefly, he asked if we would agree to him phoning Ray's specialist. After consulting with him, he said:

"We are both of the opinion that we should recommend immediate admission to a hospital, preferably the one you know already. We would book a room for you there."

Ray agreed to everything and a room was reserved for him for the next day.

"OK, we'll transfer our holiday from the hotel to the hospital," said my husband with a grin, still wanting to appear optimistic and in a good mood. I also tried to smile. Slowly, we strolled back to the hotel. In front of the hotel, Ray rested on a bench while I went to prepare for our departure.

"That really was a short holiday in the Black Forest!" was my comment on the way home. I had really wanted my words to sound light-hearted, but that did not succeed, especially as there was a cloudburst and the heavy rain started drumming on our car. This situation reflected my mood. I just wanted to start crying my heart out.

"Now we're back on familiar territory. Wake up, my dear! We're back home." Relieved, I parked at the entrance to the garage, happy to have got back home without any problems.

"It's good to be here." I nodded to Ray. We sat on the sofa and drank some ginger tea.

"You're right. Here, everything's familiar. Here people know us. And we know them. That's helpful. Here, we are in the right place."

In that night, there was something like a dark cloth over my thoughts. I tried to push it aside by deciding to be pleased that Ray and I were lying side by side, in familiar surroundings. The next morning I drove him to the hospital. The doctors had numerous examinations done, and I stayed with him until they were all over.

On the evening, when we spoke to each other on the phone, he told me more about them. But there were still no results. And neither were there the next morning, when I visited him again. He was radiant with optimism. "I feel better. Look, the swelling has gone down a bit. But I still haven't been given any results of the tests." I didn't have a good feeling.

"Why don't we go outside for a bit? It's such a beautiful day", I said. We sat down on the terrace and held our faces out to the sun. My husband told me about nice conversations he had had with another patient and seemed to be relaxed. I just listened, although deep down inside I was thinking we should talk about the events of the last days. But Ray's quiet optimism put these thoughts aside.

When I got home from the hospital, I informed Noe about the current situation. My words probably transmitted the seriousness of the situation to her. She said she would be coming for the weekend.

Ray still had medical examinations and tests. I felt sorry for him, but that did nothing to change the situation. "Everything will be fine", he comforts me on the telephone. "So you'll have to wait until Friday for the results?"

"Yes, that's fine with me." I admired his patience.

On friday afternoon, just after Noe had arrived, someone from Inner Medicine phoned us. "You can come and pick up your husband today." I was very amazed and asked:

"Would it be possible for you to let us know the results of the medical tests and examinations?"

"Please drop by the secretaries' office when you pick him up."

Not expecting anything unusual, I asked Noe if she would like to fetch her father.

"Yes, of course!" Noe liked driving and I felt relieved because I needed the time to prepare our meal. Late in the afternoon, they arrived.

"It's so nice to have you back again," I whispered into my husband's ear, as we embraced. Extremely happy to have my husband and daughter around, I forgot to ask about the results. We sat round the dining-room table with a cup of coffee and a piece of homemade cake, chatting with each other, feeling relaxed.

It was not until Ray was retiring for his sleep that I remembered and asked Noe casually as I was clearing the crockery away: "And what was it like in the hospital? What was the result of the consultation? Have you brought the results from the secretary with you?"

Noe looked down, which seemed suspicious, as I knew our daughter to be as carefree as her father. "They didn't give me anything in writing. Instead there was a short consultation." I turned round in astonishment. "They told me there was nothing else they could do for Dad. We should enjoy a few more pleasant days together."

I gasped in amazement, held my breath, the upper part of my body dropping into the direction of her words. "What? They told you that? That was their report? I don't believe it! Please tell me it isn't true!"

Noe seemed to be apathetic. She remained silent. My astonishment developed into anger at the way they had burdened our daughter. "They could have phoned and told me personally!" More silence in the living room, where our dear daughter was sitting.

I continued ranting and raving. I still could not understand the words and their meaning. I was already thinking I should get in touch with a responsible doctor, but continued ranting and raving: "They discharged Ray with these words?"

Parallel to all this, I had started to think about how I could get hold of a doctor on a Friday late afternoon. My thoughts went in all directions. In a matter of a few words, our daughter had been told about Ray's situation, which was apparently without any prospects and probably meant he would be dying soon, with the advice that we should enjoy a few nice days together.

"Does Dad know about this? Did they talk to him, too?"

"Dad hasn't told me anything about it. In the car, we just talked generally. He asked me what I was doing in my studies at the moment."

"And what shall we do now?"

Noe shrugged her shoulders, short of ideas. I took a few deep breaths to clear my head. We were silent. "Come what may, we'll go with him on this difficult way. Come what may." Noe nodded.

"I must try to get hold of our family doctor to talk to him about it." This idea was my only glimmer of hope.

"Let's ask Dad what he thinks." I went into the bedroom and suggested ringing up our family doctor. He agreed that we could ask him to call and see us the same evening.

We were very fortunate because the doctor's mobile number was given on the answering machine recording. I felt relieved and told him about the present situation. The doctor's voice showed that such things were routine for him. He said he would come right away. He concluded the conversation with the words: "I don't know whether you know this or not, but I have had further training to be a palliative doctor."

This was new to me. He had had training in the art of helping people who were not expecting to live much longer. With a feeling of great relief I let him in at the door. He sat down next to Ray, shook hands with him and let him talk. After that, he asked him: "And what is your wish?"

Ray thought he would like to get in touch with a clinic that would be willing to give him further treatment. He had not yet given up. "I don't want to leave any stones unturned," he said in a definite tone.

The family doctor gave us a list of clinics that he assumed would admit Ray. Among them was an anthroposophical clinic. To my great surprise, Ray asked me to phone them and ask for a place for him there.

"Ray, who always prefers standard medicine, would like to go to an anthroposophical clinic?" I could hardly believe it. The doctor promised to send a referral. They promptly agreed to admit him the following week. Ray was satisfied with the way he had chosen. "If you should need me, I'm available to you day and night." These words were by way of farewell. Ray looked at him thankfully. You could see that these words were doing him good.

As I was accompanying the doctor to the front door, he turned round and spoke quietly to me: "Are you aware that your husband is in a palliative situation?"

I nodded silently, although, deep down, I was not aware of the full extent of his words. I did not succeed in accepting the thought that my beloved husband had only a short time to live. I was still hoping there had been a misunderstanding, a mistake, although an inner voice was reminding me of the doctors' clear statements and that we would have to be prepared for Ray's death. My brain was still not assimilating this information, rather strongly affirming that my husband would continue to live at my side.

Noe and I had a quick discussion. She decided to postpone her practical work in a consulate so she could be available for her father.

"I think that's very generous of you, Noe. You know how much your father loves you." After a pause for thought, I added: "And also it would make it easier for me if we could stand together in this difficult situation.

We could be with him alternately, talk to each other about it and support each other. Who knows what will be happening in the next weeks?"

The days prior to Ray's admission to the clinic were like a present: having time with each other in our familiar surroundings. Yet I still had one heartfelt wish: "Ray," I said, "I would like to have a celebration of Holy Communion in a small group. Here in our flat. What do you think?" I was remembering the Celebrations of Holy Communion we had had with my brother and with my father, when they had been ill. These celebrations had been lovely, lifted burdens and done us good.

My dear husband asked for time to think about it and phoned his dear friend, Phil, who had married us. "I've decided, Chris. We'll have the celebration next week with Phil, Ria and Eric."

That removed a stone from my heart. Beaming all over my face, I was looking forward to the fulfilment of my heartfelt wish for a special celebration of Holy Communion in times of sickness.

The special afternoon drew nearer. Noe had come to join us. Phil and his wife, and Eric were standing at the door with a twig of almond blossom, a bunch of brightly coloured flowers, candles, a cross and a chalice.

We put more candles in Ray's field of vision. He was lying on the sofa. Noe brought a lot of daisies she had found on a walk. She put the yellow and white flowers into a bowl of water, around a daffodil flower, and put it on the table for him. Everything was decorated festively.

The chalice was ready, also a basket with pieces of bread.

We started the celebration with the song about the flowering almond tree, which reminds us by its blossoms that the love that is in everything will continue to live. Phil spoke about the love that knows no end, with well chosen, tender words. We took time to think about it while listening to one of Brahms' sonatas for violin and piano. Ria read verses from Ecclesiastes for us out of the Bible. Everything has its time and each thing we plan beneath Heaven has its hour.

While we were taking Communion, I felt our souls were united. Ray's face was radiant because of this celebration that was specially for him. It was as though I could see his happy heart reflected on his face.

I was so enthusiastic about this celebration that it was a long time before I could sleep. Ray was already asleep and I wanted to tell somebody about my feelings, so I phoned my girlfriend in Berlin. As always, Hanna was interested in every detail.

"How did Ray cope with it?"

"He seemed to be unusually emotional, all his senses alert, listening intensively to the words, texts and music."

"Did you have the impression that he understood the reason for the celebration?"

"I really can't say. It's probably like that with all of us. We don't realise that we could die soon. We just hope things will turn out differently."

"I can understand that. Most probably he isn't looking any different."

"But his body has changed a lot. His cheeks are very hollow, his abdomen is all puffed up. He lies down a lot, but is still living in our midst and aware of everyday events. I enjoy that. I'm enjoying every moment and am so thankful for our time together."

"My thoughts are with you." Hanna's interest in our life and our conversations in this hard time strengthened my heart.

This clinic was a lucky chance for Ray, who immediately felt at home there and liked all the doctors and nurses. They were friendly and cared for him lovingly. To my great surprise, he enjoyed the massages, the compresses, the ointments; he even looked forward to them all.

Noe and I were with him alternately. We rented a room in the upper storey of the hospital, to be near him. With a circular e-mail, I informed all relatives and friends who were close to him as to how he was, with the result that some of them came to visit him, maybe to bid him farewell in their inner thoughts. Ray was pleased about every visit.

In the meantime, he was dependent on a wheelchair, which we pushed through the garden every day, where there were countless spring flowers. On the edge of the grounds were almond trees with their pale pink blossoms in full splendour. In the streams that had been formed there, was the sound of water, frogs were croaking. It was a small paradise where we went every day. Mostly, Ray was as radiant as the sun.

"Isn't that beautiful?" He asked me to take a photo of him in the bright sunshine under one of the wonderfully blossoming almond trees. "This is my new home," he wrote under the photo, and asked me to send it to all his friends.

In spite of all the wonderful things Ray experienced in the anthroposophical clinic, his physical condition declined visibly. Some days later, he asked me to write down various pieces of news and to read his incoming mails to him. He listened enthusiastically to recorded books, instead of reading them for himself.

After talking frankly to the chief consultant, my husband decided to go back home. It seemed that he preferred to be in familiar surroundings, and it spurred him on.

"I'll manage the journey home," he said to give himself courage.

"Your husband will only live for a few more days," a male nurse, whom I met in the library, whispered to me, "I can feel that when I massage his body. There are clear signals."

I just nodded my head slightly, closed my eyes and breathed in and out deeply, already suspecting what was going to happen to me. When Ray was asleep, death was visible on his face, with his yellowish complexion, pale as ash, his cheeks and eyes looking so hollow, his bony arms and hands. Ray was also changing mentally. He did not like to be alone for a single moment. We remained with him right until he was discharged. It was only in the moments that he was sleeping that I had the time to organise all the support we would need at home. The hospital's social services were a great help here.

On the day when Ray was taken back home by ambulance, I drove on ahead in my car, because I wanted to sort things out in the flat before his arrival. "Will that work out all right?" I was rather nervous. But it worked perfectly. The hospital bed I had ordered, a walking frame, a wheelchair, and an extra layer for the toilet seat were delivered punctually. Just before the ambulance arrived with Ray, his hospital bed was standing, as he had wished, in the middle of our living room, with his favourite bed linen in light, delicate colours. A big bunch of spring flowers, which I had bought on the way home, was nearby.

Now Ray was lying in the hospital bed at home and already asleep. The journey had been strenuous for him, but he seemed to be stronger than in the days before.

I was expecting various specialists to come round: the family doctor, someone from the hospice service, also someone from the social services and a physiotherapist. They had all promised to come. The family doctor came in his lunch break and arrived almost at the same time as a lady doctor from the mobile hospice service. Together, they talked to Ray, examined him and prescribed an incredibly large amount of medicines.

"Please call us any time, and we'll come immediately," they promised before leaving. Their words calmed me down in the difficult situation. When the social services arrived in the early evening and arranged for Ray's care regularly in the morning and the evening, it was reassuring. Last of all, a nice, young physiotherapist appeared at our front door. She stroked Ray's swollen legs, gently smiled at him and said: "I'll give you a massage to help you with lymph drainage, now." In the middle of her work, she took a short break, looked lovingly at my husband and said: "If it's all right with you, I'll come round every evening to massage him, also on my days off."

I felt my eyes watering with tears. "Thank you very much", Ray and I answered both together.

In the meantime, Noe had arrived. She gave her father a bunch of flowers to hold and sat down beside him. It seemed as though she did not want to go away from him again. Ray was happy. Noe's presence was a relief to me.

In the evening, Ray went for a short walk round our apartment, supported by his walking frame.

"It's not quite the same as it was before, but it is good to be back at home," he said, beaming all over his face. "By the way. Do you know what I would like to eat? Pancakes filled with spinach and feta cheese."

"Yes, that's fine. That whets my appetite, too. What about you, Noe?" Noe nodded. I went off to buy the ingredients in the bio-shop round the corner and to get the prescribed medicines from the chemist's.

"What a good thing that both of us are here. Ray can't be left alone," I thought when I was on the way. On this first evening, the three of us sat round the

143

dining room table, eating the pancakes and talking about the work Noe had taken on in the students' parliament. I could see from Ray's face that he was enjoying his meal, which made me pleased. "Here, as dessert there's a pancake filled with pieces of banana and chocolate sauce for each of us." Once again, it became clear to me that a good meal strengthens the soul as well as the body. We had a good laugh at Noe's chocolaty face!

With Ray's return, our apartment became a meeting point for doctors, nurses, friends and relatives. Ray's sister had also come over from the USA, to stand by him. I sometimes made use of visits for a bit of time off for myself. It helped me to relax when I called friends, wrote mails, dosed off to sleep or went out for a short walk. It was clear to me that I was not as strong as I outwardly appeared to be. Ray's increasing weakness and imminent death were taking their toll on me inwardly. On the other hand, there was my wish to be fully available for my husband. Ray was gradually needing care, encouragement, signs of love and special food round the clock. Noe made use of Ray's sister being here to take a day off.

"Boil everything and make a puree of it, the fruit, too. There's nothing else your husband can digest," was the family doctor's advice the next day. I did my best. As soon as his third day back home, Ray's condition worsened. He ate and spoke less and less, lost weight and got cold. We turned the heating up, as each extra bed covering was too heavy for him. Sometimes I lay down beside him to keep him warm, whispering encouraging words into his ear, stroking him softly. I had the courage to talk about the future.

"Ray, wherever you are, wherever I am, my love for you will never fade. *We will be tied together with the band of love.*"

The next day, a Saturday, two of his best friends from his youth had planned to come. In the morning, after waking up, I had an idea: "Perhaps that would be a good chance to go to the botanical garden together?" "His garden", as he affectionately called it, was only a few minutes' walk from our house. "These friends are strong enough to get the wheelchair up the hill and push it through the garden." Of that I was certain. After I had got up, I presented this idea to my husband and asked if he thought it was feasible. After he had nodded weakly, I told his two friends about my idea, and it was their wish to carry it out.

"Then let us go out on a journey, my dear," I joked, while we were wrapping him up well to protect his weakened body, although it was a warm and sunny day. The botanical garden was in full splendour, the colours and shapes were breath taking. We stopped for a while, lingered, and admired the sea of red and yellow tulips that was spread out before us. Then we went on a bit further to admire the violet, bead-like blossoms of the Judas tree, pointed at the thick roof formed by the blossoms of the Japanese cherry tree, with countless insects flying around it. We sat down on a bench, with Ray's wheelchair next to us. I could not help feeling sad. I thought sadly about his imminent departure, and I closed my eyes in order not to show my tears.

Up to then Ray had not spoken a single word. Unexpectedly, he turned round towards me. I instinctively put my head down to him and listened to

145

his wish with great amazement, spoken in a very quiet voice. "Would you go and get me an ice, you know, the sort I loved eating as a child?" He described in detail an ice-lolly and told me where I could buy it. I agreed straight away and set off on my errand. A short time later, we all enjoyed our ice-lolly.

In the night from Sunday to Monday, I woke up around midnight, wakened by an inner restlessness. I hurried into the living room, where Noe was lying on the sofa near Ray's bed. When I switched the light on, she looked up, disturbed from a deep sleep. We saw Ray lying rather unconsciously, making an unusual gurgling noise and blood coming out from his nose.

The same afternoon, the doctor from the hospice service had given me instructions as to how to provide for relief in case of emergency. I did my best, but without any success in alleviating the symptoms, as my husband was instinctively resisting.

"Noe, I don't know any other way of helping him." As if looking for help, I looked at her. She just looked irritated. I felt panic rising up in myself, and just could not hear this gurgling noise from my husband any longer. I needed a clear head to think. I went into the kitchen and thought about what to do next. "I know what. We'll phone the hospice service's duty nurse. She did say we could phone at any hour of the day or night."

Indeed, somebody answered the phone after the first ring and reacted instantly, after I had described the situation to her: "I'll be round as soon as possible."

Within a quarter of an hour she was standing with us. We looked at her wide-eyed, wanting help. Thanks to her routine knowledge as a hospital nurse, with our help she moved Ray from lying on his back to lying on one side, to make his breathing easier. Then she phoned the hospice doctor and checked with her. In that time, Noe and I stood at the side of the bed, stroking Ray's body gently and speaking words of comfort to him.

The nurse went quietly to the back of the living room and gave us instructions in a quiet, peaceful voice. She certainly knew about Ray's condition. I was still so preoccupied with keeping him well at the time, that it took time for me to realise what we would be having to cope with. With this heartfelt, delicate assistance, I soon felt able to give my husband the sensitive help he needed. My heart became one with his heart.

"Ray, I love you. Our love is a tie that lasts for ever."

In the background, we could hear, very quietly, Dietrich Bonhoeffer's song that Ray liked so much:

"Surrounded by the powers of good, we await whatever might happen in comfort. God is with us in the evening and in the morning, and most certainly at the dawn of every new day."

In this night, Ray breathed his last breath.

The palliative nurse opened the door to the terrace, to give his soul space, as she put it. Carefully, we went onto the terrace and looked with awe at the starry sky. It was as though I were feeling Ray's soul, now free in a vast expanse.

Noe and I chose a fairly new polo sweater and a comfortable pair of trousers to dress Ray in. We put his hands together and placed a small bunch of the flower forget-me-not on them, which I had gathered on a walk the previous afternoon.

"Now it's time for me to go," the palliative nurse said by way of farewell. I felt indescribably thankful to her, as she had accompanied Ray's last minutes in a wonderful way. Noe withdrew. I felt a deep need to be near my husband, who now lay at peace in front of me. I stroked him and spoke to him.

"Ray, I love you with all my heart." My hand lay on his. I stroked his skin. "You are still here. Still with us." I felt at one with him and prayed: "God, please go with my husband on his way. Bless him. Be with us every day and fill our hearts with love and thankfulness. Amen."

It was not until the first birds' cries were audible that this inner feeling passed and I listened to the voices that were singing to welcome the morning. Later, when the birds' voices subsided, angels' voices sang in their place from Handel's "The Messiah", while I read *Psalm 139* for a service.

One verse I was particularly enthusiastic about, captured my imagination, and I read it aloud: "Behind and before you besiege me, your hand ever laid upon me."

The comfort in these words helped me to an inner peace. I went to sleep on the sofa near my husband, until I was wakened by the first warm rays of the early morning sun falling on me. I looked towards my husband, whose face radiated with an inner peace. I dressed and walked out of the house, up the hill to the castle park. To our favourite bench for two and felt Ray lying beside me.

"Let us dream, Ray, of our journeys to Bali. Let us go to the restaurant Kopi Bali, to order *Gulai Kambing* and enjoy the meal together."

In my imagination, I felt his body next to me, his hand holding mine. I smiled at the early morning sky. On the way back, I went through the vast, spring meadow and picked flowers for my husband.

In our flat, I again started to play the CD with Handel's oratorio, "The Messiah" and, to the sound of the music, I decorated the room with flowers, pictures and hearts.

Suddenly Noe was standing next to me. We embraced each other, standing in awe beside Ray's dead body, while Handel's *"Hallelujah Chorus"* was resonating through the room.

I felt it was a blessing to have Ray still with us. Several times, when I was alone with him, often in the night or morning hours, I sat down by him and sang hymns from my hymnbook, which he liked, read psalms, Bible passages and poems from it. I often spoke to him, thanked him for our time together and his love.

The third day after his death belonged to us: Noe, Ray's sister and me. It was the day of farewell to his body before it was placed in a coffin to be taken to the crematorium. In a short ceremony, we blessed Ray and asked for comfort for us, prayed *the Lord's Prayer*, and Noe read a passage from Ecclesiastes: *"There is a time for everything, and a season for every activity under heaven: a time to be born and a time to die."*

We sang the Shalom Ben-Chorine, which was composed in 1942 and we had sung it at the special communion service: *"Friends, that the almond twig blossoms and grows again and again, is a sign that love will remain."*

Love remains; all three of us felt that it was so. We talked about it and again expressed our deep thankfulness that Ray had walked with us for a part of his way.

Busyness distracts
from the pain of separation!

We do various jobs together

"Tell me it's not true. Please tell me that Ray's coming back." I was hopelessly in despair, shouted at my sister, who had only been able to get a place on a flight to Germany after her brother-in-law had died. She, too, was in despair, because she had not been able to bid him farewell. We two mourners sat in the flat, paying no attention to the difference between day and night. Our despair kept us awake.

"I can still see clearly how they put the coffin with Ray's body into the hearse and drove to the crematorium. But now it ought to be time for him to come back." The irrationality of my words I did not notice.

My sister did her best to cope with my inability to be comforted and said nothing about her own condition of mourning. She comforted me, led me gently back to reality, when I seemed to be drifting away into the depths of mourning.

"Tell me, Ordi, have I gone crazy?"

My sister looked at me tenderly, but also strictly. She stabilised me in my desperate situation, aroused in me the courage to go on the path forwards. She, too, was aware that I had, with iron control, managed mostly to keep a cool head for a long time. Now I had fallen into a hole. My sister never went away from my side. Noe had travelled back to Frankfurt for a few days' practical work necessary for her studies. In this time, my sister tempted me to go for walks, on hikes, for breakfast in a cafe, because she knew these things would give me something else to think about. Then came the blissful month of May, showing itself at its best: radiant, blossoming, with birds twittering, the perfume of flowers and an indescribable splendour of colour.

At the weekend, we were all together again and did the most necessary jobs: Ray's sister, my sister, Noe and I contacted banks, authorities, got in touch with institutions, friends and relatives.

"Isn't this intensive time of mourning hard enough? Must all these bureaucratic demands come in addition? Without you, it would be too much for me."

"We'll do all we can. The rest we'll postpone until later on." I was thankful that Noe had inherited her father's pragmatism. And the desire for pleasure.

"After work comes the pleasure," was the motto my sister gave us. And as it was almost early evening, she said: "Let us bring matters to a close for now. What about going to the marketplace? I'm hungry." Her idea was well received by us.

"I'm glad that we've decided to have the funeral service later. That gives us some time to think about how we would like to do it." Even in the restaurant, eating a coated trout, my thoughts could not keep away from all the jobs we still had to do. "Maybe we could share the different tasks?"

Noe reacted to this immediately: "I'll design the death announcement for the paper," she offered straight away.

"And I'll organise the meal afterwards," my sister added.

"I could take over the decoration," Ray's sister, who had already selected an urn made of light maple wood, decided.

"Left over for me, then, is the organisation of the funeral service. I'll start doing that tomorrow."

I was very thankful that Ray and I had in the last year written down what we wished concerning his medical treatment in the last days, the time before his death, the death announcement in the paper, the funeral service together with the form and place of burial. That served me as orientation. But I still felt helpless in all, I had to manage.

"We'll manage it together!" Noe laid her hand on my shoulder and looked at me encouragingly. It was comforting, to hear this. Her words made my work easier. So we arranged the different tasks together in that extremely busy week before the funeral.

I asked some good friends if they would be willing to make some contribution to the service. Ray's good friend, Phil, the former Dean, said he would take the service. I was very pleased about Ria's offer to read some poetic texts. I loved listening to her reading texts; she had a voice that did one good. Gabi, another good friend, offered to play the flute, and her partner the piano. We had to get together a few times to agree on texts, contents, hymns and musical accompaniment.

On the afternoon of the funeral service, the cemetery chapel was decorated with laurel bushes and fresh spring flowers in many different shades of blue. A photo of Ray had been placed centrally. A long-standing friend of his had taken it a few years before on a spring hike. You could see the sun in Ray's face. He was smiling at the people looking at the photo in a wonderful way. Right next to the photo was the urn of light maple wood with his ashes.

The seats in the chapel were hardly sufficient for all the people who came. First, Phil sang a solo for Ray, a poem by Eduard Moerike that he had set to music.

May we begin with him
Who moves moons and stars
Along blue canopies
Of the sky, of heaven.
You, Father, counsel us!
Guide and direct our lives!
Lord, may in your hands

154

Be the beginning and the end,
Everything in its place.

Accompanied on the piano, we sang the hymns my husband had requested as loudly as if we had wanted to sing our mourning away. Phil's funeral address was filled with humility. He gave us a few moments to think about all our memories of times together.

These moments were accompanied by Gabi, with meditative tones on her flute. Almost without us noticing, she inserted an extract from *the Internationale*, just as Ray might have wanted her to. At the time, I must have appeared to be disturbed by it, but during my preparation for the service, I had thought about Ray's wish and found it to be good. And Gabi had found a place for it in her free interpretation.

After the service, some of the participants thanked us for the sensitive, heartfelt and dignified farewell celebration. During the service, I already announced Ray's wish that everybody should consider themselves to be invited to a celebration of life at the conclusion of the service. We had booked a cosy restaurant for it where there was hardly enough room, as so many people had accepted his invitation. The staff had to get more food ready in a hurry. Somebody had added roses to the photo of Ray. Next to it, there was a book for friends and acquaintances to write their memories and good wishes in.

"I'm so thankful for the celebration of life afterwards," I said to my sister opposite me over coffee.

Ordi nodded agreement. "Yes, for us as relatives, it was balsam for the soul, wasn't it?"

I looked around. Noe was surrounded by her aunts and her grandma. Ray's sister was sitting with her relatives. All his friends from his youth sat together on a big table. They all knew each other and looked as they enjoyed meeting again.

"It warms my heart in this time of mourning to see friends meeting again," I said to my sister. Quickly she added: "Don't forget about the delicious meal I ordered! Coffee warms the heart, too." We laughed out loud, and with us all our friends, who were sitting around us.

Right into the early evening, we talked happily. We shared moments of sadness, hearty memories, and thankfulness. It was not easy to say "Good-bye" to all the wonderful friends who loved Ray. His sister also said "Good-bye" to us, because she was flying back home to the United States on the following day.

"Farewells are getting more and more difficult," I reflected after all the guests had left the restaurant. "My goodness! I am really tired! Let's drive home straight away. I have to go to bed."

Noe and I noticed how exhausted we were when we arrived back home. She went to bed early and slept through until the following evening. Ordi an me met at the dining room table, to eat the leftovers from the day before.

I was aware of a black, open wound developing inside me, which I suppressed, as I was still in my family circle. Noe, my sister and I sat together round the dining room table, also on the following days, eating and chatting with each other. We reviewed the events and impressions of the previous days. We enjoyed being together.

It was not until it was time for Noe to leave that I was overcome with sadness; the black wound was working its way to the surface. It was not easy to bid our daughter farewell, because I had got used to her refreshing presence, her support and working with her as a team. I recalled the hard time we had managed together in the last weeks and months.

"Thank you Noe, for bearing with me all the good and beautiful things as well as the difficult and sad things, with your wonderful nature. This time has united us. My heart is with you, wherever you may be."

Noe nodded slightly and looked away, probably because she did not want to be overwhelmed with her feelings. I embraced her and kissed her. We decided that we would go together to her cousin's wedding, which Ray had been looking forward to so much. By then, she would be doing her next practical unit in Berlin.

"After the wedding I'll come and visit you in Berlin."

"Yes, please visit me. Then we'll be able to celebrate Dad's birthday together."

Before our daughter left, I quoted the words from the Bible that had become important to us: *"There is a time for everything, and a season for every activity under heaven: a time to be born and a time to die, ,..."* I looked into the eyes of our daughter and said emphatically: *"Dance, Noe, dance!"*

Fortunately, my sister was still with me. She kept on enticing me: "Come on, let's do something nice together."

One afternoon, we drove to a nearby, mediaeval town, ambled along the narrow streets, admiring the trees in blossom and the flowers. We sat down at a street cafe. As it was just by the marketplace, we could watch the people strolling along.

I enjoyed having my sister with me; we were very close. In her presence, I was able to suppress my feelings concerning my dear husband's death.

"I'd like to be happy, to fly away from the trauma of death," I confided one evening. It was never easy for her to think of a suitable answer, other than to distract me.

Again and again, she insisted: "Come on, let's do something together!"

I felt better with this, as her words drew mw out of my lethargy. We went on long walks in beautiful nature, across the cemetery, on paths that were familiar to us from childhood days. And somehow or other, each time my sister caught sight of a delightful restaurant nearby.

"What about this garden restaurant?"

With the continuing wonderful spring weather, we were motivated to go to a beer garden, a street cafe or a garden restaurant.

"All good things come to an end."

"That's our proverb just now," my sister said in attempt to joke, yet we were both sad that the time had come to an end and wept in each other's arms. It was clear that we would not see each other for a long time, as we lived so far apart.

Chaos in the world of feelings!

In the midst of darkness and confusion

After my sister had also set off for home, I felt increasingly lonely in the quiet of our flat. The inevitable came: my black wound burst open, first taking away any motivation I might have had.

"Why am I falling back into a state of deep mourning, as if the farewell rituals, comforting words and conversations had not taken place?" I could find no answer to the question I had asked myself. My despair remained, also the weeping and lamenting.

"Ray, I miss you so much. Where are you?" Sometimes it was as though Ray were still in the flat. That is not surprising, I thought, as everything that had belonged to him was still in its place, as though it were waiting for him. The smell of his body was still there, in his clothes, his bed linen, and his pillow.

Sometimes I called for him loudly. "Where are you, Ray? Come back!"

Fortunately, in these crazy moments, I was called back to reality by my inner voice of reason. "Ray has died, don't forget!"

But this argumentation did not always convince me. Sometimes I was not able or willing to follow this reasoning. I was fascinated by the thought of meeting up with my husband. But where was he? I walked through the flat, looking for him, occasionally even sure I had seen him. On waking in the mornings, I found myself looking up the staircase, waiting for him, his embrace, his kiss, his song that he sang to me each morning: "Good morning, my darling, let me give you a kiss!"

In the absence of his voice, I sang the tune to myself. But reality warned me against getting absorbed in these unreal visions.

"Ray – is – dead," I constantly made clear to myself, sometimes like a mantra, as though I were hard of hearing. At the same time, I was quarrelling with myself: "If only I could come to believe in his death! I was there when he gave his last breath, also in the two days before we laid him in his coffin, also in front of his urn when he was given the final blessing. Why is my brain suppressing all that? Why do I see Ray alive before me, as though my intensive desire had brought him back to life? "

My critical discussions on my situation did not lead to the clarity I had expected. No, the chaotic feelings in my head were rather enforced. But I did not give up judging myself, until one day I heard an inner appeal, which seemed to bring hope: "Allow yourself to come to rest. Take time to come to terms with Ray's death." I nodded every time this sentence surfaced in me. It was convincing, for time heals wounds. I knew that in theory, but not in practice.

With short steps, I walked towards the goal, even if it cost me power and effort. I planned times for rest, meditated, prayed, read a book, walked round the cemetery, met up with friends for coffee. I took great pains to stay in the present, being aware of each moment, avoiding looking back at the past. I had a certain amount of success in this and at such moments even felt a small spark of happiness.

But I was not successful every day. On some days, I could find no way of getting my head clear. Then I was bombarded with all the *"Why …?" questions*. "Why was Ray only allowed to reach the age of sixty-one? Why have all our dreams come to nought? Why do I have to continue my way through life on my own?" First, I asked myself these questions, sometimes in a complaining tone. But nobody gave me any answers. Everything remained silent. My questions remained unanswered.

In my despair, I prayed, pleaded with God. From him, too, there came no answers, which increased my laments: "Our dreams have come to nought! Our plans for the future have gone, the desires of our hearts are destroyed, and what have you got to say about it all?"

I was fully aware of my anger, my words became more passionate and my accusation was more reproachful: "Why have you taken Ray's life away, which he so much wanted to keep? Why did another member of the family have to die much too soon? God, are you not willing to give us something good?"

In one of these situations of great despair, I reached for my Bible. I looked for the book of Job, because I could remember that he, too, had been in an extremely desperate situation. I wanted to find out how he had dealt with this problem. His story impressed me right from the first line of the text. His situation was significantly different from mine, for from this righteous and noble man everything he had was taken from him. He accepted the painful losses for a long time, before he, too, complained, finally admitting his sin and his impatience. God rewarded him with happiness in life and a long life.

Involuntarily, I compared his story with mine and was sure that Job showed more patience, even though everything that he loved had been taken from him. Was it the same in my case?

My beloved husband had died and I had nearly fallen into despair. However, my sister, Noe, Ray's mother and sister, dear friends and certainly other dear people were still with me, which I seemed to have forgotten. The fact that Job had found his way out of the dark valley with his unshakable faith in God and was rewarded with a long and happy life also gave me food for thought. It showed me that I should look beyond my present feelings. I looked critically at my situation and asked myself if I would rather find my way out of my dark hole, to look at the future positively. But I could see that I could not succeed in doing that at the moment. I was still at the beginning of the way of grief. It would take time.

In spite of all that, Job's story had given me a ray of light. It was comforting to know that he had suffered, too. His story came to a happy end because of his faith in God. That pointed to a way for my next steps out of the darkness.

I made myself an active programme with morning walks in the woods, planning not to think about the past or the future, but to be fully aware of the point of time I was in.

Instead of complaining, I listened to the voices of the birds, stood by trees and admired their stature, felt their bark. Walking along, I looked up to the sky every now and again and was happy about the light from the sun. The good mood I brought home with me often lasted right into the afternoon.

On one of my morning walks, I experienced something very impressive. Fully absorbed in thinking about my husband, I heard a voice saying to me: "Where Ray is now, he is well." I stood still, shook my head, as though I were wanting to shake these words off and looked up to the sky incredibly. There was nothing there to see, but this thought changed my view of Ray's death. I became aware that it was quite possible that Ray could now be quite well again. "Maybe Ray would rather not come back to the earthly life?" This question remained with me in the following days, giving me the change of perspective I needed. I was conscious of the possibility that he might be thinking differently from me and not wanting to come back.

"Ray, are you happy up there?" I asked, looking up to the sky. I decided not to complain any more, but instead to make a special place in the living room to remind me of him, with a lovely photo of him smiling sweetly. With small stones, I formed a heart round the frame. Beside it, I placed a small bowl of red roses, to remind me that we often used to give each other roses. Being connected with my husband in this way, visibly, was healing and set my mind at rest. Sometimes, I laughed at my husband on the photo cheekily. My daily walks, which often led me through paths in the cemetery, strengthened my inner feelings, because the almond trees were still in flower and the plants on the graves radiated bright yellow and orange tones.

"This season is as beautiful as a dream," I murmured while walking past and felt my heart rejoicing.

On some days, when I was feeling stronger emotionally, I cycled to the weekly market to buy freshly harvested vegetables from the farmers' stalls. Generally, I met various friends there. I had the impression that they did not know what they should say to me. Often I was asked with an embarrassed smile how I was getting on.

"You know, living without Ray is so painful that I would not wish this pain on anyone else at all."

That usually brought the conversations to an abrupt end. I realised that it was difficult for others to know what to say to me. When I was invited to birthday celebrations, I said very little. Without Ray at my side, I felt like an outsider in the midst of good friends and acquaintances. I could not get used to being a widow and found it so difficult to adopt this position. I also thought it did not suit me at all. During a phone call with my sister, I described my situation to her.

"We used to do everything together, and now I'm alone." Just this one sentence moved me to tears, probably out of self-pity. "I miss Ray so much, especially when I'm with other couples."

"Don't force yourself to do anything. If accepting these invitations isn't good for you at the moment, then don't bother going. Other times will come, when you will feel more comfortable in social gatherings." My sister spoke from experience, as she had also gone through this valley of despond when he husband had died suddenly from a heart attack.

"I now resolve not to have a guilty conscience if I decline invitations and prefer to be alone at home instead."

"Do that! And if you need me, ring me up."

For a long time I thought about our conversation. I felt that my own company was sufficient for me for the time being. My steps were still short, sometimes I stumbled, but despite this, I continued going my way. Some days I sat in the black hole again, afraid that I would never come out of it, but there were other days, when I was full of the joys of life, making me laugh and dance.

In the mornings, when I listened to the birds twittering, walked barefoot through the grass or admired the blossoms of the fruit trees in my garden, I could feel the life around me.

"Is it all right for me to feel well? Is it permissible for me to be pleased, to laugh out loud, now in the first intensive phase of the mourning process? What will other people think of me when they see me being joyful?" These questions ran through my head in the moments when I was feeling happy and soon gave me a guilty conscience. Indeed, I became reluctant to show my joy of life to others, the tears, which still came seemed more appropriate. Particularly on Sundays in the services, my voice often could not get any further and tears ran down my cheeks. There in the church I felt a deep longing for my Ray, who was no longer sitting next to me, smiling at me or touching me gently. I felt comfortable in black clothes, rummaged through the shops for them. I couldn't have enough of black around me. Until one day, when I asked myself: "What would happen if I suddenly felt like wearing bright colours? Would I have the courage to wear bright colours now, just after Ray's death? And, what would the people think, the ones who knew us?"

Actually, I had got used to being seen and addressed as a widow who deserved all sympathy. I heard sentences like: "I wish you much strength for this difficult time." These words did not give me any strength at all and sympathetic looks only served to arouse my self-pity. And even more, I felt that I been locked in the "mourning" department.

The next time we phoned each other I told my sister about my thoughts, which she compared with her own experience. "You know, anybody who loses someone close they have loved, faces enormous challenges. If you live these out in public by wearing black clothes, this is acknowledged by the others. It is as though you were living in a socially acceptable space for the protection of those in mourning. But any expression of the joys of life in this time makes others feel uncertain. It might well be that you fall out of the pattern by laughing loudly or dancing. It's perfectly correct to be aware of this dilemma."

I became increasingly aware of the many different facets the death of the marriage partner can bring. In addition to the loss, there are countless changes in everyday life, changes also in relationships and friendships.

"I think your image will change as you yourself change. Be it in public, the neighbourhood or in clubs and social life. At first you're the widow who needs sympathy and later on they see you as a single person."

"Oh dear!" I groaned. That was reason enough for my sister to comfort me. "You will grow into these roles." I groaned again.

"You know, I can well do without the loss of my husband, all the resultant changes, and the torture of changes in feelings."

"Maybe it would be good for you to get away from it all for a time?"

"I'll think about that." On that note, we concluded our telephone conversation, which had given me something to think about. A little while later, I received an invitation to the big, national church congress. Ray, Noe and I had good memories of the last one with the various options that we found convincing. As this one was going to be near to us, I contemplated going to it.

"God will bring my soul to rest," was what I hoped to get from the congress. One of my friends told me she had already sent off a booking. We went to Stuttgart by train. I had asked one of my husband's friends from his youth if I could stay at his flat, as I knew he had a large flat that was situated centrally. He agreed and said that he would also have two more women as guests in that time. That was all right with me, so I accepted his offer. The room I had was ideal, near to the events in the town centre. We arranged to meet in the evenings and conclude the day with a glass of wine.

The various events were a challenge. On the first evening, a young man's fine gesture of letting me share his song book for the opening service brought me to tears. And afterwards while going through "Market of Possibilities", where different churches introduce their activities, I felt so lonely at the stall belonging to a church I knew that tears started to flow.

"At home I have more control of myself," I thought. Yet, as I had decided to come to this congress, I wanted to go through the whole palette of emotions. A musical group waved to me as I was strolling past the stalls, wanting me to sing with them. I sat down with them and they promptly tuned up with the hymn Ray had wanted for his funeral: *"My time is in Your hands. Now I can be at peace, at peace in You. You make me secure. You can change everything. Give me a firm heart. Make it firm in you."*

Again, I felt challenged, but wanted to go through with it this time without crying. I did manage to sing with them, despite a feeling of insecurity and a lump in my throat, and I was proud I had managed it.

It was not until an evening service on a green meadow, with countless candles looking like the stars in the sky, that I felt calm in the midst of the many people who were singing, praying and listening to words of hope. When it had finished, my host rang me on my mobile phone and asked where I was and if we could meet.

"Yes, that would be fine." We found our way to each other in the crowd and drank a glass of wine together.

"The atmosphere in the time of the church congress is something very special," said Ron, who otherwise did not have much to do with the church.

"That is why I had the courage to book to come to this big event of faith without Ray." Ron laid his arm on mine in sympathy and gave me an encouraging look.

During the next three days, I chose from the enormous list of offers mainly things that would challenge me intellectually: theological questions, Bible expositions, social and global themes of current interest. I did go to the odd event that was more for the soul. One of them was about reading passages from the Bible, interpreting them and dancing. Because I felt like dancing, I ended up in a small, rather cramped hall. For a while, I stood around shyly and without any courage at the edge of the dancing room. Gradually, I started to dance the interpretation of the Bible passage. And, as was to be expected, I wept ceaselessly.

"Just cry, if it does you good. Nobody knows you here," I comforted myself and continued dancing.

The congress programme had something on offer for all senses. In some moments, I felt a strengthening, spiritual feeling of fellowship. Back home, my emotions felt more balanced than before, even though my mourning was still with me. I still felt extremely insecure, hurt, and desperate. Wanting distraction, I absorbed myself in the books I had bought at the congress.

At some time or other, a somewhat unclear message found its way to me, gradually becoming clearer: *"Go to Bali. It would be good for you."*

"Go to Bali? Now? In my labile condition?" My questions were unconvincing, as a firm certainty had set itself up against all doubts. I asked my friend Hanna for advice. She soon strengthened me for my intention.

"Perhaps there is some sense in a change of location. A change of climate can work wonders. You meet other people, another culture, other landscapes. All that can have a positive effect. Do it! You know Bali. You will meet people who you can rely on a hundred per cent."

From then on, I started thinking about whether I would have the courage for this journey. I remembered my friend Suryani with her experience with patients in difficult situations in their lives. I contacted her by e-mail and told her I was thinking of going to Bali in a few weeks.

"Oh, please, would you like to stay with us? All my family welcome you," was her short answer, which I was very pleased about.

171

Next, I spoke to Noe about my plans, and she was also encouraging about my trip to Bali. "If you feel that it is right for you, do it. I'd do it! What's keeping you at home? I'll get along all right. I'm busy with my practical units anyway. I could keep an eye on our flat. So don't worry. Just get on the plane!"

Following the inner voice!
The journey to Bali

Hypnotherapy and Meditation

At last! We were almost at Denpasar Airport. The flight had seemed to be endless, which made me nervous. Yet, when I saw the island through the window, my heart jumped for joy, but at the same time, I was feeling apprehensive because I was travelling without my beloved Ray.

"What will happen to me during these six weeks?" I thought anxiously.

On leaving the plane I felt a humid heat suddenly coming over me, which almost took my breath away. I stood still, recognised my labile condition, placed my hand on the top part of my chest and took a few deep breaths.

"Slowly, Chris," I told myself and went to the arrivals hall at a leisurely pace to get through the customs formalities. "And how am I to find Suryani now?" In front of me there were numerous Balinese men trying to offer the newly arrived tourists a taxi or accommodation. "Taxi, taxi! Please, madam, a taxi!" I nodded with my head to one side, which means "No" on Bali. I did not expect to meet my friend in this crowd.

Courageously pulling my suitcase past all the men with their calls, I went in the direction of the short-term parking spaces, making it clear again and again that I did not need a taxi. "Sudah." "I've already got one." That had the desired effect.

Suddenly Yaya appeared, coming out of the crowd. With a beaming smile, my friend's son came up to me with open arms. "Selamat datang!" "A hearty welcome!"

"Terima kasih, Yaya. Saya senang!" "I'm pleased to be here, thank you, Yaya."

With our embrace, my apprehension disappeared, especially when I saw my friend Suryani. She, too, took me in her arms, holding me tight for a long time. Now, in my experienced friend's arms, my emotions surfaced, my tears flowed down my cheeks. Suryani laid her hand carefully on my arm and reminded me that Balinese people did not show their emotions, at least not in public. I swallowed hard, took a few deep breaths, held my head up and tried to smile. "Everything OK?"

I nodded. Deep down, I was relieved to have arrived safely to be with them on Bali. Yaya gave me a look of encouragement, took my suitcase and turned round. We followed him to the car. My thoughts drifted back again, as Suryani was gesturing to show me that I should keep my tears under control. It was like that on Bali, people smiled instead of crying. Perhaps I would learn here to keep my emotions in balance, which had recently been going up and down like a roller coaster, and I thought that would be good. But to learn something, you need a good atmosphere, which I knew quite well as a teacher, and Bali had a relaxed atmosphere, of which we had been convinced more than once. I also felt at ease in Suryani's big family. There was always something going on, but each of us could feel free to withdraw to his or her room. During the week, my friend worked as a doctor for mental health and a hypnotherapist, and at the weekends as a meditation instructress. She had already given me and Ray a short session of hypnotherapy, and we had been enthusiastic about it.

In the meantime, the car had turned onto the fast road into the capital city. As usual on the island of Bali, the traffic was chaotic, with traffic jams on all the streets.

"What's going on in your family?" More than three years had passed since our last visit there. I was sure that there were new things I should know about.

"Twenty-two grandchildren up to now." The proud grandmother's eyes were radiant, as though she had won some sort of battle. Yes, her six sons also showed their enthusiasm about the number of their children and she felt they were confirming her opinion that the blessing of children made you happy in everything else, too. She was also happy about her sons' success in influencing the political life of the small island.

"Wow! Congratulations!" I was quite surprised at the increasing number of her grandchildren, remembering that last time there had been sixteen. "Different countries, different customs." My mother used to say this, teaching her children to meet other people and cultures with respect and interest.

Here we are! The high bougainvillea bushes were showing their countless pink flowers over the high wall that surrounded the whole compound. The car hooted as a sign that the gate should be opened from the inside. It was already late afternoon, the whole family was at home. Suryani's husband beamed all over his face when he saw me. Four grandsons, who were living in the house, aged between four and twelve, walked around me curiously. They thought that my luggage might contain a small present for them.

"Now you need peace and relaxation," my friend said after I had been welcomed. Actually, I was feeling really lively, but accepted her suggestion just the same, looking round to see where my room would be in the big house. It occurred to me that I ought to make use of their communication facilities to contact my dear ones und went back to the living-room, where Suryani made an enticing offer: "What about a relaxation massage tomorrow morning? An hour and a half. If you would like that, I would ask my masseuse to come."

I nodded approval. I thought the idea was great. "Bagus sekali!" – "Great!"

Back in my room, I unpacked my suitcase and then took a cold shower, as the tropical heat had been opening my pores. I put on light and loose clothing and opened the door to the balcony. The sultry air pressed me back into the room; the noise from the cars and motor cycles was also unpleasant, so I shut the door firmly and switched the air conditioning on. I was just settling down, when my handphone made a noise and there was a message from Noe on it.

"Hallo, Mami, has all gone well? Love, Noe."

I was so pleased about her greeting that I wrote back:

"Dear Noe! Thanks for thinking of me. Everything went well on the trip to Bali. Now, I'm already at Suryani's place. But I'm tired and wanting some sleep. How are you doing? Greetings. Mami"

"Huh", I was still thinking about Noe's unexpected question. I was feeling happy and thought of my sister. Straight away I wrote to her:

"Greetings from Bali! Have arrived safely at Suryani's place. Lots of love from your sister."

My sister also seemed to have her handphone within reach, as she had marked my message as already read.

"Dear Chris, I'm pleased the journey went well! In my thoughts I was with you. Give my regards to Suryani and her family. Greetings, O."

I lay down on the enormous bed and thought about it all. "Perhaps my sister had been waiting for news from me. What a good thing the internet is, giving me contact to my dear ones all over the world in the shortest time."

With these thoughts, I must have fallen asleep, because when my eyes opened I was surrounded by dark night. I groped my way in the direction of the balcony, where I could see a ray of light coming through the door, from the street lighting, and opened the door. At this late hour, there was a slight breeze. It was not so oppressive, the traffic noise and the daytime busyness had decreased. I walked onto the balcony, opened my arms in the direction of the sky over me and took a deep breath. I looked in vain for familiar constellations of stars.

"Of course, it's the starry sky on the other side of the equator," I murmured to myself, rather disappointed, "I forgot about that." The Great Bear, which I always used for orientation, was not there. Yet my home was far away. And Ray was not there. I began to feel I had got lost between two worlds. Into the wideness of the night sky, I dreamt about pictures of things we'd experienced together, got absorbed in them until they seemed to be real. Ray appeared.

"Ray?" "I'm with you," I heard him say, *not knowing where his voice was coming from. But that was not important to me. "If*

only you were with me in reality, Ray. I'm missing you so much!"
I could have cried. I breathed the night air in with deep breaths.
After a short time of silence, Ray turned to me again. *"Darling,
we have shared so many lovely things together. It is all still there.
The love, the memory of it all."* I could accept that. In my
thoughts, I went one time more back to our cleansing ceremony
that Suryani had invited us to. I smiled and whispered: *"Do you
know, the moment when we stood hand in hand in front of the
high priest was a special one for me. The two of us were one. It
was as though we were celebrating Holy Communion together,
concentrating wholly on the ceremony." "Yes, my dear, it was
really a special moment. I am very thankful to our friend Suryani
for that special experience we had not been expecting, because we
had no idea of what was going to happen." "I felt enchanted by his
singing, the bell he was ringing, the magic of the incense sticks."
"Do you know, before or after this experience I never saw your
eyes shining like that? You seemed to me to have been flooded in
light." "You also had this gleam in your eyes, my dear."* During
this conversation, I did not only hear my dear husband, I also felt
his hand in mine. *"Our time together was so wonderful, Ray. We
can't let it be over,"* I whispered to him as he was gradually
disappearing. I prayed: *"Good God, do not let my husband go
away from my side. Undo all that's happened."* But around me
all was quiet.

Sadly, I walked back from the balcony and lay down
on my bed. I felt like crying, Ray's death was so painful,
my heart was breaking, I was seized by a light dizziness,
which made me afraid. It was nearly midnight when I
went to sleep.

Early in the morning, the street noises mingled with
my dreams until I finally woke up. First, I had to get my

179

bearings. "Oh, I'm in Bali! In the house belonging to Suryani's family." My watch told me it was five o'clock, too early to get up. "Go back to sleep, sleep as long as you need to," I told myself gently, turning over onto my side. The masseuse would be coming later on in the morning and I did not have any appointments before that. The room temperature was still bearable, so I actually slept another four hours until my hunger woke me.

"Get on the way," my stomach rumbled and sent me in the direction of the kitchen.

"They're probably all at work and the children at school."

But immediately a voice came out of the kitchen: "Selamat pagi Chris! Apa kabar? Mau sarapan ?" Two young household workers had discovered me, welcomed me and asked if I would like to have breakfast. Their faces were radiant. We knew each other already, as they had both been working in the house for some years. Suryani had most probably asked them to look after me.

I said "Good morning", too and answered their questions straight away.

"I'm fine, thank you. Yes, I would like to have breakfast. That's a good idea."Mau minum Teh?"

"Yes, please, some tea with ginger in it."

Both of them pointed at the big, round table in the middle of the large kitchen. In the middle of it were, as always, various small bowls and plates with all kinds of good things on them. On that day I discovered boiled chicken in coconut and curry sauce, spicy fried fish in chili, garlic, onions and coconut oil, lightly boiled spinach with ginger, fried tofu and tempeh with chili and tomatoes.

"That looks delicious," my stomach said to me. I went up to the rice pot, that was next to the sideboard and which I knew to contain boiled rice at any time of the day or night for anyone to take some to go with any meal whatsoever. The Balinese eat things lukewarm.

My stomach was already used to that, also to the substantial breakfast. I liked all their food and I loved the wide selection of dishes.

Putu, one of the helpers, cut a ripe watermelon for me and placed it in front of me on the table. The black tea with the slices of ginger was already steaming in front of me.

"Mhhh, enak." "Delicious." The melon was sweet and most juicy. It made me wake up properly, look around me and smile at the two women.

Wawan, Suryani's other son, who lived in the house together with his wife Heny, and their four sons, came to keep me company at the kitchen table. He owned a car workshop, which he used for restoring old Mercedes Benz cars, until they looked as bright as new. He was a great fan of this brand and always talked about it. And that day was no exception. While we were helping ourselves to rice and the various dishes, we chatted about the Mercedes Benz Center in Stuttgart they visited a year before. Like Yaya, also Wawan was an easy-going type, well balanced, friendly and extremely proud of his family of six.

I had almost forgotten the time because of our conversation. Suddenly there was a ring at the gate. My massage appointment! The helpers opened the door.

"Should I put on a lot of pressure, or would you prefer less?"

"A lot of pressure please, so that you loosen my stiff muscles." Dewi was obviously capable of doing that. As she told me later on, she had worked as a masseuse in a convalescent sanatorium in southeast Europe. There, people wanted a lot of pressure.

"Auuuh," I shouted more than once. My muscles were apparently a bit too stiff.

"Your muscle is strong like a man," was her reaction to my complaints. She really pressed hard. In my imagination, I saw her as a vamp pressing hard south-eastern European men's bodies to make them soft. Fortunately, her strength decreased. Her fingers glided more softly and gently over my body.

"That does me good," I managed to say as a sign of enjoyment during the last phase of the body experience. Yet, after the massage, I lay on the bed exhausted and nodded off to sleep for a short time. Later, when I was sitting on a bench at the front of the house, I discovered Dewi with her driver, absorbed in conversation.

"Mau minum Teh?" I offered them some tea. They accepted the offer with thanks. I boiled some black tea with pieces of fresh ginger, served it and sat down next to them. The rather shy chatting at the beginning developed into a jolly round of anecdotes, in which Dewi displayed something of her talent as a comedian.

She reported in detail situations she had experienced as a masseuse in Russia and Turkey, imitating the voices and gestures of her bosses and patients so convincingly that we laughed tears.

Unobtrusively, Suryani had joined us and was happy, too. We got her to join in the conversation and she, too waved good-bye to Dewi and her driver.

"That was a wonderful idea of yours, my dear one. Thank you. Dewi's massage was absolutely necessary. I submitted wholly to her hands and now I'm feeling totally relaxed."

"I'm glad about that. The main thing is that you should be feeling well. I also enjoy Dewi's massages. She comes to me every week."

"I envy you," and thought, "a masseuse who comes into the house for around two hours a week is a wonderful body relaxation."

"I need the relaxing massage, because I have a lot of patients at the moment."

I could quite imagine how much good the relaxation massages did her, after a day of hard work occupying herself with her patients and their problems.

"So, now I'll have a shower and rest a while. See you later!"

Suryani's hint the evening before that I would certainly need a lot of rest and sleep was a help to me. I was aware of a great need of rest.

Lying on my bed, visions of Dewi's massage went through my head again. She did her job admirably, had great knowledge and an enormous portion of humour, which definitely relieved her everyday life. Slowly, my thoughts drifted from Dewi to my beloved husband.

"Our holidays on Bali were always connected with relaxation massages," I said to him. "Can you remember that in our bungalow complex in Legian, the older Balinese ladies received each guest with the sentence: Massage! You want massage?" We took advantage of the offer and before our arrival we looked forward to our massages on the terrace of our bungalow. The stone under us was warm, the sun was shining. Wasn't that wonderful?" "Lovely," said my husband reflectively. "We also felt sorry for the women who were working for the upkeep of their whole families." I smiled at him. "I used to hear contented noises coming from you during the massages!" "Tell-tale!" he replied.

Slowly I got used to having my dear husband with me during my daydreams. With loving thoughts of him, I went off to sleep. This time, I was wakened by a knock on my door.

"Chris, I've just had a phone call asking me to go to a sick friend. Yaya will drive you out for a meal this evening. He'll soon be fetching you."

"That's all right. It will be nice to go out with Yaya," I replied, showing understanding for her situation.

I had some time before it would be time for the evening meal, so I continued lying on my bed. My thoughts drifted back to the time when her six sons were aged between twelve and twenty-two. They were a perfect team. Each time we visited them, they were enthusiastically occupied with a particular pastime, all together. At the start of our trips there, they had formed a band together, with each one playing a different instrument. The constant sound of the basses and rock songs resounding through the house was still in my ears. When Ray and I were there again, the practice room did not exist any more. Instead, they had become a basketball team, playing basketball every free minute.

Their yard had become the pitch. They shouted and laughed during the game and soon they were playing so perfectly that they were influencing the city's basketball team. They were successful and were soon playing against other schools, later against teams from other Indonesian islands. The advantage they had was that they were all a head taller than the other players, with perfect teamwork, always happy and cheerful. We observed their progress enthusiastically and were just as proud of them as their parents were. A few years later, the basketball hype had come to an end; they had discovered the computer and were experimenting with it. The oldest ones were studying, so it was quieter in the house. One of the sons, Wiwin, was continuing to play basketball as a professional and became a trainer in due course. Four of her sons decided to study engineering. Yaya, the middle one, decided to follow in the his famous mother's footsteps. He kept near to her, studied psychology as she had done, and accompanied her on all her professional activities. That was the reason why we had got to now Yaya well. Whether at home on Bali or in Germany with us. For Suryani's professional success brought various invitations to conferences and congresses abroad with it. On all these journeys, she was accompanied by her son Yaya and her husband, who was also a professor. The family made use of their journeys for getting to know the culture of the country they were visiting. Here in Germany, too, they had a good look inside our university, got to know a nursery school with its educational concept, visited our school to observe different teachers, classes and styles of teaching and to talk to the teachers. They were always interested in the culture, education, medicine, psychiatry and psychology of a country. They communicated something of their experiences abroad on Bali in their lectures, books and articles, in courses and personal conversations. Their house also became a meeting point for specialists from all over the world whom they had got to know on their travels. In their house, we felt like members of their family. And whenever they were in Germany, they were also part of our family.

I particularly remembered one experience, when Yaya surprised us with a very personal question: "What can I do to get to know a good woman to be my wife? How does that go in your country? Can you give me a good tip?" Ray and I looked at each other. We were not used to questions like this from young people in Germany. Our daughter would never have asked us anything like this; she was quite independent and never consulted us as to her choice of friends. Well, what advice should we give to this young man from Bali? The cultural differences between young people influenced by western culture and those on Bali were great! First, we shrugged our shoulders helplessly; then Ray decided on a strategic answer:

"Be honest," he said full of conviction, "honesty is the trump card in a partnership." And I advised him with: "Smile". Simply because I loved smiling people and was of the opinion that a smile from a young man usually had a positive effect. Intelligence, talent, ambition and charm he had in plenty just as his brothers did.

On our next trip to Bali, Ray tapped me lightly on the side when Suryani told us that Yaya was going to get married. "Look here, it seems that our advice has been successful," he whispered to me.

Yayas family soon grew to six people. For me, it was the confirmation that his mother's idea that giving the island Bali successful descendants, was taking effect.

I had dressed up for the evening out. Yaya, his wife Tess and their youngest son fetched me with their car.

"How was your day?"

"Oh good! Dewi gave me a super relaxing massage. After it I was nothing but tired.""And which relaxing restaurant shall we drive to now?" he asked me with a charming smile.

"I'll leave that up to both of you," I answered promptly. "You know the area around better than I do."

"What about a cosy place by the beach where they grill fresh fish? Would you like that?"

"A freshly caught grilled fish? That would be fantastic!" I beamed all over my face and started to look forward to the promising evening menu. My stomach seemed to be caught up in the anticipation. It was rumbling in satisfaction.

"I'd much prefer to have a place with a view of the sea," I said as we were walking from the car to the beach. "So we will have the chance to watch the sunset."

Yaya laughed, showing his gleaming white teeth and countered: "I've already reserved the most beautiful place with the best view of the sunset for you."

Suddenly, I was not interested in the menu any more. What caught my attention was rather the cosy place beneath palm trees, directly beside the lightly coloured, sandy beach. From here, I looked over the vast sea, which was reflecting the sun in a powerful shade of orange.

"A truly wonderful place, taken from a picture book. Do you come here often?"

"Sometimes, occasionally at weekends. The children like playing on the nice, flat sandy beach, as Raja is doing now." He pointed at Tess, who had run after her son, because he was running towards the water.

"You are fortunate. You live in a most beautiful part of the earth."

"Yes, we Balinese know that we live in Paradise."

I wanted to investigate this part of paradise. Remarking a short "I'll be back right away," and ran barefoot towards the sea. The fine sand under my feet tickled me. I was not used to this any more as we had not been here for years, because the long journey would have been too much for Ray.

The water was pleasantly warm. Walking forward, the water splashed upwards in front of me. I was happy to see the drops of water coming up. But it was strenuous. I stood still, looking over the vast sea, up to the horizon, which was just merging with the dark orange sun. Admiring this theatrical performance from Nature, I concentrated on standing upright, breathing in and out at regular intervals. I was completely aware of myself. The strong rays from the sun pierced into my closed eyes. To my surprise, I became aware of my dearest husband, as though he were standing in front of me; with my mind's eye I saw him. He spoke to me:

"Are you feeling the warm evening wind on your skin, my dear one?" "Ray, are you there?" He ignored my question. "I have happy memories of our walks together on the beaches here on Bali." As in a film, pictures of our evening walks passed in front of my inner eye, with us wading barefoot through the gentle waves, then sitting down on the firm sand, while the sun was sending its most beautiful rays across the sea. "Yes," I answered dreamily, "I like remembering that, my dear." "Do you remember the restaurant that we liked to go to after sunset, our restaurant?" "You mean the romantic one? The garden was lit up with candles, the flowering bushes had a sweet perfume." "I remember how lovingly we looked at each other." "Ray, please come back," I called softly over the sea. I felt the soft waves tickle my feet and became aware of my surroundings. Quickly, I turned and walked back to the table where Tess and Yaya were sitting.

They both seemed to have observed me all the time and laughed at me quite openly when I returned to the

189

table. I knew that Yaya would not want to allude to my sadness, but rather help me to catch on to his joy.

"Chris, what about a freshly caught Mahi Mahi?"

"Good idea, Yaya! Let us order Mahi Mahi. I'm looking forward to the meal already." Reality was catching up with me. My stomach was giving clear signs of hunger. Before the grilled fish was brought to us, we conversed in the typical Balinese way on light-hearted, joyful subjects, with hearty laughter.

After our evening excursion, I lay satisfied on my bed and thought about the last few hours. This evening had been a special one: a nice evening with Yaya, Tess and Raja by the beach, an impressive sunset and absolutely delicious fish.

"What more do I want?" went through my head. Promptly came the answer: "I definitely want my husband back again!"

Since the feeling of encountering him on the beach, I just could not get Ray out of my mind. Now, in the quiet of the evening, he appeared again.

"Ray, please stay with me. I'm longing for you. Let us, as we always do, share our experiences, communicate with words, gestures." "My dear, I'm here!" His words made me peaceful and allowed me to wallow in my memories, to tell him about my impressions. Just as we had always done. "This evening I noticed once again how uncomplicated the Balinese are, especially with their children. Did you also notice that? I don't notice any rules, orders, conditions or threats. The children do what they would like to do. Yaya is a typical Balinese father, who accepts them with a laugh, shows his happiness, affection and love." Happily I

registered how Ray was getting into the conversation. *"You know how fascinated I am when fathers take their sons on their lap and show them how to play in a gamelan. With the bodily closeness, the children are taught how to play it. There is no conductor to show them what to play, no, they just listen to each other, watch each other and play without sheet music. That's how the children learn it from their fathers. That is the way the next generation is taught on Bali Isn't it fantastic to learn an instrument by imitation, feeling the rhythm, listening?"* Ray sounded enthusiastic and it was as though I were hearing in the background the metallic sounds of a gamelan orchestra. Ray was in form. He continued: *"And do you remember the mighty temple ceremony here in the capital city, with Suryani's daughter-in-law Heny? The intensity and volume of the gamelan music went through my bones and marrow. It must have affected others like that, for suddenly people around us were falling down in a trance."* *"I remember that well, because we were clinging onto each other, to avoid being caught up in it all. Under no circumstances did I want to fall in a trance."* Ray laughed. *"We survived it! For several hours we stood tightly pressed in a crowd."* *"Yes, Balinese temple ceremonies go on endlessly."* The impressive pictures and sounds had found their place in my memories. Ray was pressed close to me at the temple festival. *"How good it was, being together,"* I whispered before going to sleep.

The weekend! For decades, my friend had been inviting anyone interested to an enormous atrium building on Saturdays, to take part in her meditation.

"How many times have I participated in all the years of our friendship?" I asked my friend on the way there.

191

"And how often have you been here in the decades I've been offering the chance of these meditations?", she asked me back. We laughed because both of us could not remember.

"Well, be that as it may, we did not stay away from any of your events when we were here."

That was the way it was. Before setting off on our journey, we were looking forward to the Saturday meditation, which included gymnastics, song and dance. And especially Suryani's contributions before, between and after the exercises. She told us about her everyday life as a doctor, her trips abroad, giving advice on a healthy lifestyle.

"My concept is to activate the Balinese in expressing their emotions, which tradition tells them to suppress. They should be active in sorting out their problems and not constantly cover them up."

I chuckled to myself, because that was the thing I admired about the Balinese. I knew the western culture all too well, which was too emotional and aggressive for me.

"At home people sometimes express their dissatisfaction and problems too explicitly, which is not always advantageous when living together with others. The Balinese live out their emotions in the countless temple ceremonies."

"Yes, it may be so, but too often they hide their negative emotions, because our culture does not wish them to show them, and they become depressive. Quite a few Balinese come to us in the psychiatric department.

It's much better to show them ways of expressing emotions and relaxing, don't you think?"

"You are the specialist here, recognised, greatly valued, for many people a guru. Not only for the Balinese, as you always say, but also for international guests. Your house is a meeting point for international specialists. Even on German TV there was a report on your work with schizophrenics, who you help in your Suryani Institute." My friend smiled at me and said: *"What I do anybody can do."*

"But you have the press and TV on your side. They publish your opinion, your commentaries, your lectures and all your activities. You can be proud of this success."

She nodded. "Yes, all of that is good."

In the meantime, we had arrived at the place where the event was to take place. She got out and went up to the hundred or so people who were greeting her respectfully. A team of helpers were also putting microphones and loudspeakers in their places. I went cautiously, smiling in a friendly way at all and sundry, to the upper end of the atrium, hoping not to be conspicuous there. I was not sure about my emotions, being here without Ray for the first time.

We started off with gymnastic exercises done to music and demonstrated by a group of women. It was fun to experience rhythm and movement in this large group. Yet I was soon short of breath because the midday heat was finding its way into the atrium. After the music had died down, my friend took the microphone in her hand, welcomed everybody, introduced her theme "The Expression of Emotions" and soon started practical exercises. She gave us instructions for letting each vowel sound resound all together with a strong voice coming from the diaphragm and with a long breath. Our voices rang out mightily. Some were already weeping with "A" at the beginning. Maybe that was influencing me? For quite unexpectedly with "U" , instead of a singing voice, a lamenting shout which made my stomach tremble came up from my chest area, turning into sobbing. My inner control reacted quickly and stopped the emotional outburst.

"Don't show your inner self to the people here," my inner voice of reason told me. I looked around. They were all occupied with themselves and seemed to be uttering the consonants, loudly lamenting, shouting or weeping, with no reluctance at all. That gave me the courage to let my emotions out again, but a bit more decently than the first time. After the exercise, I remained standing with my eyes closed and felt that my body was coming to rest. Yet Suryani was already giving direction for a relaxation exercise to be done in a lying position. With regular, deep breathing, our bodies came to rest. During this exercise, I came to think about my body as seen externally. I was aware of the ground I was lying on, the space outside and inside the open atrium building, felt the pleasant warmth on my skin, breathed the sweet scent in that seemed to come from frangipani flowers, heard the birds twittering in the trees nearby.

Suryani's pleasant, deep voice concluded the relaxation exercise that was doing so much good, and continued with the next task. "Go into small groups," she said, "and tell each other how you felt in the last two exercises."

"Oh no! Not that in addition! I can't and won't talk about that to others," I was certain. I would have liked to make myself invisible. But to my dismay, three young Balinese who spoke good English rushed up to me, sat down next to me and talked without any inhibitions about their thoughts and emotions. I hoped that it would be sufficient to show I was feeling it with them, to distract them from my own feelings, as I did not feel capable of talking about my feelings of grief. I was simply afraid I might burst into uncontrollable tears. Fortunately, my friend ended the talking in groups, and I did not have to say anything. Without any break, she started with a meditation, speaking in a rather deeper voice.

"Sit upright, close your eyes slowly. Concentrate on your nose. Notice how breathing in lets energy flow into your body and how it flows out again while breathing out. Take time to continue feeling this. Notice how the energy from outside flows into your whole body, right down to the tips of your toes. Keep observing this for a while. Notice how the energy from outside flows into your body, right into the palms of your hands. Concentrate on this energy for a while. Now feel the energy from outside flowing into your abdomen."

Suryani guided our attention to further points of concentration in our bodies, before she concluded the meditation that had lasted for about twenty minutes, telling us to open our eyes slowly and stretch our limbs.

"Beneficial, really beneficial," I heard voices around me say. Satisfied faces confirmed this. For me, the sitting position for the meditation had been rather uncomfortable. My body was no longer as agile as those of the Balinese participants were. It simply did not like sitting cross-legged for so long.

"Next time I'll bring my meditation cushion with me, so I feel better sitting," I resolved.

A pianist started playing simple but joyful songs that everyone sang, clapped and moved rhythmically to. I restricted my participation to the rhythmic movements and a lalala. There was only one song that I knew, and I loved it, too. Suryani had taught it to me years ago.

"Disini senang, disana senang, di mana mana hatiku senang." "I like it here, I like it there, anywhere where my heart is I like to be."

The simple words and the joyful tune made me as enthusiastic as the other participants, whose faces were beaming with the singing, clapping and rhythmic movements.

"Suryani's concept is reaching the people," I thought. "She will certainly go home satisfied. The participants expressed their emotions, seeming totally relaxed and happy."

Time flew quickly. It was already afternoon when we were setting off for home. We stopped at a small *Warung*, a simple kiosk selling packets of food. Rice with different vegetables. We ordered that, a bit of everything. The saleswoman packed our boiled rice in a bag, added half boiled eggs, some spinach, beans, soy shoots, fried tofu and finely chopped chicken, with roasted coconut flakes scattered over it.

"The big portions of meat in Germany you don't find on Bali," she said by way of apology, giving me one of the meals.

"Meat is not so important to me, but could you ask for a large portion of sambal?"

I loved this hot accompaniment, the paste made of finely chopped chilies, shallots, cloves of garlic, with some coconut oil rubbed into it in the mortar, spiced with salt from the sea, some shrimp paste and lime leaves.

"Sambal spices the dish and disinfects the stomach, because it is so hot," my friend explained to me, but I had known that for a long time.

At home, while we were resting in our rooms, I discovered a message from Noe on my handy.

> *"How are you, Mami? What are you doing? Have you settled in on your favourite island? A big hug! Noe."*

My heart jumped for joy over our daughter's message. I wanted to reply straight away:

> *"Hi, nice to hear from you! Don't worry, Noe. I'm being well looked after in Suryani's family. What about you? Is everything OK? Love, Mami."*

My thoughts drifted to Noe and then on to my sister in the States. So I sent her again a message.

"Hi, Ordi, is everything OK with you? I feel at home here with Suryani's family. Love."

Immediately, a reply came onto my display:

"Be glad that you're in a warm part of the world. Here it's cool and rainy. Unpleasant. Otherwise, everything's OK. Take care of yourself! My wish for you is that you soon feel better. Greetings, also from all the friends here, whom I tell about you."

What a super invention the internet is, giving us such swift contact to each other, especially when we're far away from each other. Lying on my bed, I was overcome with longing for my dear husband. I closed my eyes and concentrated on my breathing, my thoughts wandering back into past times.

"Oh, Ray, don't leave me, stay by my side. For ever." My feelings were completely with him, I felt him lying beside me. "Were you at the meditation today?" "Yes, it was good." "Do you still remember the first time? We knew hardly anything about meditation, we simply weren't interested. But we didn't want to disappoint Suryani when she offered to take us to her public meditation. We had no idea as to what to expect. And at the beginning I, at least, was feeling right out of place. It took time for me to take advantage of what was happening. It wasn't even difficult for me to meditate, although my scepticism and my fear stood in the way. No, I felt peaceful and relaxed afterwards, suddenly smiling the way the Balinese do." I laughed. "That's

198

similar to the way it went with me. I was rather afraid it could take me away from my Christian faith. But that didn't happen. During the meditation, I felt I was connected with our triune God. It's remained like that up to today." "It's always a help to know where you belong. You know my doubts concerning the Christian faith." "You make that clear to everyone, Ray. Despite that, I was always happy when you sat next to me at the Sunday service, we prayed or took Communion together."

Ray seemed satisfied, lying next to me. I was happy to have him by my side. With this feeling, I nodded off to sleep.

That night I woke up several times. My heart was thumping. Fearfully, I got up, went onto the balcony, expanded the top part of my body and breathed deeply. After that, I felt better. I observed the stars in the night sky and thought about the following morning.

"Probably my heart is beating in this way because I'm starting with hypnotherapy." Although I wanted this short therapy because it promised to relieve my problem, I was apprehensive about it. On my way back to bed, I encouraged myself: "Get help for your grief. Trust your friend's competence. Trust God. It will get better."

Apparently, my clear words were being effective, for I then slept right through to the next morning, when the late morning heat was coming through the window. My friend wanted to be back by midday. Until then, she would be working in her practice.

"I've still got time for a good morning shower and a delicious breakfast," I said to myself encouragingly and got out of bed. Downstairs in the kitchen there was already a cup of tea with pieces of ginger. I took a plate, filled it with warm rice, vegetables and tofu, putting some of the sambal spice on top of it all.

"This will strengthen me for the day."

"Where would you like to lie?" asked Suryani, who unintentionally was being like a therapist and making me feel like a client. I could not accept that. We were in my room, an agreeable place for hypnotherapy, I thought.

First, she talked to me about the treatment, described what would be happening and asked me a few background questions about things she needed to know in advance. After my initial nervousness, I felt increasingly more peaceful and concentrated.

"Are you ready?"

I slipped into a lying position in which I felt comfortable. My therapist sat at the foot of my bed, at a distance. She spoke to me slowly, in a comforting tone of voice and gave me enough time to follow her instructions between her sentences: "Breathe in and out slowly. Follow each breath with your full attention. Remain completely with each breath that is flowing through your body. Now feel your muscles, as they relax. Now turn your attention to the soles of your feet. Feel the energy from breathing in and out slowly."

I could follow her words well. My everyday thoughts disappeared quickly. Her words were already familiar to me from her meditation. I concentrated on my breath, the way it was going from my head to the soles of my feet. In this first phase of the hypnotherapy, I felt relaxed. The   therapist led me into deep relaxation by means of breathing in and out. I felt as though I were sinking deeply and heavily into my bed. Although my consciousness ebbed, I still heard her voice clearly.

"Now I'm going to lead you into your past. You will see a situation in front of you, in which you are very happy. Give me a sign when you have put yourself into a situation like this one."

I managed to see an abstract situation in front of me, in which I felt left alone.

"Describe this situation to me and how you are experiencing it. Express your feelings."

This task was difficult. I noticed that my consciousness was still controlling my emotions. I gave Suryani a sign. She led me a step further back and helped me to overcome my inner barrier.

"Now leave this unhappy situation. Take strong breaths, in and out," her voice led me after I had seen the unhappy situation and told her about it.

"The power of the Holy Spirit is going with you in this difficult situation. The Spirit of God is with you. You are not alone. You feel the strength. It is helping you. You will certainly overcome your unhappy situation. Now you know exactly how to proceed. Be active! Change the unhappy situation. Accept help from other people, until your situation has changed to become a good one."

Her words gave me a feeling of strength. I saw myself rising from the valley of the negative to the height of the positive. I felt that I was being protected by the Holy Spirit on this way. Other people suddenly came and accompanied me, helping me to climb to the heights. I heard the therapist's voice as a distant one.

"Tell me what you and the others are doing about it."

As if disturbed by her words, I stopped the activity I had begun. I felt that I would rather remain sitting in my cave, because it was more comfortable for me. I wanted to tarry in the depths of my grief that would cost me less strength, was not so strenuous as running off to climb the mountain. It was problematic for me to tell her about this inner conflict and so I kept quiet. But my therapist was persistent:

"You have the Spirit of God. You have a living body. You have dear people around you who will help you. So leave your negative place! Become active! Now!" she demanded.

My body still resisted the strenuous action. With her supporting words, I tried to do it in short spurts, which I soon stopped, for they were costing me too much strength. Suryani still did not give up, demanding that I should become active. It took some time before I was convinced. With help from God and the anonymous people, I made myself an inner scaffolding, which gradually went upwards. With her unchanging words always in my ears, telling me not to reduce my efforts but to continue going upwards. They were effective, my will was roused and gave me the strength to climb up the scaffolding slowly. Suddenly, I felt less burdened from the feeling of loneliness and being left alone. I was feeling lighter. That spurred me on. I knew that my activity was able to overcome depths. With God's help and support from the other people, I could climb from the depths to the heights. Then I was able to give my therapist a signal. I was on the way up. But there was more to do.

"Now you have left your dark room! You have people around you. They like you. They are glad to see you. Feel that. Feel the joy around you; leave the picture of your negative emotion behind. See the positive. Open your eyes, open your heart. You are carrying the Spirit of God around in you! You have friends. You are important to them. They need you!"

I felt this step was like a radical change of perspective. It was a fresh way of looking at myself, surrounded by people who liked me, who needed me just as much as I needed them. In my deep grief I had excluded them, confided in only a few. Now it was a matter for my heart and my love.

She demanded: "Describe the pictures that you see! How are you feeling?"

I felt myself under pressure, having been asked yet again to be honest about myself. That was not easy, but I tried. "I'm relieved because I have managed to leave my valley of loneliness behind me." This one sentence cost me a lot of strength. I was deep in concentration, watching the pictures in front of me. "I'm feeling some sort of relationship. The love of God is with me." Again, I was deep in concentration and needed time to find some words.

"I'm feeling connected to the people around me. They are looking at me with affection; they are supporting me. I am feeling great thankfulness growing in me."

"Now concentrate on your breathing – in and out. Breathe deeply. Remain with your inner picture of the people surrounding you, standing alongside you. Feel the joy of life developing and growing every time you breathe in. Give me a signal when you notice that this is happening."

With this step, too, I needed some time to feel the joy of life that was developing from the concerted energy and strength. It was not easy to give a signal because I did not want to lose my inner picture of a fellowship that was strengthening me and of happiness. In the following steps, I felt Suryani's strong bond with me. That challenged me to follow her instructions. Although I trusted her enormously, I was increasing my trust in my own mental power and my ability to imagine. Suryani helped me to imagine people who with hand and heart were willing to go with me on my difficult path.

"Now feel the energy flowing through your nose into your body and flowing through your whole body. Follow each breath. Now pictures are coming into you again. You see Ray. He is coming towards you. You meet each other. You feel attached to each other. In this state, remind yourself of situations which you have experienced together, look together at pictures of common experiences."

Meeting Ray here in my therapy was hard to accept. It took time for me to become aware of him and very slowly walk up to him and feel him. When we looked into each other's eyes a mighty feeling of affection went right through me. Smiling, our lips met. We stroked each other: our faces, our hair, our backs, and embraced each other. Each breath felt warm. I lost all feeling of time. I did not feel like following Suryani's deep voice when she said: "Your way together has now come to an end. Ray will now bid you farewell and go on his way. God will go with him and be with him. You can rely on him finding a good place."

For me that sounded like a sign to scream inside myself, to stand against it, for not one cell in my body wanted to separate itself from my dear husband. On the contrary, I wished to have this inner relationship for ever. Our wish to grow old together came to the surface again. That wish left no room for separation, as Suryani was demanding now. She was thinking it would not be any problem to let my husband go.

"Take a look at the path that is in front of Ray. Each of you, look at the path in front of you. Chris. *Look at your different ways.*"

"Why should I look at two different paths, which I don't want to have?" my inner being vehemently resisted her instruction, but she did not relent.

"Bid each other farewell. You will always remain united in your love, even now when your ways are separating. Find some sort of farewell ritual."

I was not yet willing to let go of my husband. I walked with him on his way until her voice called me back.

"Settle for a farewell ritual and go your separate ways."

This part of the therapy went against my feelings, my will, even against my interests. But the therapist was most obstinate und did not give up. I had to yield, that was obvious.

"The tie of love connects us with each other, no matter which ways we go." With this sentence, I enticed myself out of my refusal. Very gradually, I got used to the idea of a farewell. With very tiny steps, I walked towards my husband. When I was standing in front of him, I felt his heart with my hands, looked him in the eye and gave him a blessing for his way. Ray looked at me intensively, nodded gently and said in a soft voice: *"May your way be blessed, too, my love."*

Our hands held each other firmly, our looks touched each other. We were breathing in the same rhythm. Although we were connected with each other, I sensed our separation was coming. Cautiously, we withdrew our looks and our hands from each other. I turned over and behind my back, I felt Ray turning over, too.

"Now look at the path in front of you. Look at it carefully. Take steps on it, consciously and firmly. God has prepared this way for you. Do the task He has for you. Your ways are the ones God wants and blesses."

I still hesitated, took one step cautiously, stopped, turned round to look at my husband who was walking on his way to the light. I bowed my head, looked at my way and walked on it, hesitantly and with slow steps.

My therapist gave me time for this process before bringing me back into the world of reality, with short pauses for breathing. "Now leave your inner pictures behind. Guide your consciousness to your breathing which is flowing through your nose. Become aware of your body. Feel the surface you are lying on. Move your muscles very slowly. Open your eyes and look around the room we are in."

I followed the instructions, but inside I could not manage to separate myself from my world of deep feelings. My picture of the way together did not go away. But it divided into two separate ways going independently, each in a different direction. This picture I stored in my memory.

"How are you?" With this question, Suryani brought me back from my other world. I was aware of it and said nothing to describe how I was feeling, as I could not manage it. As an answer, she just got a smile. I blinked, stretched my body and sat up.

"Thank you, my dear; I thank you with all my heart for going with me in my deep grief and sending me on my way. My wish is to go on my new way soon, with courageous steps." My therapist beamed at me with her broad smile. I went up to her and embraced her.

Outside, the sun was shining at us in its full splendour. The frangipani bush was sending a fruity, sweet perfume through our noses. We stood in the garden and gazed at the trees and bushes with their different structures, colours and shapes. Each tree seemed to be standing by itself, but at the same time connected with the others. Sometimes, one died and a new one was planted. Beneath the shade of an old mango tree, we took refuge from the intensive rays of the sun.

"With all my heart, I thank you for your help."

"You are welcome."

"I'll withdraw now and come to rest. We'll see each other again tomorrow morning. Have a refreshing evening." Carrying a big bottle of water under my arm, I went to my room.

"Just lie down, dose, sleep," I was saying to myself, when I unexpectedly heard Ray's voice:

"Do you remember," he started, but I turned round. Our farewell was still in my mind, also the picture of our different ways.

Looking for a place to relax!

Walking and mindfulness

The next morning, my friend and I talked at the breakfast table about the way her grandchildren were being brought up.

"You know, I'm not satisfied with a lot of things the little ones do. But I don't intervene. They will find their own ways. It's all right for them to go on diversions. It is important to me that they are creative, play musical instruments, do sports and express themselves with art. It doesn't always have to be the computer."

I chuckled, because I knew her dissatisfaction when the children spent too much time in front of the television, the notebook or a mobile phone.

"What are your plans for the coming days?" I changed the subject, suspecting she would have a full diary.

"There's quite a bit to do," she replied.

"I think I'll go to *'Three Brothers bungalows'* for a few days. They'll certainly have room for me."

This typical balinese bungalow complex that was being run by the third generation was part of my standard programme, because the big garden with its old trees and numerous bushes with their splendid flowers reminded me of Paradise. Also, the luscious nature attracted countless birds with their songs and giant butterflies with brightly patterned wings. Whenever I looked down at the stream running through part of the compound from the small bridge, goldfish came towards me with open mouths. I liked to stroll on the narrow paths, looking at the bungalows that were built in a traditional style and the religious statues standing on either side of the paths. Most of all I liked the oval swimming pool, which was surrounded by frangipani, bougainvillea and hibiscus. In the shade of an coconut palm, I used to lie on the edge of it on one of the comfortable sun loungers in the heat of the day. In the evenings, I used to walk to the beach to enjoy one of Bali's wonderful sunsets.

Suryani smiled understandingly. She knew my weakness for the Three brothers bungalows by the sea. "Yaya will drive you. He has some time around midday today," she said and was already dialling his number. Yaya lived almost next door with his family and it seemed that he was always available for his mother.

While I was packing my suitcase, I thought of our daughter. She was definitely well occupied with her practical units. But I was worried about how she was taking the death of her dear father. She was also close by him when he gave his last breath, just as I was. Basically, I was worried about her, but I knew at the same time that she was going her own way. This young woman in her mid-twenties, very busy, surrounded by a lot of dear people. I remembered conversations with her about our grief, in which she was silently crying. Yet she took after her father, who was always emphasising: "Everything's all right, my dear."

On a recent visit to her in Berlin, we had celebrated Ray's birthday with an evening meal. We talked about the last days with him with such delicate, loving words, that my heart felt quite warm.

"Noe is definitely coping with Ray's death in a different way than I am." I was sure about that and decided to write a message for her:

> *Dear Noe, How are you? My thoughts are with you. Today I'm going to the Three brothers bungalows. I'm l looking forward to some long walks on the beach. With Love!*

Just as I was about to leave, I heard the signal announcing her answer:

> *Oh, I envy you! I really would love to be with you on the beach. But Berlin is super cool! I love it! But Mami, enjoy your days at the beach. Noe.*

"Oh, it is nice to feel this closeness to each other despite the far distance between us," I felt happy. Thinking of Noe, I carried my suitcase in front of the house and waited for the car.

Yaya was indeed a busy man, as a Doctor of Psychiatry, at the University and at the Psychiatric Clinic. Despite all that, he was taking time to accompany me to the bungalow campus.

"Thank you for your radiant smile, young man. It 's infectious!" I called to him by way of greeting. I knew Suryani's son hardly other than relaxed and smiling.

On arriving at the balinese bungalow complex, Yaya went straight to the reception, enquired about a room for me, went through the formalities and accompanied me to my room.

With the remark "A good place for you," he nodded approval to me.

"My heart thanks you," I said, putting my hands on my heart.

"Not at all. It's a pleasure for me. You're part of our family. Whenever we come to Germany, you help us, too," he replied.

"That's true. We are pleased every time you visit us."

"Let me know if you need anything. See you soon!" I accompanied him back to his car, waved as he was driving off and went to the reception on my way back.

"You come alone," one of the helpers observed as he went past. "Where is your husband?"

That was my first challenge. Up to then they had concentrated only on filling in the forms and not noticed I had come alone. Involuntarily, the question had set my tears going. I swallowed, as I did not want to display my grief in public.

"He is in Heaven!" I tried to state the fact briefly, without any big display of emotions and pointed up to Heaven.

"I am sorry." I could see that he sympathised. Relieved to have survived this question, I was sure that from then on all the reception staff would be informed.

But the subject was not yet closed. In the afternoon, the women from the district who were trying to sell hand-made things and offer massages, to help the family income, called to me loudly: "We know you."

"Yes, we know you, too," I called back.

"You take massage later, yes?" And a bit later I was asked: "Where is your husband?" One of these women had noticed that Ray was not with me. I told her, too, that he was in Heaven. "Oh, I am very sorry!"

With a sympathetic look on her face, she came over to me and put her hand on my arm. In the next moment, she was offering her service. "You massage now?"

I nodded, thinking how good a relaxing massage would be for me. And half an hour later I was lying on a comfortable sun lounger in the shade of a coconut palm, enjoying a massage with her feet. She relaxed me and made me tired, so that I stayed lying there until late in the afternoon. Sometimes I swam a few rounds in the swimming pool.

Towards evening, when the sun was showing its light orange colour for the evening, I got up, to be on the beach by sunset. This beach was famous for its spectacular sunsets. With a bit of luck, one could see a full spectrum of colours, from light yellow, to bright orange, dark red and violet. During our holidays here together, an evening walk on the beach at sunset was a must.

While I was dreamily sitting in the white sand, intoxicated by the powerful colours over the sea, my thoughts drifted back to past times:

"Ray, where are you?" I whispered. The orange-red sun that was getting darker sank into the sea. "Ray is dead," my subconscious told me, leading to a piercing pain. I cried, my tears dropping down into the sand. Slowly it became darker. The sun bade farewell for that day. From my inner eye, the picture of our separate ways emerged and at the same time, I heard Suryani's voice: "Ray is dead. Now you are going on separate ways. Accept that!" "I can't," I countered in despair and felt myself resisting being alone and death with its finality. As though she knew about my thoughts and feelings, I heard her again, saying: "It needs time and work to overcome the death of a dear person." "You're right, and that's why I'm here."

"Madam, you need light?" Unobserved, a man selling torches had come up to me. I shook my head in a friendly manner and set off to go back.

The next morning, I woke up early. "The beach is calling," an inner voice was reminding me to go through my daily plan for movement. "Get on with it. It will help you to have better thoughts."

That, too, was our tradition. We made use of the early morning hours for running and meditating on the beach, because the heat was unbearable as soon as the late morning.

I looked at my watch. It showed quarter past six. "A good time for starting to run, so as to be back by the late morning," I thought, pushed the thin sheet away and tiptoed to the terrace to find out what temperature would be waiting for me outside.

I was received by a gentle, morning warmth. The first rays of the morning sun were descending through the trees and dazzling me. In a reflex action, I shut my eyes. In that way, I could enjoy this glorious moment with all my senses. I heard the stream splashing as it flowed past my bungalow, heard the cocks in the near surroundings who all seemed to be crowing to tell the morning to come. Only the loud motorcycle on the main road nearby was louder. I breathed deeply and, to my surprise, there was no stinking from the motorcycle, but a nice, sweet perfume that I smelled. Interested to know more, I opened my eyes and discovered quite near me several tall bushes with plenty of frangipani flowers on them.

"This is Bali, the way I love it. Full of light, nature and sweet perfumes." I felt good all over, took deep breaths before stretching my arms up to the early morning sky. I yawned out loud and started singing the german hymn: "Each morning is so fresh and new." This hymn was still with me while I was putting on my sports clothes, walking through the lonely garden, along the road to a narrow path that ended on the beach.

"In my experience, things are happening on the long, sandy beach, so I won't be alone." It was like that, too. A few fishermen were standing up to their hips in the softly splashing waves, their eyes fixed on their fishing rods. Joggers who were equipped like professionals panted as they passed by, various dog-owners were proudly walking their dogs on the lead, young Balinese women were enjoying the early sun and throwing themselves with loud shouts into the shallow water. And also, those walking for the sheer pleasure of it, like me, were strolling along the beach.

Quickly I took off my shoes and hid them under a bush. The sand still had the coolness from the night in it. Tiny grains of sand tickled the soles of my feet. I enjoyed the light massage, as I was rolling my foot from the heel to the tips of my toes at every step. My friend's announcement during her meditation came into my mind and inspired me to do a walking meditation. I wanted to be free of my burdensome thoughts.

"I'm breathing regularly, in and out, feeling the sand under my feet." For a time I concentrated on my breathing and rolling my feet, while walking, saying to myself:

"I am thinking entirely of myself, breathing in and out. If thoughts come, I let them fly on like the clouds in the sky."

My steps adapted automatically to the pace of my breathing. The surroundings became less and less important until they disappeared from my consciousness. The breathing became lighter and in the pace of my steps. How far I walked like this, I do not know, I was so deeply concentrated on the meditative walking. I stopped, looked round and asked myself what had taken me out of my meditation.

"Oh, I've got here," I exclaimed loudly. I recognised right behind me the restaurant where Ray and I had experienced many a romantic sunset with a glass of white wine. I went in the direction of this restaurant through the soft sand, stood in front of it dreamily, before sitting down.

"Ray," I started hesitantly, "are you near me?" Instead of an answer, I felt him putting his arm round me and I cuddled up to him. Dreamily, we looked over the sea. "What stories would the sea and the vast sky tell us if they could talk?" Ray smiled at me tenderly and gave me a light kiss on the tip of my nose. "Unimaginable things,"he whispered and nodded significantly. "I understand," I breathed out, closed my eyes and softly stroked his slim arms up to his long fingers. In front of us, the blue of the sea was uniting with the blue of the sky.

I must have nodded off to sleep, blinked into the sun and felt a heavy grief inside me."Oh, Ray, I miss you so much, our tenderness, embraces, our words and gestures of love."

Dissatisfied because I was still clinging on to my dear husband, I stood up abruptly, shook the sand from my clothes and marched back quickly, as if I was wanting to run away from my grief, telling myself again and again:

"I won't allow my mourning to have a place here." I ran through the water that was shallow enough for paddling and it splashed up in the shape of an arch.

"Walk on your way, Chris!" my reason told me. Not until I was out of breath did I stop and continue at a slower pace. My pounding heart came to rest.

"A meditation would be a good conclusion for my morning tour, to cleanse my thoughts and come back into the here and now." I looked round to find a suitable place and found one in the shade of a palm tree. With my feet, I piled sand up to form a stool, sat down on it, put myself in the position for meditation and started to concentrate on my breathing.

"Now direct all your attention towards one point that is about one metre away from you," said Suryani's voice inside me. Words and phrases for meditation were fixed inside me. But as the view over the sea was having such a calming effect on me, I fixed my attention on that.

"The sea gives me energy; the morning sun is glittering in the soft waves and driving my sadness away."

I felt a deep breath lifting the upper part of my body and putting it down again.

"If your eyelids get heavy, close your eyes slowly. Concentrate all your thoughts on your nose. Feel the energy from your surroundings flowing into your body, strengthening you, and then nourishing the surroundings when you breathe out. Keep your concentration entirely on yourself. You feel peace in yourself."

"Wonderful," I blurted out after the heat of the day had concluded the meditation in its own way. I opened my eyes and saw above me the endless blue sky. "Thank you for giving us the morning," I sang this german song, my mother used to sing. Walking on with it in my mind, I looked for the bush on the beach where I had put my shoes. That was not exactly easy.

"I should really know all the buildings. I have been here so often," I was sure. But I noticed the changes in the buildings, especially here in the tourist area. Each time we came to Bali, we needed time to get our bearings again.

"Our Bali, as we got to love it, is continually disappearing," Ray had complained on our last trip. "The prospect of making big money is enticing. The rice farmers are selling their fields either to big investors, who want to build hotels on them or to private persons from western countries, who want to have an elegant bungalow near the beach."

"How true," I thought on recalling his words. "The Indonesian currency is so low in value compared to the western currencies that it's easy to buy up the island. Where is justice? And in addition, the Balinese people's income in reduced because the millions are being consumed by the rich investors, as package tours prevent tourists from having their accommodation with the native inhabitants, who then have no income from it. This puts them in a dilemma. They find it hard to earn their living, especially with increasing prices for food and education."

I suddenly noticed the bungee jumping tower. "I recognise that," I thought and walked up to it. "My shoes must be near here." Indeed, not far away I found the bush with my shoes underneath it. In the bungalow campus, I walked in the direction of the breakfast restaurant.

"Wonderful, the table by the pool is free."

At the counter, I quickly ordered the Balinese breakfast with red rice, helped myself to a cup of tea and sat down at this table in the shade of a coconut palm. I was looking forward to the breakfast. I loved this traditional Balinese morning dish, sweetened with natural dark palm sugar and boiled in coconut milk with the fresh fruit that was served with it, the delicious papaya, the delicate bananas that tasted different from the ones we ate at home, the fresh pineapple and the mango with its fruity sweetness.

With these thoughts an "oh!" of enjoyment escaped from me, which made me smile. For me, it was an absolute joy to the senses for me to stay here on the bungalow campus. My pleasure reached its summit when I could eat the typical Balinese breakfast by the pool and watch the light and shadow by the water and in the splendour of nature. The light wind made the water in the pool glitter with a silvery blue. The flowering bushes were in a warm shade of green and each flower like a drop of colour. Even the otherwise monotonous brown trunks of the coconut palms the rays of the sun had transformed into a sunny-yellow light brown. You could hear the wind rustling in the light green palm leaves.

"The rays of the sun have a wonderful effect on me. All colours are radiant, showing themselves at their best, which is enchanting." Dreamily, I looked up at the rustling palm leaves and hardly noticed the young Balinese woman who was serving my breakfast for me with a relaxed smile.

In the dish with the boiled red rice, the freshly grated coconut looked like snow in the sun. The fruit on the second plate glowed bright yellow and orange. A fantastic color and shape experience!

"How much I have been looking forward to this!"

You hardly find the sweet red rice dish in restaurants. Women sell this sweet dish in the morning bazaars. I always look out for seated women with a large saucepan in front of them, which is covered with banana leaves. They pack the red rice, which they cover with grated, fresh coconut and drops of homemade syrup made from natural palm sugar, artistically in banana leaves and hold the package together with a small stick taken from a palm leaf. If you are lucky, they make a spoon from a banana leaf folded into two.

"In things like this, you can see how ecological the Balinese were before the island was swamped with western plastics. It seems to me that they haven't yet understood the difference between a product of nature and plastic, because some Balinese women throw their plastic rubbish away in nature, just as they used to do with products from nature. They seem to ignore the fact that the plastic rubbish does not decay with the weather to become manure."

After the delicious breakfast I spent the whole afternoon in a deck chair with a book, under a coconut palm, interrupted only by swimming round the pool a few times. As usual, the older Balinese women came and offered me their massages. "You massage, Chris! Massage good. Good for you, Chris." I nodded, because I knew how the gentle massage would really spoil my skin. By no means as enjoyable as caresses, but better than nothing. And I also loved the smell of the freshly pressed coconut oil which the women used.

On this evening, I was too tired to walk to the beach again. Instead, I sat down in the restaurant. Rather shyly, I looked for a suitable place and decided for a place in the corner. I had hardly finished off the mixed salad with shrimps, when a rather dreamy-looking woman from Australia sat next to me and engaged me in small talk, which I found quite pleasant. Soon she started talking about her problem. Her boyfriend had jilted her. She lamented her loss.I could not help chuckling secretly, as it was basically similar to what had been bothering me: separation due to Ray's death. I could really sympathise with her, which seemed visibly relieved and showered me with good wishes, which did me good.

"A good deed every day," I recited to myself while on the way to my room passing the lights in the garden, smelling the scent of the flowers. Up in the room, I discovered a short message on my mobile phone.

Chris, how are you? Is everything all right? Suryani

I was very pleased about these words from my good friend and wrote back immediately:

> *Oh! Thank you for thinking about me. The walks on q the beach are working wonders. Looking forward to seeing you soon! Chris.*

"And our daughter?", my thoughts turned to her, "how is she doing?" I asked myself und decided to send her a message.

> *Dear Noe, is everything all right? Sunny greetings to you from the beach. It would be even better if you were here.*

Noe answered that she was in the process of sorting out the papers from her practical unit. Despite that, she liked the capital city.

> *Berlin is simply fantastic. Just the same, I'd like the sun in Bali more. But ... you know.*

Laying on the bed. My thoughts were still with Noe in Berlin, lingered there for a while and then drifted back to reflect on the past day.

"The sun here has a healing effect on me, especially in this place where I am only outside in the sun, by the water, under trees, with my skin hardly covered up."

The next morning went in a similar way to the previous one. I woke up early, tiptoed onto the balcony and admired the way the sun's early rays were making the gigantic, old mango tree's leaves so radiant. I quickly put my sports clothing on, hurried to the beach and ran with light feet on the beach, through the shallow seawater that was splashing up in the shape of an arch. I laughed.

"Isn't that lovely?" I was thrilled. But soon I was out of breath, slackened my speed, stopped, felt the morning dew around my feet, felt the cooling, fine beads of sand massaging my feet. The sound of the waves was regular and gentle. This concentration on my feet interrupted the cycle of my thoughts about Ray's death. Now, concentrating on the present, I felt thankful. My look went up to the delicate blue morning sky.

> *"Thank you, God, for letting me experience nature with all my senses. Thank you that in this way I am forgetting my endless grief."*

I felt like having a meditation, looked on the sand for a suitable place and found not far away my meditation place from the previous day, still rising up out of the sand. I went up to it, sat down and looked over the vast sea. In the soft colours of the water, the rays of the sun were glittering like small, golden stars. Slowly I closed my eyes, took the energy from the enchanting surroundings into me and concentrated on my breathing for some time.

The meditation had its after-effects while I was eating my breakfast in a cheerful mood. A gentle morning wind was moving the palm leaves.

My programme for the rest of the day was similar to that of the day before. I alternated between the deck chair and the pool, enjoyed another massage with the feet and was almost asleep, when I heard a voice not far from me speaking my language: "Would you like to do something this evening?"

I raised my head and thought: "This question is unfortunately not meant for me." But I listened to the conversation.

"If we only knew where something is going on here."

I sat up and discovered two women at the edge of the pool. In a reflex reaction, I got up, went over to them and spoke in german language: "Hallo, ich höre eine mir bekannte Sprache! " "Hello, your language sounds very familar to me."

Pleasantly surprised, the two women turned to me. We soon got into conversation. Anna and Dorit introduced themselves and told me it was their first time on Bali. They had come from Germany the evening before.

"Everything is still new to us. We didn't have time to read the travel guide, so we don't have any plans. What about you?"

"I've been coming to Bali again and again for more than twenty years now and this bungalow complex is a must for me each time." I probably wanted to show them how competent I was, also hoping that we could do things together. And, indeed, the conversation went in this direction. We were soon arranging to meet for the evening.

"So, seven o'clock at the reception?"

"Fantastic! We're looking forward to going out with you."

I waved to Anna and Dorit and strolled along the garden path towards my bungalow. As I entered my room, my mobile phone squeaked. There was a message from Noe. My heart was really joyful.

> *What have you been doing today? Can you stand the heat? Here, it is cool and rainy. I would much prefer to be with you on Bali. Love.*

Quickly I answered:

> *Hi, Noe! I'm so happy to get a message from you. Here, the water and shade help me through the heat. I am looking forward to this evening. Guess why? I have a date with two German women. Will tell you about it later. Warm greetings from Bali to you!*

Express your emotions!

A passionate song of mourning

Out of anticipation, I was standing at the reception fifteen minutes before the appointed time and chatting to the people there. My Indonesian vocabulary was sufficient for that.

"Cantik!" "Beautiful! " said the man on duty and looked behind me.

When I turned round, Anna and Dorit were standing next to me, looking really chic.

"Hallo, the man is right! You're looking beautiful tonight!"

"You look great too," they answered promptly and laughed. In this good mood, we set off.

"My husband and I, we …, ," I could have started each of my sentences in this way, as I was telling them about the romantic places we had discovered. The women were curious and wanted to get to know these places. I led them away from the noise of the main road onto a road where no traffic was allowed, by the beach. The soft background music emphasised the peace and quiet here. It came over from the gardens of the restaurants with their romantic candlelight.

"It is a great fun, to stroll around here." Anna's enthusiastic comment made me happy.

"Here at the front is where our favourite restaurant must be!" We discovered the tropical garden, lit only by candles, which sparkled with each of the crystal glasses on the tables. The enchanting atmosphere was enhanced by a musician who was playing soft music on a Balinese bamboo recorder.

"It could hardly be more idyllic," said Dorit enthusiastically. I was pleased about the compliment and that I had fulfilled their wishes with my recommendation.

"This is really a holistic programme for spoiling people," Anna gave us a dreamy look.

"Can you hear the sound of the waves?" Slowly we turned our ears towards the sea and listened, fascinated to the steady sound of the waves. We didn't notice the young balinese woman in a dress that reminded of the famous Balinese temple dancers. She handed us the menu with a graceful movement, smiled.

"Chris, tell us what you're going to order."

"A freshly caught fish with hot sambal sauce, rice and vegetables."

Dorit looked at the pictures on the menu: "I like the look of the fried rice with chicken and the side salad. And for dessert, I'd like vanilla ice with tropical fruits."

"What does 'Nasi Campur' mean?" Anna asked me. "'Nasi' is rice in Indonesian and 'Campur' means mixed. It's boiled or slightly fried chicken, roasted peanuts, fried, coated tempeh or tofu, hard boiled eggs cut in half, and, if you wish, spiced with the hot sambal sauce."

"That sounds interesting."

"It also tastes excellent. It's eaten almost every day and each kitchen varies the ingredients."

Our dinner tasted delicious. Anna and Dorit enjoyed it and nodded approvingly at each other. I was feeling very happy. I wasn't by myself at the place where I had spent such a wonderful dream of an evening with Ray. Again and again, my thoughts wallowed in sweet memories which threatened to become dark ones if I were to get absorbed in them. The other two seemed to be noticing this; they knew about me and diverted me, asking about life on Bali, and I enjoyed telling them about my experiences.

"Well, I feel like having some entertainment after this oasis of peace," said Anna as we were leaving the restaurant.

"Not experienced enough yet? OK. Let me think about it." I remembered a bar with a small stage, which was sometimes used for performances by musicians from all over the world. "Would you like to experience a jam session?"

"That sounds interesting." Both ladies were enthusiastic and I tried to think where this bar exactly was.

"It can't be far away. Because we lingered there on our way back to the bungalow campus. The hot rhythms were enticing. I hope the shop is still there. In Bali, you have to expect changes everywhere you go."

"Let's have a try!" Anna encouraged us. So we courageously set off to look for it.

"Taxi, you need taxi?" Every few metres we were invited to make use of the services of the countless private taxi drivers. But we decided to walk, and observed the night life at the same time. Now, in the month of July, it was very hectic, with a lot of tourists strolling through the streets of the district where all the pleasure was.

"There is a lot going on here," remarked Dorit, and Anna nodded.

"Yes, the southern part of Bali is very touristy." I also was amazed at how many tourists were pushing their way into the clubs, bars and restaurants, which I had nothing to do with in my bungalow campus or on the beach.

"Where do all the people come from?"

"Here in the southern part of Bali, you find a lot of tourist. Most of them come from Australia; for them it's only a short way to come here. But more and more tourists come from countries like the US, Russia, Japan, China, India and of course from Europe. This beautiful island is a magnet for everyone," I laughed.

"What a contrast to the cozy place at *three brothers bungalows* and the promenade by the beach!"

"Yes, Bali is very versatile," I explained to the Anna and Dorit, who were here for the first time. Unexpectedly, I discovered the bar I was looking for.

"Come on in! The best places for you." A good-looking young man came up to us, smiling, and led us charmingly to a table near the stage.

"What does one order here?"

"Bintang," I decided. "The best is to drink Balinese beer to relieve your thirst."

Slowly, we became aware of what was going on around us. At the tables, young people were chatting and seemed to be hardly noticing the musician who was sitting on the stage. He reminded me of the music students from Java, Indonesia's main island, which has several universities with good reputations, with his ponytail and intellectual glasses.

I listened to his experimental playing on a violin. I got to like it more because he was bringing sounds from his instrument that I was not accustomed to. There were dark, delicate, soft, sentimental and squeaky sounds to be heard, some of them melodious, some reminding me in a fragmentary way of a tune I knew.

Dorit and Anna also liked his music; they kept on beaming at me. This music increasingly touched my soul. I felt captured and attracted by his way of playing the violin. He started so sing that sounded like: "Ain't no sunshine...". The young musician played parts of the song and sang the words in fragments.

231

"Isn't he experimenting in a wonderful way!"

While we were listening, we made comments on the effect his playing was having on us. I was already singing with him in my mind, at first quite enthusiastically and beating time happily, but then my feeling changed. Overwhelmed by my grief, I sang: "There is no sunshine since he is gone!" I found these words, which had changed with my deep feelings of mourning, intensive and painful. The lamenting sounds from the violin emphasised my feelings. Suddenly I got up from my chair. "Can I sing with you?" I had jumped onto the stage, hurried up to the violin player with big steps and almost overwhelmed him with my question.

Without any words, he gave me a microphone without taking his concentration away from his very sensitive performance. The grief in me was only too present. I sat down on the chair next to him and closed my eyes. The singing came out of my heard. *"He is gone. No sunshine since he is gone. He is gone. No sunshine."*

My voice had dark tones, sounded weepy, tortured, rustling, and hopeful, and went well with the sounds coming from the violin. All my memories of Ray, my pain at the finality of his death transformed themselves into a tune. I lived out my feelings, immersed myself into the condition of a trance. The lamenting sounds of the violin guided my voice.

The musician then referred to my fragments of the words. "No sunshine since she's gone."

"Since he is gone. I feel no sunshine, since he is gone." Again and again. Our singing took up the fragments of the text. The violin played between them,

232

found connections and then went in different directions. A fascinating play on tunes was unfolding. I gave myself completely into my feelings. Dived into a dreamlike state. The plaintive violin guided me. "No sunshine since he is gone." It seemed, I couldn't stop.

It really was not easy to separate myself from my inner concentration, not even while the audience was clapping. I could only slowly open my eyes, look at the violinist gently, bow and put my hand on my heart as a sign of thanks. It was not until then that I stood up and thoughtfully went back to my place.

"Heavenly! You were so much absorbed in yourself." Anna beamed at me. Dorit was still clapping and nodding towards me in acknowledgement.

"Are you often singing in front of audiences?"

As yet, I could not give an answer. I was still seized by the depth of my experience. I needed time to come back to reality. After a few deep breaths, I managed it.

"Dorit, normally I don't sing in public, and this time wasn't planned either. Something pushed me on the stage. The singing just came out of me."

That night, I lay awake for a long time. My adrenalin level was high! Pictures of the evening were still fluttering around in my head.

"As if a husk had burst open," I whispered to myself, "My feelings turned into a song. But, what was special about the young musician? He touched my heart through the plaintive sound of his violin." With these thoughts I fell asleep.

"That was a very impressive evening, Chris! First the romantic dinner and then the song out from your heart. Thank you for that!"

We had arranged to have breakfast together the next morning.

"*The song out of the heart* is a good name for it! Right! It seemed that the sound of the violin opened my deep emotions."

"You both have been really impressive." Anna praised our performance once again. The previous evening gave us a lot to talk about and put the spice on our breakfast, which made it unusually long and drawn out. Sooner or later, my thoughts were drifting in the direction of my deck chair. I was still tired from the last nights experience.

But Anna brought me back to the matter in hand with a further question: "Do you know what I noticed this morning when I went to the reception? One of the women working here was putting little baskets made from palm leaves, decorated with flowers and rice, on the path. What was that for?"

"Those were presents for their Hindu gods that they worship. Connected with them is a wish for a blessing or a request for success or forgiveness. With a gracious movement of the hand, they spread holy water on each of the sacrificial gifts and send their wish, together with the delicately smelling smoke from the joss sticks, up to heaven."

"That's exciting! I think it's remarkable how they live out their faith so visibly. Not like us Christians. We go to church to pray, and otherwise we save it for the privacy of our own room."

I had heard this argument before. Had not Noe spoken like this?

"If we do it at all," Dorit continued. "My impression is that our faith in God is very much on the decrease. Going to church on Sundays is not fashionable nowadays. The churches are only filled on special occasions such as the high festivals of Easter and Christmas. Then the old traditions still have an effect."

Anna was interested in the practice of Bali Hinduism, which was not really comparable with Indian Hinduism.

"Do you know, the Balinese include their ancestor worship, ancient traditions and religious performances in their religious faith?"

"And why do people put their sacrificial gifts on the footpaths?"

"They place them in front of the house, the shop, some place where they want to ask for the blessing. Each of their gods has a particular place: the lower ones at a lower level. For the higher gods, the gifts are placed on small steles or a small temple. The higher the god, the higher the place for the gift. Once or twice a day they place the gifts on special places on the site of their house. But not just there; they also ask for blessing on their rice field, car or motorcycle."

"They also sacrifice to their gods on rice fields?"

"Yes, when they are planting they ask for the blessing of a good harvest, and if the harvest is good, they offer up thanks with gifts: they entwine some ears of rice with yellow and white cloths and symbolically lay leaves from flowers, rice, cooked food, small sweet things on the ground for the lower gods. Nearby, on the temple steles, they sacrifice to the higher gods."

"That sounds fascinating! We don't know anything about that in Christianity," Anna observed.

"I'm not so sure," was my spontaneous reaction. "We don't do it with visible presents, but we ask God for His blessing on our plans, request His blessing on sad occasions like illness or death, just as on joyful occasions like a wedding, the birth of a child or a birthday. And sometimes we address God spontaneously and thank Him for something that we hadn't hoped for. We often use the expression *Thank God*, and sometimes we really mean it, when we are relieved that something has turned out well. Or don't you also ask for forgiveness for mistakes you have made?"

"I think our communication with God is modified, not always in the foreground and occasionally subconscious."

They thought about my words. Dorit sat up. "Well, the two religions certainly can't be compared directly. But I think certain elements of faith can be compared with each other."

"I'm always rather sceptical when Balinese tell me that they, the Hindus, and we Christians ultimately believe in the same god. 'There is only one God' I often hear. Maybe they mean that the highest instance in all religions is the one God."

Again, there was a short pause. Dorit nodded. "Yes, that sounds strange to me. We pray to one God, the triune God, Father, Son and Holy Spirit at the same time. On Bali they pray to different gods concerned with different matters."

"The almighty most probably stands behind these deities."

"Perhaps the people who say that, Chris, mean the universal God, who unites all people in their faith?"

"I don't quite agree with this view. I'm afraid I'm not familiar enough with Hinduism and Islam. But maybe you're right: ideally, it could be so. In Heaven there are no walls, no borders, and therefore no border posts to exclude, are there?"

"I've never been aware of any border posts in Heaven," Anna blurted out with a laugh. Dorit continued the argumentation: "Despite this, people obsessed with religion fight against others with a different faith in this world. You find it happening everywhere and at all times. Isn't that crazy?"

Anna made use of her pause for breath to supplement the statement. "You find exclusion for reason of having a different religion everywhere. And, in the worst case, coupled with greed for power or money. Look at Syria, Afghanistan and Nigeria. When I see something like that, I can't have any positive view of religions."

I only listened to the account of her position with half an ear. My thoughts had latched on to Balinese Hinduism. "Let's talk about the positive examples of religion. Here on Bali I meet their faith as communal, peaceful, colourful, very artistic and, above all, public. How deep the faith is in each individual and whether it's felt to be a collective duty by some, is hard to say. But it is clear that the Balinese live out their spirituality with a certain mysticism, which we don't encounter in our modern society. We just don't have it. That might be the reason why the island is attracting so many tourists from western lands. They feel at home, and individuals live out the spiritual and mystic side of their lives here. Meditation and yoga centres are coming out of the ground like mushrooms, probably because the form of Hinduism on Bali has a special atmosphere."

Anna and Dorit looked at each other uncertainly.

"What attracted you to Bali? Was it the spirituality here?" I asked, suddenly curious to know.

"No, it was just chance, the travel organisation's special offer. But we are surprised and fascinated at the same time to see how intensively faith is lived out here. As a tourist, you can't help noticing it."

I could understand what made the two of them so enthusiastic. "I, too, am fascinated at the way the people on Bali live out their faith and include me in it. Yes, there's no way of escaping it. Here I glean inspiration for my Christian faith, strange as that might sound."

Dorit returned to the subject of tourism. "Tell me, Chris, are there really so many yoga schools and yoga hotels with yoga courses that you told us about before?"

"If you take a drive to Ubud, you won't be able to get away from this trend. I don't take advantage of these offers, but practise meditation with my Balinese friend. But the run on Yoga courses and such like is great!

Ultimately, it's good business as the courses and retreats aren't exactly cheap. They are offered mainly by people from western countries, whom you must pay accordingly."

"That's good for those who want to make their profit from it, also the organisers and also those who find that yoga does them good."

I was feeling tired from the conversation, although the subject was so interesting. My eyes turned yet again to the deck chairs. One in particular, under the coconut palms, seemed to be smiling at me invitingly. The massage women already stood by the pool, offering a massage. "My dear ones, it's time to go to my deck chair!"

"We'll walk through the shopping streets. Perhaps we'll find some nice souvenir."

"It may be that we won't meet again. Today you're going on to the artists' town Ubud and tomorrow my friend's son is fetching me. So it's time for farewells."

"It was a great enrichment for our holiday to have met you, Chris. Thank you very much. You're a wonderful woman. I'm sure you'll be successful on your new way. I wish you much happiness."

"I also say, thank you Chris. The chance of getting to know you was fantastic!"

"Yes, it was wonderful to get to know you ladies. Thank you for your company."

We embraced each other as good friends and waved as we went in our different directions.

Later on, dosing in the deck chair, pictures of our short, intensive encounter went by: The breakfast conversations, *my song out of the heart,* our romantic dinner with the sound of the waves, the dear words of farewell. My heart felt warmed and comforted.

"Ray, you were definitely with us," I whispered to myself, got up and dived into the cool water to refresh my body and mind.

The inner voice says:
Take a break!

A retreat with peace, quiet, deep feelings

"Can I leave you like this or do you still need me?" Yaya, my friend Suryani's son, put my luggage down.

"That's all right, Yaya. I'm very thankful to you for driving me to Wayan."

The past weekend had been filled with activities in Suryani's house. The sons of Wawan and Heny had asked me to cook Spaghetti alla Carbonara for them. That entailed driving to the nearest supermarket which, to my amazement, was hardly different from our supermarkets in Germany. Back home, three of the sons enthusiastically agreed to help me with the cooking. They chopped onions and ham, flavoured the sauce and kept looking into the pot to see if the spaghetti was done or not. All went well. The plates were distributed and the members of the family sat on their chairs expectantly. "Enak," "delicious", was the unanimous comment as they stuffed it in and helped themselves to some more. "Yes, it tastes so good because we cooked it all together," I remarked and everyone nodded in agreement.

On the Saturday morning, it was time for Suryani's public meditation again. When we drove up to the atrium, about a hundred people were waiting for the master of this art once again. You could see their anticipation at the prospect of moving about all together, singing and clapping, lying down to relax and meditate and listening to her recommendations for healthy living. I observed her ability in showing enthusiasm, especially when it came to singing simple, joyful songs together.

After the event, we were sitting in larger groups on the warm ground, when somebody passed 'Balinese fast food' round. Packed in a paper bag were rice, fine strips of chicken, some water spinach, hot sambal and roasted peanuts.

"It's a good feeling to be eating together in good company," I said to the Dutch woman who had joined us after the event.

My positive feeling changed yet again when I was resting on my bed in the afternoon. Something dark moved inside me and darkened my mood. I wanted to get away from it, got up to see what the others in the house were doing and met my friend who immediately noticed my grief: "Would you like to meditate on the beach tomorrow morning?"

"That would be a good idea." I was always open for a morning meditation on the beach with her, no matter what mood I was in. With great anticipation, I went to sleep with pleasant thoughts. Early on the Sunday morning a full car set off. Cok Alit, Yaya and two friends of Suryani's were also with us.

"On Bali, lots of people fit into a car," I thought chuckling to myself as we set off. The mood was cheerful.

"Probably they are all looking forward to sitting in the warm sand for half an hour and enjoying the morning atmosphere. At least, that's how I'm feeling," I thought while the others were nattering in Balinese.

Our party sat in a semi-circle with its open side facing the sea and the horizon. There was a light wind, the sea was splashing lightly while we were concentrating on our breathing and meditating.

Around us, it was full of life. Balinese families were going for walks on the beach, swimming in the sea or sitting together on the warm sand. We also strolled barefoot over the warm, soft sand after our meditation.

"Do you all feel as refreshed as I do?" asked Suryani. "The sea air and the grains of sand give support to the effects of the meditation and make it something special."

I nodded assent, because I found any meditation on the beach with her to be pure joy.

After our return back home, the family quickly gathered together round the breakfast table, on which the cook had already placed various delicacies in small dishes. Fried fish, chicken in curry sauce, water spinach, soya done as a vegetable, crispy fried tempeh and tofu with a sweet sambal sauce, roasted peanuts and my favourite sauce.

"I love your homemade sauce! How do you make it?" They explained to me: "That is sambal mata, raw sambal. You cut chili, onions, garlic and pepperoni very finely, add salt, a little dried shrimp paste and fresh pieces of lime to it, mix it all with coconut oil, maybe mix a few drops of water with it, that's all."

"I'll make a note of the recipe and make sambal sauce at home."

"Here, take some more if it's not too hot for you." The family was pleased that I was praising the food and passed the sauce to me, which I greedily poured over my rice. I knew that tears would come into my eyes from it, but I was ready for that. During the meal, I realised that I had quickly got used to the traditional Balinese breakfast and was not missing bread, butter and jam for one minute.

As if by some tacit agreement, everyone retired to their rooms after the breakfast together. I lay down on my bed and soon dosed off to sleep. But my sleep was restless. There was something working inside me. Probably my grief. "Don't let it come to the surface just now. Better to get some sleep," I dictated to myself and tried hard to go back to sleep. Yet the heavy feeling in my tummy gave me no peace.

"Think about your grief," I heard while half asleep. "Take a time out of it all, away from all activities. Have some peace and quiet until you've put everything in order within yourself. No distractions! Concentrate on what has to be worked through. Carpe diem!"

This clear message did not go away. I sat up, ready for an inner dialogue. "OK. I have heard the order to withdraw, to give myself time, peace and quiet to come to terms with my grief after Ray's death."

I thought about it. "What about accepting this message?" I lay down again, pulled the cover over my head and tried to sleep again. But something was still working in me. My willingness to go on this inner way grew and developed into a certainty. My thoughts seemed to be flying over a territory, as if they were looking for a place, until they found one. "Wayan!"

The message was clear. I knew Wayan already a long time. Ray and I had had a friendship with the painter over many years. We got to know each other because at an exhibition where the artists were present we had been fascinated by his works of art. He invited us to come and see more of his works. Some time or other, we thought of him coming over to visit us. We had in mind an exhibition and workshops, which he as a lecturer at an art college would certainly enjoy doing. His time in Germany gave him ideas; he was successful with his art, which later gave him advantages in his profession. His time with us strengthened our friendship and from then on, on each of our trips to Bali for several weeks, Ray and I used to rent one of his spacious flats near the artists' town of Ubud. We loved the life in his family, with the grandparents and

245

employees. It felt almost like home. From his more peacefully situated campus, we liked to go on tours through small, traditional villages and over landscapes of rice fields.

"Perhaps I should go along with my feeling and take a room at Wayan's place? Maybe that would be the right place for me?" The longer I thought about it, the more my inner voice assented to this idea. My sleep was over. A plan had been made. "I must tell Suryani about it."

In the living room, I came across my friend.

"Do that. I think it is good for you. Take time for yourself to relax," was her reaction. She spurred on my intention and we were soon dialling Wayan's phone number. "Chris here."

"Hello, nice of you to call. Where are you? Do you intend to come here?"

"Can you read thoughts?" I asked with a laugh. When I had been informing people of Ray's death, I had also informed Wayan by e-mail. I told him about the time I was spending with my friend's family and my thoughts on taking a room at his place.

His invitation spurted out of him: "At any time! Your apartment became vacant yesterday. Come on. We're looking forward to having you here."

This words opened up my heart! He had called the flat that we normally rented 'my apartment'! And this flat was vacant just now?

"That sounds really good," I said after the phone call. "My inner voice tells me, this place will be the right one for me now." My friend beamed at me. I dialled the number of my balinese friend again and booked my flat for the next day.

"You'll be working during the week, and I'll be looked after by Wayans family."

"I think that's a good choices, Chris. Tomorrow, Yaya will drive you", said Suryani. I already knew that sentence!

"Yet again, your good son. What would you do without him?" I laughed.

The drive passed quickly. Yaya was a good conversationalist. We laughed a lot. After we had left the city traffic behind us, we drove through the more rural regions with rice fields and rivers in deep canyons, before we arrived in Penestanan near Ubud.

We dragged my luggage for the last three hundred metres, because only a narrow drive led to Wayan's property. We were out of breath when we stood in front of his wife, Made.

"Nice to meet you, Chris!" Her soft embrace and her sad smile brought my grief back again. Tears ran down my cheeks and formed small, dark marks on the ground. I quickly wiped them away. On Bali, one does not cry, and I quickly introduced Yaya to her, who was standing by my luggage. She led us to the big dining table, where some guests were taking a late breakfast. Ketut, her sister brought a glass of water for each of us.

"May I introduce our guests? Here are Laura and her husband from Hungary. She is editor of a travel magazine and writing a report about Bali. I think you know Mio from Sydney already, because she comes several times a year to accompany meditation courses and works for a restaurant as a food designer." She pointed out three women who were in lively conversation.

"This is Emma from Holland and Paola from Milan. Both are staying with us for the first time. And here is Claire, our good friend from Switzerland, who is unfortunately leaving us in a few days. Claire lived here for a month."

The women waved at me in a friendly way and beamed, quite relaxed. Paola called happily: "Welcome here at this beautiful place!"

"Thank you!" I waved at them all, turned round to Yaya and went on in the direction of my flat.

"They give you a hearty welcome here, as if you were one of the family." Yaya still seemed to be impressed while we were climbing the steps to my flat.

"That's right. Perhaps it's influenced by the rural life here. In the city, you keep yourselves in with high walls and hardly greet each other, don't you?" Yaya laughed. "You know, guests come here who are open for this friendly, family atmosphere. They enjoy the company and especially living together with Wayan's pleasant and friendly family. Probably the peace and the luscious green also influence their choice to come here, as in the evenings you hear the frogs croaking, the ducks quacking, the chickens cackling and the dogs barking. Not to forget that geckos have a loud call," I added.

Meanwhile, we were standing on my balcony. Yaya looked over the vast garden, the artistic sculptures, the stream near the house, and nodded: "This is the ideal place for you, Chris. Here you can withdraw and find your balance again."

I was thinking about his words and felt, he was right. Then I changed the subject. "Be careful when driving back home! In the rural area here, people and dogs walk on the road."

"Thank you for being so anxious about me," he laughed, and bade me farewell with a short embrace. I waved to him again from the balcony. "You take care of yourself, Chris. Phone us at any time if you need us. OK?"

"Thank youuu," I called to after him, turned round and looked at my apartment. The balcony was furnished like a living room. On one side a comfortable sofa set. In front, where the green trees and bushes grew, enough space for yoga exercises and meditation. On the other side of the balcony a large desk with a cute floor lamp. And above everything a roof of reeds, to protect from sun and rain. I dropped relaxed down onto the bamboo sofa.

"I feel, that's the right place for me, to find my inner strength again," I thought and cuddled into my cushion. The sun made me feel warm. I looked into the coconut palms, with their fruits pressing closely against each other. The wind was moving in the filigree leaves that were shimmering in a yellow and silver green. What a present, the magnificent tropical nature. I felt a deep gratitude, looking into the vast, bright blue sky. After a while, I felt like having a meditation: Sittingt at the edge of the sofa, straightening my spinal column, putting my hands together on my lap, expanding my chest and concentrating on my breathing in and out through my nose. Slowly, I closed my eyes, focused on my chest and felt it rising and falling. My concentration wandered slowly upwards from my feet through my legs. "The muscles in my feet are relaxing," I said slowly with my inner voice and continued through my legs to my hips, the trunk, my shoulders, my arms, right up to the fingertips. Slowly, I felt more relaxed.

How long I remained sitting like that, I could not say. But I was not feeling the burden of the past days any more just then. After a prayer of thanks, I slowly stood up, went into the bedroom, lay down under the mosquito net and quickly went off to sleep.

When I woke up, the sun was setting, the orange shades of the evening light were becoming lighter, giving way to a green-grey tone that was becoming increasingly darker. Now the evening mood came over the birds, insects, geese and chickens. They resounded through the night with their humming, gabbling, cackling and crowing. I closed my eyes in order to identify the different voices. Here, in the middle of this varied concert, I felt at home, accepted, in a place that I was familiar with. The sound on my mobile phone told me that there was a short message from Suryani.

Everything went well?

As it always was when I got a message from a dear relative or friend, my heart leapt with joy. I answered quickly:

*Yes, I am well. Thank you for everything my dear. I am
ready for my retreat. Lots of love, Chris*

I knew why I had chosen Wayan's place. Not for
spending time with the family and all the others who
were living here, at least not at the beginning. My inner
voice gave me the clear direction that I should devote
myself to the final farewell from my dear husband. In
the hypnotherapy, I had already been led onto my way,
which now needed to be taken, even though it was hard
at the moment. Therefore, I had a clear aim. Yet a fine
inner voice whispered to me: *"The way is the destination."*

Nature heals!

A new start every morning

On the first days of my retreat, my morning walks were dominant, and they often went on until later in the morning. I sidled past the guests' table, ordered breakfast in my room and continued the day as a retreat. I dwelt on my thoughts and tried to accept any feelings that surfaced: grief, anger, despair, helplessness.

I did experience satisfaction and inner joy whenever I set off early in the morning to take a long walk in the surrounding nature. Mostly, I chose lonely paths, which went past rice fields, where the rice farmers were working; I would linger there for a time, looking at the luscious, tropical landscape all round me: Green. Yellow-green. Green with a white light. Bright Bali-green. Watching the shining colours which the morning sun was producing as if by magic, my heart rose up to a higher level.

On this first day in the interior of the island, I had woken up before sunrise and noticed a deep feeling of grief in my breast that made my breathing harder. My instinct advised me to take some deep breaths. I closed my eyes and concentrated on my nose, breathed in and out with regular breaths until the heavy feeling of grief went away. "Thank God!" I prayed and remained in my lying position for an other while.

"Right, get up, go on your way, walk through the warm and tropical nature. This will help you to start the day positive." I noticed that my instinct for survival was still working well. Quickly I threw the thin bed covering to the side, crawled out of bed under the mosquito net and felt satisfied. I opened the balcony door, went out and listened.

In the distance the cocks were crowing, the crickets chirping loudly; Wayan's father seemed to be letting his chickens and ducks out of their night quarters. He was talking to them in a loud voice and they were

"Nature heals." I felt that clearly at this moment when I was all ears and my thoughts were gradually leaving me. The fresh morning wind on my skin then made me aware of my body. I dressed and set off. Behind the last row of houses on the village street was the beginning of the path to the rice fields, which I followed. Hardly a hundred metres further on, the rice fields appeared, lit up with the light green colour from the sun. I continued my walk and did not stop until I was totally surrounded by rice fields. In front of me stood a rice farmer with his naked legs up to the ankles in the flooded earth, raking his field. Next to him, another one was using a long bamboo rod to drive birds away that were trying to get at the ripe grains. Crowds of them flew up into the air, only to pounce on the next ear of rice. While I was strolling a bit further on, I came across two thin, wiry rice farmers, their skin tanned by the sun. I could tell by their gestures that they were talking about their respective harvests.

As a silent observer of the morning life on the fringe of the rice fields, I felt quite at ease. Now there were only narrow paths between the different fields, on which I was trying to keep my balance, until I came to a wider path again. I felt he soft grass all round my legs.

"Today, if I'm lucky, I'll get a view of the holy mountain, the volcano called *Gunung Agung,* in the distance," I thought and looked for a suitable place. Because it was so clear that morning, the chances were good. "There it is! The holy mountain!"

I stopped to contemplate it solemnly. The volcano standing out from its surroundings reminded me of a humpback whale. On that morning, it fitted into the rather misty colours in the distance with its light grey colouring. The background was delicate; it was as on a throne in the distance, but the volcano was still dangerous. In recent years, it had made the island tremble several times and spat out fire. People and villages near it had had to be evacuated and the airport had cancelled its flights.

My thoughts drifted involuntarily back to the times when Ray and I had walked through the tropical landscape in the mornings, hoping to get a view of the holy mountain. I felt my longing for Ray surfacing.

"Come on, let's continue to walk together, hand in hand, Ray," I said to comfort myself and let my imagination show me that my dear husband was with me. That was successful, indeed. I felt his nearness, his long, gentle fingers around my hand. With a feeling of deep closeness, I continued walking along the paths through the rice fields. When I met a rice farmer coming towards me on an old bicycle, my husband went from my side, leaving a quiet, soulful smile on my lips.

Returning to my apartment, I was hoping to meet my good friend, Wayan and as luck would have it, I did. I found him sitting on his seat at the big table and having breakfast. When he saw me, he got up and came up to me with open arms.

"Hi, Chris, how are you?" His sensitive voice touched my heart We embraced each other. I wept silently, came out of the embrace and told him about Ray's last days, his death and my mourning.

"Wayan, I'm having difficulty in getting over the loss," I complained and wiped the tears from my cheek with the back of my hand. He looked at me full of sympathy and said nothing.

"You know, Chris, we Balinese feel these things in a different way," he began cautiously. "When someone dies here, we are full of hope because the person we love is coming to God. We are convinced that things are much better for him there."

I nodded silently. Yes, we Christians believe, too, that the deceased is being well looked after in the presence of God; we believe in the resurrection from the dead and eternal life. And yet, the ones left behind still mourn; at funerals and afterwards, many tears are shed. With what he had said, he reminded me that on Bali joy and hope predominate.

"Probably he wants to comfort me and help me to find my way out of my valley of tears," I thought to myself. I wanted to relax and think about his words, so I said "Good-bye" to him. Upstairs, on my sofa, looking into the palm trees from my balcony, my thoughts went round. I thought of the balinese culture, to hold back tears and to put joy in the foreground, because they know the deceased is with God.

"And what's about me? I'm caught in my grief. Everything is circling around me, around my grief." I realised our cultural difference and how far away I was, to feel the joy that Ray was with God.

Sitting on my sofa, in the evening light, I saw in my mind's eye a balinese burning ceremony, to which we were invited by friends. "It's a bit like a festival," Ray had said as we were looking at the splendid procession from the edge of the road, with the extravagantly carved wooden towers containing the bones of the dead. They were decorated with golden, red and white cloths. Friends and relatives were carrying them through the streets on thick bamboo poles. They repeatedly raced enthusiastically in circles, to shake off any evil spirits. In addition, the *gamelan orchestra* was dominating the mood with the high tones of its brass instruments playing at high speed. At the place where the ceremony was to take place, the priest, with help from others, carried out a lot of symbolic acts that we did not understand, and it all took a long time. Eventually, the corpse was transferred to gigantic wooden horses that had been covered with black cloth, which were then set alight to burn the bones. The whole ceremony took more than half a day. It started in the morning at the home of the family with the blessing of the corpse from the priest and the washing of the corpse by close relatives. Early in the afternoon, a procession was formed to go through the streets of the village, accompanied by the *gamelan orchestra,* with a lot of people going with them. The cremation lasted until late afternoon, and not until then was the ceremony over. I did not remember seeing any sign of mourning, as we do at our funerals.

"Ray was quite close to the mark when he said that a burning ceremony on Bali was more like a festival than a funeral such as we are accustomed to," went through my head.

"And I have come on the journey to Bali to come to terms with my grief." Slowly, I was becoming aware of the paradox situation: Coming to Bali to come to terms with my grief arising from Christian tradition, when the Hindus have different ways of dealing with death. "Will I maybe succeed in coming to terms with my grief on this island, under the influence of the Balinese culture? I imagine it could help me to focus my attention on Ray and the joy because he is being well looked after in the presence of God. Will I perhaps come to the conclusion that our two cultures are not so far away from each other in regard to death?" I called to mind a scene during our funeral service, when a friend of ours put his arm on mine and explained to me: "Ray is better off. He's with God now."

At the time, I nodded out of politeness, but without understanding what he meant by it, as my thoughts were governed entirely by the feeling of loss. I was grieving over the loss of our happiness, our wish to grow old together and to live out our dreams together.

To a certain extent, we celebrate our mourning. We show the bereaved our sympathy, let them know we feel with them. We talk about the so-called year of mourning, emphasise that we must come to terms with our grief. On Bali, however, there is no such tradition of mourning. Here death is accepted as a part of life.

"I don't know what it's like in individual cases. Yet, if one has got good karma, been brilliant at doing good deeds, similar to our Ten Commandments, then one will be with God. If that's not a reason for joy …," I murmured to myself and switched round.

"But now I'm here on Bali. My friend told me in the hypnotherapy to bid my husband farewell and go my own way without him. 'God will take care of Ray,' she had said; yet this way is painful for me. I would still rather not walk it alone. I don't like the idea of a final farewell from Ray." I was well aware of that. To reconcile myself to it, I added: "I'll go my own way, for better or worse." For a while, I thought about what I had said. Then I added: *"Days of light and clarity will come; I feel that and am fairly sure of it."*

Backsliding!

A heavy fall with a injury

The first days after my arrival I lived just a day at a time, guided by my feelings and my momentary needs. Most of the time I spent on the balcony. I sat or lay on the comfortable, upholstered sun lounger and gazed into the filigree coconut leaves that changed with the sunlight from light green to orange green. Behind them, the broad, dark green leaves of the mango tree. From further down, the exotic perfume of the *cempaka flowers* drifted into my nose.

I woke up when the cocks crowed and took that as a signal that it was time to get up, opened the door to the balcony, letting the morning coolness in. On the first look through the green splendour in front of my balcony into the light blue morning sky, I felt well and truly surrounded by tropical nature. This feeling made it easier for me to experience the morning with all my senses. Sometimes I was very sad, but then I usually sent it away with my gymnastics, or a meditation. I opened my arms wide in the direction of the sky, shook myself awake, stretched the upper part of my body and breathed in and out firmly, before sitting down for a meditation, concentrating entirely on my breathing. Mostly I finished my morning ritual with the Lord's Prayer. After breakfast, which I had brought to me on the balcony, I sometimes remained seated on my favourite place, observing the life in the high bushes and trees. Delicate squirrels with grey and brown stripes would jump around almost like acrobats on the filigree coconut palm leaves, as though they were playing a catching game. Exotic butterflies would enjoy the nectar of the bright red hibiscus flowers, reaching graciously into the flowers and then going on to the next flower. When I bent over the edge of the balcony balustrade, I could watch the chickens leading their young out for a walk with busy cackling, picking up anything that was eatable from the ground, almost nervously trying to get the young ones to imitate them. They took hardly any notice of the pineapples that were growing almost on the ground, seeming to be sitting on thrones in the midst of elegant, pointed leaves. The goldfish in the softly rushing stream that meandered its way through the garden seemed to be noticing me whenever I looked down from the balcony, because they stretched their wide open mouths above the surface of the water and made noises which made me think they were hoping I would feed them.

My observations could continue for hours. Occasionally, I sat on the sofa in the evening, when the chirping crickets and the barking watchdogs were encroaching on the silence. Everything I observed, heard and smelt from the big balcony distracted me from the pain of my grief. Mostly, at least. Sometimes a feeling of grief came over me that started around my stomach. It moved over my chest into the lung and made my breathing flatter. Until the colours inside me darkened, making me tired and floppy.

Each time, it was a challenge for me to go through with it. With deep, regular breathing, I slowly raised myself up again and started to move my limbs. Sometimes I said a hopeful prayer.

"Today the path up in the heights is calling!" an inner voice called to me one morning. Indeed, I felt ready to tackle this particular hiking route. It went over a high ridge with a spectacular view on either side of the narrow path, went down into ravines and gave the chance of a wide view of the sky. I quickly put on my sports clothes and set off. The night before, it had rained. The earth was soft, the morning air exceptionally cool. The paved path seemed to be slippery, so I walked down carefully on the steps to the Hindu temple that were overgrown with moss. My inner voice warned me to be careful with my steps because of previous bad experiences with Bali's streets and lanes, which could be uneven and have unexpected holes. At the bottom, I walked over a bridge that crossed a river that was moving with mighty, roaring masses of water, climbed carefully up the broad steps that led to the path on the top. Up there, the earth was still moist with a few puddles. Again and again, I stopped to admire the landscape. The high, thick grass on the side of the path was shining like silk, continuing right down the ravine, which had old, gnarled trees growing on either side. That morning, the firmament was like an endless tent roof illuminated with light blue.

While I was observing all this, my mood changed surprisingly. It was as though a dark cloth was coming from my stomach over my chest. Not able to resist the strength of this feeling, I closed my eyes, breathed deeply, feeling each breath consciously. I felt anger and fury coming up in me because I was standing alone and not hand in hand with my husband. My grief and aggression were soon searching for an outlet.

I complained to God: "God! Where are you? Why are you letting me stand here alone? Why are you making me suffer? What have we done wrong? Why did Ray have to die so soon? Why have you shortened our years together like this? You have destroyed our wishes, our yearnings. I don't understand it!"

Completely absorbed in my painful questions, I lamented right up to the firmament until my voice could do no more and I cried bitterly. I felt disappointed, left alone, helpless. Sobbing, I called up to Heaven again, as though I were expecting an immediate, comforting answer or a cure for my pain: "Oh, hear me, God, help me!" But there was nobody to give me answer.

Resigned, I looked down at the earth. I did not give up my questioning. I shouted to myself: "Ray, come back to me! Let me feel your hand in mine, see your eyes, hear your voice. I'm yearning for you!"

Time went by. Slowly, I recovered and went on with heavy steps. In the distance, I could see houses situated apart from each other, but it soon became clear that they were a small village by the street. My steps and my bearing had become normal again. I was amazed at the decorative houses, skilfully presenting talents in art and woodcarving. In front of a food stall, a Warung, there were young coconuts on the ground that seemed to be smiling at me.

The saleswoman, an elderly woman was standing behind the stall in conversation with a school child. I waited for a while, wished her a good morning and pointed at a coconut with a questioning look.

"Selamat pagi Ibu, ada Kelapa muda? "

"Mau?" I nodded to show I would like to drink the milk from this young coconut. Its owner fetched a small, rusty hatchet and made a hole in the outer layer that was just the right size for putting a drinking straw through it. She then gave me the young coconut. In the meantime, I had sat down on a narrow bench in front of the kiosk. Like someone who was dying of thirst, I sucked the coconut milk out through the straw and enjoyed the refreshment from it.

"Absolutely delicious!" Gradually I became aware that my emotional outbreak had been strenuous.The coconut milk soon had an effect, refreshing and strengthening me. I looked around me. On the street children and teenagers were hurrying past, some dressed in school uniform, others in hotel uniform. Some stopped briefly to buy sweets and water. Older people were ambling more slowly to the Warung to buy basic food items and chatting with each other. Motorcyclists were riding through the puddles and making high fountains spring up.

"Life in this remote village is very interesting!" went through my head. I felt that I was in the midst of it all, even though I was no more than a silent observer. I had drunk all the milk from the young coconut, paid, nodded at the saleswoman by way of farewell and set off on the way back. This went at first on a flat street alongside the village by the road, soon went into a slope and continued as a narrow, rather rough path leading to the top of the hill. Again, I was fascinated by unbeatable views. Amazed, I stopped again and again. On either side of the path, high grass was growing. In the light of the sun, it looked like silk and the wind blew gently over it. The palm trees and the gigantic deciduous trees on the edge of the ravine were growing in a downward direction, into the ravine. The sky was like a tent roof over this play of nature.

As had already happened on the way there, I was again overcome with the blocking feeling of grief. As a reflex action, I breathed more deeply. Without any success. So I had to accept my grief so it would not bring me out of balance again. I looked for a place where I could sit down and found a big stone very near me. I felt heavy; my head was sinking down, tears were flowing and dripping onto the ground. Like it was just a heap of misery, left in the lurch by God and the world.

"Ray, I'd like to be with you!" something shouted in me, "No matter where you are now." More heavy tears dropped onto the ground. This time, the voice of reason reacted quickly and admonished me: "Your weeping, your shouting and complaining is all very well! But don't forget that you are not only experiencing grief. You have also been given good things. Look round, you are sitting in the midst of this splendid nature. That is God's gift! You are on a beautiful island with dear people round you who like and support you. Yes, you do experience pain, mourning, disappointment, unhappiness. But don't these things occur in anyone's life? Do you think that life is only pure happiness? Think of the sad fate of countless people. In the Bible alone, there are numerous examples. Chris, don't think God has deserted you just because you are feeling grief and loss. Be certain: God is with you in times of joy as well as in times of sorrow. He is always there. God is holding you in His hand! Take this hand. Show your trust in God!"

With closed eyes, I concentrated on my inner voice and took a deep breath. Slowly, I stood up, opened my eyes and looked up to the sky. I noticed its steel blue colour. This sky was not disturbed by any clouds. "Over me the sky has this lovely steel blue colour und inside me everything is dark." I shook my body as if I were wanting to shake the dark colour away. My look was still in the direction of the sky. With cautious steps, I went back on the path along the heights. In some places, it was still moist and made me jump over puddles that occupied the full breadth of the path. The way went downwards and I started involuntarily to walk at a quicker and less controlled pace. Suddenly there was a big puddle in front of me. I decided to jump over it, but I slipped on the moist clay of the earth just there, fell and landed flat in the puddle.

"That as well! Just what I needed! How deeply do I have to fall?" I shouted full of annoyance. This fall into the dirt destroyed in one moment my positive resolution. I had no strength for getting up again. But my anger and self-sympathy did not help me to get up, either. With trembling legs, I stood up and looked down at myself in disgust. I was dripping wet. My trousers had started to tear. On my right knee, there was a bleeding wound, hurting me. Both hands were grazed. Continuing to walk on caused me pain.

"Now I've got visible wounds, in addition," I sighed full of pity. The way back to my room was most difficult. I was ashamed because of my dirty clothes, the torn trousers, and I was also limping from the wound on my knee.

I crawled up the stairs to my room and went straight into the bathroom. I took my dirty and torn clothes off in the shower. In addition to the water from the shower, tears were running down my face. I wept for a long time under the shower.

On my way to get into bed, I heard a sound announcing a short message on my mobile phone. "Not now!" I ignored it and spent the next hours in bed, wrapped in a big sheet. Just before going to sleep from the exhaustion, I heard rain falling loudly on the roof. "That goes nicely with my situation," was my dry comment.

It was still raining when I woke up late in the afternoon. My wounds were painful and I suspected they needed attention. I got up and dabbed them with some disinfectant that I always had with me on my travels. The wounds on my knee and my hands had widened and the wound on my knee was a few millimetres deep.

I remembered what my grandmother had said when I was a child. Whenever I came to her with wounds or grazes, she would tell me to hurry out onto the balcony to hold the wound in the sun. "The sun heals wounds." Then I followed her instructions without knowing why. Later on, I realised that the rays of the sun dried the wounds out, and maybe even disinfected them.

Yet in my condition, I did not feel like going outside to hold my wounds up to the sun. I felt endlessly tired. As though drunk with tiredness, I lay down on my favourite sofa and stared at the coconut palms. All the colours seemed to be grey, as grey as my mood. My experiences on the high path were running inside me like a film. My lamenting, my anger, my prayers, my deep fall and finally, my external wounds.

Quite clearly, I saw the pictures in front of me, until, much to my surprise, they were transformed into a kind of shape, which I could gradually recognise. Straight away, I got a creative impulse:

"*Draw!* Take a pencil and paper. Draw this motive."

Convinced by it, I stood up and went back into the room, got a soft pencil out of my luggage, then sketching paper and went back to my place. In the meantime, I could see the motive clearly with my inner eye. I concentrated on it, planted it firmly in my memory, as if I had wanted to take a photo of it. Then I sat upright as I would for a meditation and drew what I had seen on the paper.

I was the shape of a human head with the eyes fearfully wide open and a mouth open from fright, obviously calling for help and looking at the person viewing the picture. Under the chin there was a double water line, a sign of the danger of drowning and going down into the water. Above the forehead, there was a sign that the person was thinking in the form of a spiral on which a wide, flat dish was balancing. This, too, was in danger of falling down, because two balls of unequal size were moving in it.

Still in deep concentration, I put the pencil down, looked with surprise and interest at the picture in front of me, which in the meantime I had developed fond feelings for, also because it was the result of that day's adventures that were being expressed in this drawing.

A few deep breaths brought me back to reality. I leaned back a bit and contemplated the pencil drawing before me as from a certain distance, still fascinated to see how it had brought my inner thoughts to the surface. The picture was a part of me. Without thinking about it I wrote under the drawing: *"Out of balance."*

Something worse comes!

A loss with hard consequences

The sun was already standing high on the firmament when I woke up. Pains on the palms of my hands and my knee were reminding me of the accident the day before. With a certain amount of trouble, I got out of bed, limped into the bathroom, grabbed the little bottle of antiseptic fluid to disinfect my wounds again.

"Ow!" How that hurt! Feeling tortured, I got back into bed, pulled the sheet over my head and mentally separated myself from the world. I did not wake up until midday. The weather matched my mood. Big drops were splashing onto the tiles on the edge of the balcony. I limped outside.

"Yes, that's wonderful." In front of me, on the table, was my breakfast. My mood improved.

"It was probably Made who thought about me." I murmured to myself gladly. In front of me, there was a big cup of ginger tea, a plate with fried rice and vegetables and also a little bowl of freshly cut papaya, pineapple and a banana.

Thinking of the saying: "Eating and drinking keep body and soul together," I cheered myself up while enjoying one mouthful after the other.

Then I lay tired, wrapped in a warm blanket, on my favourite sofa and observed the big drops as they fell from the leaves. "Like tears," I murmured dreamily. "Even the coconut palm leaves are weeping with me." My eyelids became heavier and I went to sleep again. And on waking up, I found the situation as it had been before: It was raining heavily. I suspected that that day would not bring any further change, turned over onto my side to sleep again, when my mobile phone gave a sound. It was a message from Noe.

> *Hallo, Mami, how are you? Is everything all right? I haven't heard anything from you for a few days. Please send me a message, OK? With love, Noe.*

Her words lightened my mood. "How nice to get a sign of life. And from our daughter," my heart cried out, soon feeling a bit happier. I wrote back straight away:

> *Dear Noe, nice to hear from you! Here, everything is OK. I've come here to Wayan's place and am being well looked after. What's about you? Enjoy your days in Berlin! Soon your practical will be over. Hugs!*

"The internet is such a wonderful invention. You can send messages all over the world, as though it were no distance at all." Very quickly I got used to my mobile phone and the exchange of messages. It was clear that I did not want to do without it.

Satisfied, I thought of my dear ones in Germany and the USA. My sister had already asked about me the day before. Now I felt like sending her an answer. Because I did not want to upset her, I made no mention of my fall or my attacks of grief.

> *Hi Ordi, thanks for your message. I'm staying with Wayan for a fair bit of time. You know, it's were I feel like at home. How about you? Kisses, your sister.*

As I could have expected, she wrote back right away:

> *Hi Chris! Am so happy to hear, that everything's OK with you. I'll continue keeping my fingers crossed for you. With Love, your sister.*

"Yes, those are the coloured lights that come on in days when it's grey." Encouraged by the exchanges with my dear ones on the internet, I went to sleep again.

Early in the morning, I was awakened again by the cackling of the chickens, turned over again for a bit more sleep, but the ducks on the neighbouring rice field were quacking a lot.

"Well, that's all I'm going to get," I said to myself out loud, got out of bed, stood under the shower and contemplated my wounds, which had already formed a slight scab and were not hurting so much. "Plaster on it. Heal up," I ordered them and stood in front of the mirror to checked my body. "Can I be with other people again?" I asked critically while looking at my creased-up face. "It's all right," I gave myself the permission, because I was generally feeling better than on the last few days. All the sleep seemed to have done me good.

I heard a noise from my mobile phone and limped onto the balcony, because I was interested to know who it was from.

"I'm driving off now. Will be with you in an hour. Yaya."

I dropped down from the clouds! "What day is it today? Surely not Saturday, when it's Suryani's meditation?" But it could only have been Saturday, because on this day Yaya was coming to take me to Denpasar. In the darkness of the days before, I had paid no attention to what weekdays it was.

"OK, Yaya is fetching me right away. I am looking forward to Suryani and her meditation group. It will bring me up again, after all my pain this week."

Quickly, I limped back, looked for suitable clothing, choosing a light, long-sleeved blouse with a loose pair of summer trousers, packed my bag for my weekend outing into the capital and went cautiously down the stairs.

To celebrate my recovery, I took my breakfast at the big table, which this morning had no other guests. Made, Wayan's wife, was in the kitchen. When she saw me, she came and sat next to me, with a gentle smile. She gently put her hand on my arm. Her sensitive gestures touched me so much, that tears came into my eyes. I tried to cover it up with a smile, as under no circumstances did I want to cry. My eyes wet with tears, I smiled at her and thanked her.

"Terima kasih Made." "Thank you."

I asked her for a typical tourist breakfast which I really felt like eating that morning. "Saya mau makan bananapancake, fruitsalad dan ginger-lemon tea," I said, mixing Indonesian and English. Made was used to this and understood immediately what I wanted. She nodded with a charming smile and disappeared into the kitchen, from where enticing smells of banana pancakes were coming. A bit later, she was holding a plate under my nose.

"Your breakfast, Chris!"

"Mhhh, it smells good with cinnamon and honey on the top. Thank you, Made!" The ripe papaya and the juicy melon were also smiling at me. I enjoyed the breakfast and did not notice Yaya until he spoke to me from behind with his audible, broad smile:

"Good morning, Chris, how are you?"

"Oh, Yaya! Welcome! Nice to see you again! Do you want to share the breakfast?"

"No, thank you!" He shook his head firmly. I knew that the Balinese do not eat anything sweet for breakfast. On the other hand, he did not refuse the tea

273

Made placed in front of him. I looked at Suryani's son lovingly. For me, he was a special person, always balanced, jolly, in control of things and uninhibited. I could hardly understand the peace and friendliness he carried around with him.

I thought: "I admire him for it. I'm having difficulties in trying to conceal my disappointment and annoyance. Although I'm a cheerful person with an infectious laugh. Yet, in our culture, one shows the unpleasant emotions as well. On Bali one shows only the positive ones."

"Let's go, Suryani is waiting." We set off. As was to be expected, our mood was cheerful. Just before the capital city, we got stuck in a traffic jam for a while. I used this time to show Yaya proudly my photos of the holy mountain I had taken with my mobile phone on the early morning hike.

"Wowh, nice!" he praised me. He was himself a good photographer. So I felt praised. When we arrived in front of Suryanis house, he parked his car on the road. I got out, took my luggage from the back seat and went over the courtyard to Suryani, who was already waiting for us.

"Welcome!" We embraced each other cordially. Then she asked me to take my bag to my room straight away, as she wanted to drive off to her event.

Just before the door to my room, I stopped and looked for my mobile phone. "Where is my mobile phone?" I said aloud to myself, hurried back to the car and searched all over the inside of it. It was not long before our arrival that I had shown Yaya the photos, so it could not be far away. But it was not there. On the way from the car to the house, there was no mobile phone to be found. I became visibly nervous, ran to the room and searched through my luggage. No success.

"I'm looking for my mobile phone, have you seen it?" I asked all the members of the family that I met in the house. They shrugged their shoulders and shook their heads.

"OK, I have to look again," I remarked and went more and more nervously through the house, over the courtyard, into the car again, on the street. My mobile phone had vanished. And I was feeling more and more confused. I had no idea where I could look for my dear, faithful phone. But I did not want to be inactive about it. So I set off again. Suryani held on to me. "Sit down and relax," she ordered me and took control of the situation.

"How can she be so relaxed?" I thought, "My mobile phone cost me enough money. But the worst is: All of my connections to my family and friends were stored on the phone. Only on the phone!"

Exhausted and bereft of comfort, I sat down on the armchair. I thought about the dilemma, that my mobile phone was the only place where I had stored all the addresses, phone numbers and e-mail addresses.

Driven by the idea that my phone must be somewhere, I raced onto the street again, searched every square inch, asked the neighbours, but it had mysteriously disappeared. Full of despair, I went into my room and threw myself onto the bed.

I was still not ready to accept the situation and was assuming it would be found somewhere. My head was throbbing. I became tired.

"You can't change the situation anyway," I thought. "You have looked everywhere, at the moment you can't do anything else. Perhaps it will be found in your absence. Calm down, concentrate on the coming meditation session and relax."

I tried to achieve what I wanted with deep breathing. It worked, but I did not become really peaceful. From outside I heard a voice calling me. While driving, nobody said anything about my disaster.

The big event with Suryani and others had its desired effect. The singing together, the relaxation exercises and the meditation helped me to become more peaceful. Yet on the way back I was feeling restless again, my thoughts circled round the loss of all the numbers of my contacts. As soon as we got back, I went once more to all the places, but my mobile phone was still lost.

The others in the house registered my despair, but remained unimpressed by the situation, which irritated me. "If I were in their place, I would help to look for it. A mobile phone is something valuable," went through my head, "especially in my case. All my data have gone. Doesn't anyone sympathise with me?" I began to pity myself. The inner voice of reason gave me an explanation.

"That is a typical difference between the cultures. Accept it." Disappointed, I went upstairs, threw myself onto the bed and went straight off to sleep.

On waking up, I was already feeling better. So I went downstairs and met Yaya. We had a discussion about my problem. I asked him how he would explain the disappearance of my phone. To my great surprise, he replied spontaneously with a broad, radiant smile: "*This is Bali mysticism*. Take it as it is. Live with it."

His words irritated me completely. I wondered: "That can't be true! Does he really mean what he says?" I rolled my eyes and shook my head. I had to leave the room. I apologized and went back to my room.

Lying on my bed, I thought about his words again. "Yaya, the man with a doctor's title, lecturer at the university here, gives me mysticism as the explanation for the loss of my phone?" I hardly could understand that. Probably it was supposed to be a joke that I couldn't understand?, I asked myself. My thoughts were working at a fast rate. "Or was the loss of all my numbers and addresses possibly a sign from the gods, to stop me from concentrating on contacts with my family, and rather to concentrate on myself?" These thoughts made me laugh. The fact was that it was no longer possible to contact anybody, neither Noe nor my sister Ordi nor anyone else. I did not know anybody's address by heart and my password was also blocked in the meantime. I already tried my luck on Yaya's laptop, but because I typed things wrongly several times, they blocked my post box.

"I guess, I've lost my memory," I whispered, short of comfort. "Is that the mystical?" My despair increased. More questions ran through my mind. "How will Noe and Ordi react, when they don't get any more messages from me, when I don't answer theirs? I should at least have given them Suryani's address."

"Why didn't I… ," My thoughts were spinning. Until my inner voice comforted me: "It doesn't matter! It is like it is, Chris! You have to accept it. There is no solution in sight."

I had just decided to pull the sheet over my head and go to sleep, when there was a knock at my door. "Come, Chris, we want to go out for our evening meal!"

I gave myself a jolt, and asked: "Where do you want to go?"

"We were thinking of the Restaurant Kopi Bali."

"That's a good idea. I'll soon be ready." Suddenly I had forgotten all my problems. I jumped out of bed as all worries seemed to have flown away. This restaurant was not only my favourite one, it was the place where my beloved husband and me always ordered our favourite dish: *Gulai Kambing!* This evening brightened my dreary mood.

The chef of the restaurant felt honored, to welcome the highly respected professor Dr L.K.Suryani, her husband professor Dr. Cok Alit and family. He took the time to greet all personally. Even the cook came out of his kitchen to greet the large family.

This was my chance: I made use of this opportunity to ask the cook for his special recipe for the lamb dish, as it did not taste so good anywhere but here. I was dying to get to know about his ingredients and his tricks in their preparation. Indeed, he took my request seriously and described the way the dish was prepared with such an intensity that it made my mouth water. I was all ears.

"We take meat from lamb, which I choose myself, cut it into small pieces and put it overnight in fresh coconut milk. In this coconut milk I then simmer lemon grass and lime leaves. Various spices are also important, such as curcuma, ginger and gallants. The hot flavour from a little chili and the special taste of tamarind round off the overall taste. It is very important for the spices, meat and coconut milk to have enough time to merge with each other. We wait until the next morning until the sauce is cooked with all the ingredients for over an hour, until the meat is wonderfully tender. Then, I give the dish more flavour with further spices. But these remain my secret. Enjoy your Gulai Kambing and be convinced of the effectiveness of my spices!"

And really! Convinced by his description, I nodded to him and folded my hands in front of my chest.

"Thank you very much for telling us about your recipe. I always look forward to your wonderful dish. It was also my late husband's favourite meal."

I turned to the others again, who were smiling at me significantly. Meanwhile, our drinks were on the table. In front of me, there was a freshly mixed creamy orange mango juice, that I loved from the first sip onwards. When the *Gulai Kambing* got served, at the latest, my thoughts about my lost phone had flown away. Instead, I felt Ray sitting next to me and heard his gentle smacking of the lips as a sign that he was enjoying it. The disastrous day ended with the enjoyment of the exquisite dish and a feeling of well-being in the midst of Suryani's family.

"And, what about an early morning meditation on the beach?" asked my dear girlfriend, chuckling, before everyone retired for the night, knowing perfectly well that I would go for it. "The water gives us good energy."

"Sure," I nodded. I was only too willing to accept this offer. That night, I slept surprisingly well, right through to the morning. Perhaps because I had suppressed my thoughts on the loss of the phone with the imagination concerning the *Gulai Kambing*.

"There's a lot going on for early on a Sunday morning," I thought, observing the native inhabitants on this beach, which seemed to be exclusively for them. Our small group of meditation fans mixed with them and looked for a small place in the sand. My friend took the lead, as she always did, leading our small group with slow words into inner concentration.

"Guide your attention to the dark blue, glittering sea in front of you. If your eyelids get heavy, close your eyes and breathe regularly. Feel the sand you're sitting on, the soft warmth of the morning sun on your skin, hear the delicate, regular rushing of the waves, listen to the shrill calls of the water birds, the voices of the people passing by. Take the energy of the sea into you and trust that you will always be well looked after."

I felt my body becoming lighter, with not so many hindrances. The borderlines between my body and the surroundings seemed to be dissolving away. The deep, sonorous voice of my friend guided our concentration back to breathing in and out.

"That really was pleasant." With this thought, I opened my eyes, looked into the sky that had been lit up by the sun, the now glittering, silvery sea, and spontaneously said a prayer of thanks to Heaven: "Thank you, God, that I am part of a fellowship in these gorgeous surroundings, where I am finding rest. I feel Your love holding me up."

I was still carrying the pleasant mood of the Sunday morning inside me, when I said "Good-bye" to my family-friends after a delightful breakfast together.

"Your meditations were so good for me, Suryani. My heartfelt thanks." With an embrace, we bade each other farewell until the following weekend.

Before we drove off, Yaya handed me an old mobile phone with his and his mother's numbers stored in it.

"Just to make sure you don't get completely lost," he said with a meaningful smile.

Grief and pain find ways to process!

Writing and painting

On the balcony of my suite, sinking deeply into the cushions on the comfortable sofa, I was looking at the thick vegetation the mighty mango tree. His branches formed a deep green roof.

I longed to be close to me loved ones. "But who am I still in contact with?" I moaned. "Ray my love is dead. He is not with me any more. Yet my inner tie to him is unbroken." Just now I missed exchanging with Noe and my sister, our family. I felt so close to each of them in that moment. But: our connections were broken by the loss of my cell phone, I realised again. "And that at the sensitive time where I longed to have my family around me." My feeling of loss was painful, while I was laying on the pillows and stared into the dark of the green leaves. I knew of no way out. Felt only consternation and despair inside me.

With my hands in front of my forehead I whispered: "Why? Why just now in this time that is so difficult for me?"

Tears dropped onto the floor. I had a bad feeling in my stomach. "Somehow I'm rushing from one catastrophe to another. I seem to have got a contract for unhappiness," I lamented to myself and continued crying. "When is there going to be light on the horizon? I can't stand it any more."

Down in the world of my feelings, I dozed off. In my dreams, I heard a voice: "Wake up, you woman, get up. You are not alone. God is holding you in his hand. You will get through this difficult time. Believe that firmly."

Still half asleep, the picture of Elijah came into my mind, who had retired into the desert after a time of great unhappiness and did not believe in life any more. It was not until he heard God's voice encouraging him that he believed he could come through the difficult time. He got up and continued on his way.

"I would like to trust in God as Elijah did and continue to go on the way God has sent me on." I encouraged myself, went up, got dressed an walked barefoot on the balcony. The early morning sun was already shining on the horizon. I sat down on the sofa. Something was seething inside of me. I felt within me a strong willed to accept things and keep going. But until now, I did not succeed in standing up and going forward with courage.

"*Write!* Write down what is weighing heavily on you." Taken by surprise, I paused. "Write?" I murmured to myself. I followed the impulse as if sleepwalking, went into the room, rummaged in my rucksack to look for my exercise book and a pencil, sat down again on the comfortable sofa to follow up this impulse.

The exercise book was open in front of me on the table. I picked up the pencil. Something inside me wrote:

Losing

I lost my beloved husband.
I've lost my phone, my connection with others.
I've lost my inner peace.
I've lost the control over myself.
I'm losing my reason.
I'm feeling hopelessly lost.

After that, I put the pencil on one side, looked at what I had written and felt that the words were reinforcing my hopeless feeling of being lost. Tears dropped onto the paper, doubts came to the surface as to whether I was in a condition to continue taking the steps that would lead me further on.

"Stay with your emotions. They are OK. Write some more," my inner impulse told me.

Having

I have a great fear of the loss
of closeness,
of the familiar,
of what I love.
I have a great fear of the loss
of the ground under my feet.

Again, I interrupted my writing. "Go on, keep on writing," something whispered inside me. As in a trance, I sat with my eyes closed, listened to what was going on inside me before writing again

Gaining

I gain peace and take time.
Am I getting my trust back?

Exhausted, I leaned back and read my words, recognising the development from the first to the third poem, a sorting out, or even a reconciliation? Amazed, I realised that each word had come to me while I had been writing it down. Beyond all control.

I looked up to one extremely bright star of the morning sky, with the feeling that my body was being made clean, as it is in a shower. A bat flipped past my head. Through the coconut palm leaves glow-worms were hovering silently and sending rays of light into the darkness. I saw them as a symbol of hope, smiled with confidence and thought: "If there was a way opening up for Elijah, then a way will also open up for me. It will lead me out of my darkness into the light. I am relying on that."

The following day was somehow different. The cocks were announcing daybreak. At first hesitantly, then sleepily, then more and more powerfully. "Probably they are not driving only me out of bed and making me go into the day, but everyone else around here, too," I thought. Yet I was not unhappy about the merciless crowing from the cocks, I rather saw it as a start signal for my morning walk over the rice fields. While I was still lying in bed I was imagining the pale morning light colouring the night sky with a delicate light blue, which in a short time would become a yellowish blue from the sun.

My anticipation of this motivated me to get up quickly in order to experience the morning change of colours in the sky between the rice fields, the best place being one with a wide view into the distance.

With a bit of luck, the Balinese people's holy mountain, the volcano *Gunung Agung*, would be visible. That would be the summit in both senses of the word. Seeing the mountain was for me the high point of any morning walk.

It may be that my devotional way of looking it is influenced by the holiness the Balinese ascribe to this mountain. Their life is strongly influenced by the spiritual volcano. It is seen as the seat of the good gods in Hinduism. From it, all the fullness of life comes: water, and from that the fruitfulness in nature. Yet there is also the opposite pole: the sea. It is inhabited by demonic deities, which are designated to death.

All the Balinese live between the seat of holiness in the middle of the island and the ungodliness surrounding them. They consider it their life's work to keep a balance between the good and the evil. That means a constant maintaining of balance in their everyday lives with numerous rituals, worshipping and cleansing ceremonies, temple feasts with floral and artistic presents for the gods. This appeases the gods, and also puts the Balinese in a good position after death, giving them a good karma. For family life, the communal life in a village and the temple, this maintaining of the balance is useful. It brings inner and external peace with it and binds all the inhabitants of the island together in communities.

The daily rituals and the bright, colourful festivals in the temples fascinate the tourists from all over the world, who benefit the country, the island, the Balinese, financially – if they are given the opportunity of gaining anything from it. Me too, I am really fascinated by the mighty woodcarvings, the musical, dance and theatrical performances. I admire much more the sense of community and the apparently endless friendliness and patience of the Balinese.

All these thoughts were going through my head while I was hurrying along the still quiet village street to the turning at the end that led to the narrow path to the rice fields. Here I walked at a slower pace. I stopped again and again to enjoy the landscape formed by the rice fields. This view was stunning! I couldn't get enough of this enchanting sight. My heart was already feverish when I thought about it. And then, I was standing in front of the rice fields, radiant in their light green from the morning sun, all my senses are open wide. I continued along the narrow paths that the farmers have made between the fields belonging to different people. Whenever I looked down, the strong light green of the fresh rice plants radiated back at me. Abruptly I stopped. The field in front of me with almost ripe ears of rice was glittering in a very unusual way! I bent down, looked more closely and found the reason for it.

On every ear hung an extraordinarily large drop of dew, which was reflecting only the morning sun. Even the stem itself was also reflected in the dewdrop with its delicate light green.

"Enchanting," I exclaimed, before holding my breath reverently for a moment, "everything that the morning sun brings into the day." I was so pleased about this glass bead.

In the meantime, the sky had changed. The light yellow colour had given way to a clear light blue, which dominated and threw its light onto the plants. Taking slower steps, I strolled on, stopping repeatedly.

"Selamat pagi, Pak," I said "Good morning" to the rice farmers who were working on their fields at this early hour and they greeted me back with a long drawn out "Pagi."

My path ended suddenly, forcing me to jump over a stream, which I could walk along for a time, still looking for a clear view of the holy mountain.

Yes, behind a small hill there was a clear view. In the distance, I could see, well spread out, the *Gunung Agung* and at its height of 3000 metres it made everything else appear flat and insignificant. The morning air that was still humid gave it a milky blue-grey colour that had a soothing effect on me, although I was well aware of what sometimes came out of this volcano. The holy mountain radiated peace and might into the vast morning sky. The sun seemed to be withdrawing, to give it the honour it deserved.

"How great!", I said out loud and raised my arms to the heavens in thankfulness. I took a deep breath and felt completely happy.

Unexpectedly, Ray appeared. I sensed him behind my back. "It feels wonderful, Ray, when you are with me. Please stay with me," I whispered softly full of longing. But I immediately I wondered whether It would not be better to know that he was on his way, just where he was now. And to know that I was on my way on the earth, which was certainly a good one.

With these thoughts, I set off on the way back. Back in my room, I fetched my exercise book, took the pencil in my hand and sat down on my favourite sofa. I felt words forming inside me and wrote them down:

Different ways

Fly, my dear one, fly,
Your carriage is ready
to steer its way to the incomprehensible.
There, there, my dearest one
is where your way is going.
There it will be good.
There you will find endless joy and love.

Here, my dearest one, back here,
I will stay.
My way is leading me further on,
here on the earth.

Why are we separated? And for how long?
I find no answer to my questions.
Only know that some time I will go
to the place where you are, my dearest one.

Wherever you are,
wherever I am,
we are united.
We remain one with each other,
with the bond of our love.

As if looking at a blurred film, I looked at what I had written and only noticed my exhaustion when my eyelids were getting heavier. I felt what was going on inside me, concentrated on my breathing in and out. Unexpectedly, the breathing out gave me a lightness, like light on the horizon. It aroused in me a feeling of trust. I wanted to enjoy this present and hold on to it. I concentrated entirely on my breath. For a very long time.

When I opened my eyes and looked around me, the light wind of the early evening was rushing in the leaves of the coconut palms, in which the yellowish green light from the late afternoon was shimmering. The words I had written now appeared to me in a brighter light. I was so happy to have written my inner poem down.

On that evening, I did not leave my comfortable sofa. When I was feeling tired, I cuddled into the soft cushions there and went straight to sleep.

The next morning I woke up by a feeling of hunger. I got up with the idea of looking for the fairy in the kitchen, Ketut, and was lucky. As if she were sensing that I was wanting something edible, she asked me in a friendly tone: "Mau makan?" "Would you like something to eat?"

"Mau." Yes, I wanted something to eat and nodded to show her how pleased I was with her offer. She was already ladling a big portion of rice from the pot where there was always a supply of warm rice. She pointed at various dishes, which she had already prepared. I asked for the boiled water spinach on pieces of fried fish and at boiled soy sprouts. On top of it all, Ketut scattered hot, spicy coconut flakes, which had a brownish colour, groundnuts fried in oil and half a hard-boiled egg.

"Enak," I was already showing my enthusiasm about the first bite. "Delicious!" The cook showed her satisfaction that I was liking the food and told me in two languages that I ought to eat well in order to get strong again. "Chris, harus makan. Get strong again."

With my mouth full, I assented to her advice, again nodding my head firmly. Yes, from now on I would eat regularly and plentifully. To help my digestion, I went for a walk through the big garden. I stopped to admire each of the stone statues, Hindu deities that were supposed to keep all evil from the parcel of land. In the soft, light grey tufa stone of volcanic origin, many different details had been carved. The figures were really awe-inspiring. I walked on, alongside the stream, where the gigantic goldfish stretched out their open mouths at me.

"I can't give you anything to eat," I said loudly and hurried upstairs to my flat, intending to spend the rest of the evening at my favourite spot there.

In the darkness, I again admired with great fascination the trails of light from the glow-worms that were flitting through the bushes. In the distance, dogs were barking, keeping watch over their territories and loudly drawing attention to every movement.

"What was the reason for my trip here, to Bali?" I was trying to think back. In the first weeks after Ray's death, I could not accept the fact that my dear husband was no longer at my side and would never come back. One day a voice inside told me to go to a place where both of us had been at ease, to Bali.

"And was the decision to act according to these words a good one?" I almost felt that I was being interviewed, but I was really only interested in looking back and a possible result from it.

The change of place meant a lot of good to me. Here I felt free and independent. My sister-friend Suryani and her big family looked after me well. Also the people at Wayan's apartments. In her hypnotherapy, Suryani sent Ray and me on different ways. I was in a position to think about my body as a whole, with its emotions. *I could not have done that in my busy life at home.* Bali too had always been like a home to us. Here I felt the good company in my friend Suryani's family, also here in "my" flat at Wayan's apartment.

My thoughts wandered back again: In Suryani's hypnotherapy, I met my beloved husband again. We bade each other farewell, making ourselves available for our different ways and tasks. But now, back in reality, I found I was constantly drifting back to my deep desire to continue living with him.

"I am gradually getting used to my way, which I must take on my own. I am forming this way with everything that is good for me, for instance my daily programme of movement that helps to strengthen my body, mind and spirit. Also the meditation, the peace I allow myself to have in this way. That I could come to terms with my grief in creative ways was surprising to

293

me, and a pleasant surprise, too. The most important thing is and remains listening to my inner voice. It knows the way," I said to myself loudly, stood, and fetched myself a glass of water, which I emptied in one gulp.

In the meantime, it was dark all round me. I still could not sleep. Something was moving around in me, but I did not know what it was. I closed my eyes and listened to that inner voice. A picture was developing, not very clearly, schematically, but ready for sketching.

"*Take your colours,* brush and the sketching block." With paper, water and watercolours in front of me, I closed my eyes again, in order to concentrate on the picture. I saw colours, light colours. Slowly a shape developed, a light shape, which, I thought, was probably Ray. He appeared as a silhouette in light, in radiant, clear light. Around him, a light, delicate sky shining in delicate yellow was opening up. *"Ray is in the light!"*

I was overcome with joy, I felt certain that he was well. Relieved, I took a deep breath and concentrated on this picture. Unexpectedly, a question arose inside me: "Where am I on this picture?" I could not find myself there, not in the inner picture inside me either. As Ray was already in the light and I did not want to disturb him, I kept my distance. Heaven was not yet my place. So was it earth, then? I was thinking about my feelings and thought I had not yet arrived back on the earth, I was somewhere between the two. On a cross or a post? My heart was still bleeding from the despair arising from our final separation, drops were falling on the ground. I painted what I saw within me.

I painted Ray in a delicate light blue in a circle of white light and transparent yellow. This showed him hovering in the light sky, surrounded by a blood-red trail that went down to the earth and spread out on its surface. I hung onto this trail of red, between Heaven and earth, on a post that reminded me of a cross. Down on the earth Ray's colours were reflected: the light blue, the white, the transparent yellow. In these colours, my dear husband was still present on the earth. Exhausted from spending so much time with this intuitive painting I stood the picture up in front of me to have a good look at it.

"*Ray has hovered away, and at the same time he is still present on the earth for me.* I am suspended between the two, with a bleeding heart."

That night, I dreamt about the two of us. I looked at Ray from some distance, for his place was already in Heaven.

"That is presumably the reason why the intimate conversations with him are much more few and far between. *Ray is happy with God*," is how I interpreted my dream afterwards.

In conversation with God!

Lament, petition, pause, forgiveness, trust

"Oh, if only I could accept the fact of his death at last!" This wistful thinking came up again and again. In the meantime, I saw the two of us on separate paths, one of which went in the direction of light, but inside me, there were still feelings of resistance, despair and anger, which found their continuation with the loss of my mobile phone with all the addresses.

"*Why?* What have I done wrong?" This question arose repeatedly: "*Why me?*" Again, it seems so hard for me to accept the facts. Once again, I addressed my questions to the highest authority. "Why do I have to go through the world alone, without any contact with our daughter and my sister?"

The countless variations of this *"Why…?"* question were constantly creeping into my mind, suppressing all reason, all the positive support I was being given. As a matter of course, they were throwing me back to the start of my thoughts, back to where I had been before leaving home for Bali.

Now I brought my complaints before God. It was easy to put the blame on Him, without giving any reasons. He, the creator of Heaven, earth and all that is in them also has my destiny and my family's, too, in His hand. So why should I not reproach Him? Yes, I went even further: I turned my back on Him in a huff. But not for long, as in a few days my inner voice made its presence felt: "What is the purpose of all this complaining and turning away from God? Is it helping you?"

At least it aroused my self-pity once again and pulled me down to earth again. And I wanted to go in the opposite direction. So I tried to visualise the story of Job, hoping that would open my eyes and give me inner peace again.

Job, that pious man, had done nothing wrong and was tested in the hardest possible way. His entire herd of animals was stolen, his servants, sons and daughters all died, his house collapsed. He himself had to leave the village because of an infectious skin disease. Job brings it all before God, accuses Him and argues with Him, because he is sure that he has done nothing to deserve this harsh punishment. In this process, he comes nearer to God, his faith and relationship with Him grow.

This changed the way I was looking at my problem. I could understand how deep the pain is that is experienced on the death of a loved one. Yet, for very many people, that is not the end of it all, as they still have to experience far worse things: wars, rape, expulsion, hunger and much more.

"Is this thought helping me?" I reflected. "Yes, a little. It is giving me a more objective view of my own circumstances. I shouldn't forget about those who are suffering much worse things." That was one of the thoughts, which led on to others that showed me that I was not so badly off in my sorrow.

"I am able to travel to Bali, to take advantage of the help here, take time for myself and experience the warmth, the beauty of nature and a fascinating form of spirituality."

It was as if I were giving myself a symbolic jerk, which brought me back in the right direction and finally reconciled me with God.

On one of the following evenings, I resolved: "I will succeed. I will stop blaming God for my misfortune and then work on accepting the reality of it."

A few days after my cleansing process, I was sitting on my favourite sofa after a meditation and looking beyond the coconut palms at the night sky. The darkness became light and *a picture was formed* in front of my inner eye. I quickly stood up and fetched my paints.

The colours white, yellow, blue and black came into my mind. Intuitively, I painted two fairly long oval shapes. Around them areas of colour flooded with light, almost transparent, changing from the left edge of the picture from yellow to blue and back to yellow and to a transparent black. In the transparent blue area, there was a powerful, blue oval shape, going in an upward direction and in the black transparent area a black oval shape by the top edge of the painting.

After I had transferred my inner picture onto paper, I contemplated the watercolour for a long time, noticing a clear difference from the first watercolour. The figures were not there with their blood red and black shades. The new picture looked light, bright, and transparent.

On the reverse side of the paper, I wrote: "*Around me, things are clearing up and getting more peaceful.* The delicate blue shape, which I think represents me, is in the colour of hope. The shape representing my husband is in the colour of mourning."

I left this picture on the table. The yellow, blue and transparent black colours were just super. They showed that something had changed within me. I was feeling more trusting and hopeful; a closeness to God was developing from this. Full of thanks, I whispered:

"God, You are present, in each of us. You are in all and above all. What a comfort that is," and asked for His blessing in a special way. I wrote down what I was asking for:

Asking for a blessing

O God, do not leave us!
Be with my husband, protect and keep him.
Lead him on his way to eternal peace,
to joy without end!

O God, forgive us our trespasses!

Be at my side here on the earth.
Give me comfort and stability.
Lead me on my way.
I need to trust in You,
so I can overcome my insecurity.

O God, give us your blessing!

After praying for this blessing I felt relieved and at peace.

On the following days, I read the words I had written down again and again and they gave me great pleasure. That resulted in my steps on my hikes having more swing in them; I looked upwards and breathed more freely.

"You're making progress," was my comment as I was walking on the paths through the rice fields. At Wayan's place, people had been coming and go also new guests. On their first evening, a tune drifted up to me, which was not clear at first, but then it reminded me of something I had heard before. It was FC Liverpool's hymn, in the meantime taken on by Borussia Dortmund and other football clubs.

I heard in the silence of the night the sound that nobody has to walk alone. I was pleased about these cheering words, which I automatically applied to my situation: "I don't have to be alone," I comforted myself, "not even when I'm sad and feeling lonely, for I know at the bottom of my heart I'm being held up."

Yes, I even felt that, however far down one falls, one is always held in God's hand.

"My new way will be a good one, not always, but getting better more and more. It will happen that I'll be in despair and without hope. Its for sure that I am not alone. I believe, I am always held up by God. Always have caring people around me "

The song from the apartment below had come to an end. "It's a song that really gives you courage," I thought again. How good it is that people let this song inspire them.

"Everything changes. Nothing remains the same. The chances of experiencing better times are at least fifty per cent and can be as high as a hundred per cent." I was sitting on the balcony, laughing at myself. At the bottom of my heart, I knew that I was already climbing up the mountain again. And I wasn't alone. My family and friends were going with me. They were on my side to support me. Also there was the invisible bond that tied my heart to God, which could cope with disappointment, lamenting and anger.

With so many positive thoughts driving me on, I stood up from my comfortable sofa, hurried down the stairs and went outside. The door to the family house was open. In the evening light, I saw Made, Wayan's wife, sitting on a raffia mat. Next to her, her sister Ketut and her daughter Nyoman. In front of them were coconut leaves, that they were forming into small bowls for sacrifices, with their skilful fingers. They were talking to each other while they were working and appeared to be cheerful and relaxed. Made saw me walking past and called to me:

"Hello, Chris, come in. How are you?"

Rather shyly, I went up into their circle. They offered me a chair. I thanked and answered Made's question with a cheerful nod of the head. "And what are you doing?" I asked curiously. Made told me about their big family celebration in their house temple. Then I remembered the Balinese tradition of remembering their deceased relatives once a year with a big celebration in the house temple. "Everyone will come to honour our ancestors and ask the priest for a blessing. We women are preparing the sacrificial gifts and decorating the house temple. The men will cook the food."

I admired the skill of their fingers and the speed at which they were making one basket after the other and then placing each one in the middle of their circle. The women's friendly, relaxed mood went with me on my way.

The stars in the sky were sparkling brightly, as though inviting me to stroll through the night for a short time. Leaving Wayan's property, I walked on a path devoid of all people in the direction of the long steep flight of stairs, which led to the main road. There I stopped, not sure where to go next.

Suddenly, the light of a torch shone at me from one of the paths coming from the side. It was such of a sudden that I did not have time to feel afraid.

In the light of the torch, I made out a small woman with a very pale skin wearing a loose summer dress and with her blonde hair pinned on her head in a creative style. She smiled at me with a big, wide mouth.

"Hi, how are you?" she said to me cheerily, as if meeting under the starry sky were the most normal thing in the world. "Are you looking for the way?" She did not wait for me to answer, but explained all the paths to me that went from the place where we were.

"I am OK," I began my answer and then paused, as I had thought of something else I could say to her: "Except that I have lost my mobile phone and with it all my addresses."

I was amazed that I could blurt something like that out, on that starry night, to a complete stranger. My unhappiness over this had pushed my mourning over Ray into second place.

"Oh, by the way, my name is Sterling," she introduced herself, "and I live down there," she said pointing in the direction of Wayan's property.

With a smile, I told her that I was also living down there. Quickly we got into a conversation. I found out that she was American, a psychologist and theologian, living in a small house hidden by trees since she had retired six years previously. I immediately felt I could trust the charismatic woman. I described my situation after Ray's death, my deep mourning and, of course the loss of my mobile phone. That aroused her helper-instinct.

"Let's have a look, what we can do," she comforted me and, after a short pause for thought, she added: "Does your sister or anyone of your family have skype?" I nodded. My sister and I had already spoken to each other on skype several times. It was free of charge. We could see each other. So, this was fantastic for us. Sterling was glad I was following her train of thought.

"Chris, let's go to my house."

I accepted her suggestion. While I was following her, I thought about the situation I was in. I walked behind Sterling through the night to her house and her computer.

"So, what's the name of your sister? Maybe we'll find her on skype." We typed her name and place of residence in and were quite excited. Could she be found with this information? Involuntarily I held my breath. Some moments later, a photo of her appeared. We had found my sister! We cheered. Sterling immediately typed a message, introducing herself, telling my sister why she was writing. Also she was asking for my sisters e-mail address.

Then, we just had to wait and see if my sister would let herself in for contact in this way. I got extremely nervous. But we had to wait for an answer. So I said "Good-bye" to Sterling and hugged her heartily. She was well aware that our next meeting would be very important to me.

Back on my balcony, laying on my favourite sofa, I was amazed at the unexpected meeting with Sterling.

Kept shaking my head, because I couldn't understand how lucky I was this night. I chuckled.

The next day at midday the small, vivacious American woman was hurrying up the stairs to my apartment and calling out to me with her radiant, charming smile: "Guess, what happened, Chris. Your sister answered. *We are in contact!*" Overjoyed I gave her a big hug. Worries dropped away from me like heavy stones.

Hand in hand, we ran to her house to write an e-mail to my sister. I told her about losing my cell phone. I also asked her to write to Noe and to Ray's sister to tell them about my situation and that I would be pleased to get mails from them at Sterling's address.

From that day onwards, I visited Sterling in every afternoon to read my mails that my dear ones had sent to her address. Sterling became my contact person. She made it possible for me to be in touch with my love ones. At this time I felt like my heart was dancing a rumba. Every time I met my new american girlfriend, I hugged her full of joy.

"Incredible!" I called out back on my balcony, because of my new situation. I danced around and shouted: "*I am in touch with the world again!*"

The darkness fades -
Light shines through it!

Opening up for what is going on outside me

During my early morning hike, I decided to have breakfast with the others on one of the following days. At first, I felt rather unsure of myself and wondered if the other guests were informed as to how sensitive I was.

Thinking: "I hope nobody will ask me about it," I walked down to the long table with the heavy chairs, where some women were sitting deep in conversation.

Just greeting the group somewhat awkwardly, when behind me Emma from Holland, as she later introduced herself to me, turned up and told everybody:

"Hello, all of you! I'm just back from a super cool yoga lesson! Pure relaxation, I can tell you!" She beamed at us blissfully. As we did not react immediately, she went on: "Isn't it a wonderful day?"

My thoughts were hovering somewhere between my shyness and Emma's enthusiastic feelings of happiness, for which I envied her straight away. Yet my inner strength reacted quickly and convinced me that the start of my day was blessed. A rather plump, but apparently energetic woman at the end of the table seemed to be taking it differently and told us her story in the same manner.

"Yes! It can only be a good day. Just imagine, this morning I almost trod on a frog, that jumped up so high out of fright. As we say in Italy, when frogs jump it will be a perfect day."

"Paola! Do they really believe that in your country?"

The enthusiastic look on Emma's face changed to the opposite. The others at the table laughed heartily. I could imagine Paola almost treading on the frog, when she added emphasis to her tale with a "Quaak!"

"So you've been playing leapfrog this morning," I blurted out. We had enjoyed playing at it as children. But Paola did not react. She concentrated on Emma's yoga lesson and continued:

"Yoga? That could be good for my figure. Yesterday evening I was in the Yellow Rice Field Café and ate up a delicious chocolate cake! Perhaps I could get rid of the gained weight with some yoga." Then she reflected. "On the other hand, I'd better not do that, as I had an unpleasant situation in my first and only yoga lesson." She hardly breathed at all, gave us no time to ask questions, but continued with her reason for not wanting to go to yoga: "On that day I had so much flatulence that it was impossible for me to concentrate on the exercises. Instead, I concentrated on not letting out air at the wrong time or in the wrong direction. Fortunately, I was lying at the edge of the group near the window. Whenever the yoga instructress spoke loudly, I burped by way of comment."

After this story, too, everyone roared with laughter, which helped me to get free of my reservations and join in the merriment. With a firm voice, I ordered rice with vegetables, a plate of fruit, and ginger water, as the others were still talking to each other.

Claire from Switzerland wanted to know how Paola had found out about Wayan's guest houses.

All eyes turned to the vivacious Italian woman. It was really fun to listen to her and laugh loudly at her stories. She seemed to enjoy being cast in this role, as she started off again: "That will maybe surprise you." She paused a bit, to increase the tension. "I was actually on holiday for two weeks on the Malaysian island of Tioman. At least, that is what I had booked and my colleagues in the office in Milan will be assuming that I'm on holiday there. But after only four days on Tioman, I was bored and thought of booking a short tour. That's how I came to Bali." She looked round happily and continued: "Unfortunately, I can only be with you for five days, as my flight back to Malaysia is booked then. But I can tell you: you're absolutely super! I love all of you, I love this place. It's simply fantastic here!"

With this compliment, she won our hearts. We believed almost every word that she spoke in her cheery manner. And at the same time, she appeared to be completely sincere.

Leaving this beautiful island out of boredom and booking a tour to Bali instead was something I could not understand. It was a flight of several hours away. When I had been on that small island a few years before, I went hiking into the interior and on boat tours to tiny islands surrounded by white sand and crystal clear, turquoise coloured water, that were not far away.

"Paola, are you serious about that? You paid for a hotel room on the beautiful island of Tioman and booked a short trip to Bali out of boredom?"

"Why not? Somebody there told me Bali was really beautiful. That motivated me! *And indeed, Bali is really beautiful!*"

"And how did you find us here in this idyll, away from the town?" Claire repeated her original question.

"Oh, that was quite simple. At the airport I met a woman who told me she was going to take a taxi to Ubud. 'Ok,' I thought to myself, 'that is a possibility for me, too.' I asked her if I could join her. And when we arrived in Ubud, I had said 'Good-bye' to her. Form this on I simply followed my nose until I discovered this place."

"You really are full of surprises, Paola!" Emma said loudly. She replied immediately:

"That's what my dear colleagues in the office are always saying to me! It was they who sent me on holiday because they thought I was getting too tense.

But rest and relaxation are no use to me. I always need to have something going on."

That was underlined by everyone at the table nodding their heads. Paola was really full of fun! She was humorous and lovable at the same time! I really liked her, too. Each sentence and each facial expression fascinated me, enchanted me, so that I forgot the world around me. For that reason, I jumped when Emma suddenly asked me: "Hey, Chris, what are you doing all day long? I've hardly seen you."

I quickly thought what I could say, as I did not want to talk about my grief in this company, as I was afraid my emotions might get out of control. So I decided to tell them about my hiking.

"I go out a lot, Emma. Sometimes I set off walking just after sunrise when all you can see is the rice fields. I often stop for a while in order to observe the interesting things going on around me. With a bit of luck, I can see the volcano in the distance. That thrills me whenever it's possible. But I also admire the old rice farmers on their fields, the way they do everything by hand. Once I was shocked to see an old rice farmer walking barefoot through the deep mud on his rice field. With a metal canister fastened on his back, he was using his upper arm to pump a liquid to protect the plants – certainly poisonous – through a nozzle to spray onto the shoots that had just been planted."

I took a deep breath and continued: "Last week I spent some most interesting hours with an old man who had built a small wooden hut on the side of the road, where he was to be found during the daytime. The pictures he had painted and was displaying caught my attention and I was impressed by his manner. I sat down near him and got talking to him. Actually, he was in his hut near the rice fields to keep an eye on his cow while it was eating grass. He had tied it to the trunk of a coconut palm tree. He spent his days there painting and cultivating vanilla, cloves and coffee. All these things he offers to tourists who are walking by for sale. We drank a cup of coffee, made with his own homemade coffee."

"Do you speak Indonesian language?" Emma interrupted me.

"Only a little. The words I don't know I describe, or show what I mean with my hands and a clear facial expression." I was really in the mood for narrating and hardly wanted to stop telling them about my experiences: "Yes, and while we were talking over our cup of coffee, I discovered an old wooden xylophone. I asked him if he would play something on it for me, and he agreed. I'll never forget the way he played on this instrument. The traditional Balinese tune rang so enchantingly and full of yearning over the rice fields."

I stopped my narrative, blinked dreamily and then said: *"I experience wonderful things on my morning hikes."*

Emma's eyes were gleaming. She asked if she could come with me on the next morning. Paola too, was looking at me as if she were a hungry dog. "Chris, unfortunately I must leave the day after tomorrow. Would you take me with you tomorrow? I'd love to go on a morning hike with you. I admit that that's not my best time. I usually get up between eight and nine o'clock, but tomorrow I would make an exception!"

"OK. That's fine. Tomorrow morning at seven o'clock here at this table," was my spontaneous answer, because I liked Paola, although she did arouse doubts in me as to whether I could satisfy her expectations of an interesting morning hike. I had not said anything about my labile condition. I quickly considered changing my decision. But I had already agreed and I was the sort of person who kept her word.

As if someone had given an agreed signal, the people at the table got up and went off in different directions. All of them seemed to have a programme for the day. No wonder, for the town had some good offers. A bazaar with an endless supply of goods for tourists; countless artists who welcomed visitors. To the north of Ubud, wood carvers had settled who carved unbelievable filigree figures out of wood. There were cookery courses, language courses, as well as yoga and meditation courses, Balinese temple dance courses and various instrumental courses. No tourist needed to suffer from boredom.

On that morning, I only wanted to lie down. When we were saying "Good-bye", Claire came up to me and gave me a hug. I suspected that she was informed about my dear husband's death and my disturbed soul, as she had been a friend of Wayans's family for years. Her loving embrace felt so good that I was feeling much better when I went up to my apartment. Somehow or other, I was feeling I was as light as a feather.

In the middle of the afternoon, I woke up from a deep dream. I sat up and listened. Everything around me seemed to be silent. I was used in that silence. Because in the midday heat, not only human beings rested. The animals rested too. They became active again in the late afternoon and some in the night.

I remembered my dream. Ray visited me in my dream. He looked different. Not the way he looked as I knew him, as a tall, slim man. In this dream he appeared to me in an indefinite shape that reminded me of a cross. A radiant, pure light was coming out of him, which made him look transparent.

"How wonderful it must be for you, Ray. You seem to be surrounded with pure light," I sent my words devoutly to Heaven.

"Paint this picture." Once again, my inner voice was active, instructing me to preserve this picture as a watercolour painting. With paints and paper in front of me on the table, I concentrated on the pictures in my dream. *Not very clearly, I saw the shape with its light. It did not seem to be settled in any one place, but was hovering in a surrounding of black and blue tones.* Not until the painting was finished did I come out of my inward concentration and contemplate the result with interest. Obviously, I did not judge my work according to any artistic standards. Instead, I looked with great interest at my inner life, which was showing itself in motives and colours.

"Ray, I'm still in mourning for you, and despite this I would like to set you free for your way into the light. Can you send me some of your light to lighten up my darkness?"

For a long time I sat deep in thought, felt the connection to my beloved husband and imagined his light until I felt it extending to me and including me. The feeling of being close to him in the light, although we were in two different worlds, was just heavenly. I ended the day with a prayer of heartfelt thanks to God for all the wonderful things I had been able to experience on that day.

"Good morning! You are already up and about!" I called over to Paola who was coming up to me, albeit rather sleepily.

"Yes, today I've surprised myself! But with the prospect of our morning hike, getting up was no problem."

I chuckled, greeted her and asked: "Ready to leave?"

I set off at a brisk pace, but she put the brakes on, asking me to think about the Italian matron.

"Come on, we can surely go a bit faster!"

But Paola tripped along behind me, muttering: "I'm doing my best. But small Italians take small steps." After a short pause, she added: "But they sing fantastically!"

As if wanting to prove that, the small Italian woman started singing a song with an enchanting melody. And because I did not understand the words, I asked her for a translation into English, which she gave only fragmentarily while she was singing the song again and again. The swinging rhythm got into our blood and our steps started going in time with each other. I could not help grinning. When I pointed it out to her, she burst out laughing and that made me laugh, too. Paola sang on, from one tune to another without a break, which seemed to animate her, as she just kept on singing us both into a good mood.

In the meantime, we were walking at the same speed on a narrow path formed by small concrete blocks that were breaking in some places, showing a rushing stream below them.

"Be careful! The surface has got some big holes in it. Bali's paths can be treacherous," I warned her and told her about an accident I had had on one of my first holidays on the island, when, distracted by the spectacle of people dancing in a trance behind a wall, I had fallen into a hole that was fifty centimetres deep.

"Can you imagine that? Suddenly I found myself half a metre lower down with a smarting, open wound on my shin."

Paola seemed to be taking the warning and started walking round each hole. Fortunately, this path made of concrete blocks soon came to an end and continued as a narrow footpath through the rice fields. The delicate green idylls of the rice field amazed her.

"The wide view of the fields is urging me on!" she called, waving her arms about as if she were wanting to fly. At the same time, she was hopping along like a chicken that was in a hurry.

"What a crazy, lovable chicken," I thought, walking with a smile behind her. She was already starting to sing the next Italian songs. One of them I recognised. It reminded me of something I had experienced.

"You know, when I was studying sports, skiing was a compulsory subject. As someone who had grown up in flat country, I went for the first time to the Austrian mountains with my university. At the beginning, I did not get on too well with the skiing, but the après-ski, the party after skiing, was OK. On the way back to our quarters, we were in good spirits. My sports colleague, Romeo, an attractive Italio-German, was making his way through the deep snow beside me. He put his arm round me and sang Andreano Celentano's song: 'Una festa sui brati' into my ear. Awesome! His voice plus his beauty were disarming! " I still remembered this scene exactly. "Do you know Adriano Celentano?", I asked the italian lady.

Because she did not know him, I sang this former top hit to her. Then she remembered. We sang loudly 'Una festa sui brati' while we hiked along the rice fields. Our spirits rose. Loudly and boldly we sang the melody over and over again.

"Paola, you are putting me into a good mood. Do you know that?"

"I guess so! People often say that to me. But I'm just being myself. Nothing more."

"Do you know, today is the first time I've sung for ages?"

I was silent. Reflecting that I was not only enthusiastic about Paola, but also about myself. I was on the point of leaving my unhappiness, my pain, behind and, fantastically, I was feeling free and happy. My entertaining hiking partner interrupted my thoughts.

"Well, sing me some German songs now, Chris."

"Oh!" I hesitated. I was stuck for an answer. Several English songs came to mind, because we used to sing them as young people in the evenings, sitting round a campfire, accompanied by a guitar. But German songs? Most of the radio programmes only played English songs, only a few of them specialised in German ones. I did not like their words and tunes because they were monotonous, too simple and boring. Interesting, modern German songs are hardly ever played. Ray and I regretted that and had asked a few years previously on a guided tour of a radio station why the German music scene was hardly represented. Unfortunately, they did not give us an answer. Yet I had no peace about Paola's question about German songs. I searched my memory hard and found something: When I was a child, my parents took us children on a hike in the woods every Sunday. We always sang songs on those occasions. Now I remembered them. I sang one of them: "Anyone God wants to favour He sends into the wide world. He wants to show him His wonders in mountain and valley, in town and field." At first, I sang hesitantly, gradually becoming freer. In my mind, I was once again the child singing aloud with father, mother, brother and sister. Soon Paola was singing the refrain with me. We sang "falderie" and "faldera" alternately.

"Do you know about the German poet Joseph von Eichendorff? He wrote these words."

"No," was her brief answer while she was repeating the melody over again. Thinking about childhood songs, I thought of another song: "My father was a wanderer and it's in my blood, so I'll go a-wandering as long as I can and wave my hat." As there is a "falderie, faldera" in this song, too, the Italian woman emphasised the rhythm by hopping on one foot. I did this, too, and soon we were both singing only the "Falderie, faldera", waving our hands when it came to waving the hat.

"How beautiful life can be!" I thought as tiredness made us gradually less enthusiastic.

On the edge of a rice field, Paola stopped and looked at me questioningly. She was pointing at a sheaf of corn that was held together by a white and yellow ribbon and had small sacrifices in front of it.

"Here the rice farmer's family performed a holy ceremony to satisfy the lower evil powers and to ask the higher gods for a rich harvest. The flowers, pieces of different fruits and grains of rice are presents for the gods. Each of them is in a particular colour and pointing to a different direction in the sky." My hiking friend followed my explanation in wide-eyed astonishment.

"The lower gods are honoured with presents on the ground. Near them, on the raised shrine, the goddess of rice, Dewi Sri, is being honoured. The white cloth covering the shrine and the yellow-gold ribbon around it remind us of the rice goddess."

Filled with awe, we admired the creative sacrificial gifts in the midst of the rice landscape.

"So the Balinese are true believers and religious?" she asked. I nodded. We set off on the way back.

"Today's morning hike has been a wonderful present for me. I'll keep it in my heart and take it with me when I leave tomorrow."

I confided to her that the hike was like a present for me, too. A present from God.

"With your heartiness and joy while walking and singing together, you have awakened the joy of life in me, really."

We bade each other a hearty farewell. This wonderful italian woman had tears in her eyes and said she would rather not leave, but continue to stay here, as Bali was so beautiful. She ran up the stairs to her apartment, waving enthusiastically.

I collapsed onto my favourite sofa, needing a good rest. Spending the rest of the daytime on the balcony, after a delicious breakfast and slept for a while before reading a book, observing the life in the trees in front of my balcony. Thinking about my life with my eyes closed. About my new way as a widow, as a single woman.

While I was thinking about my journey from mourning to the light, colours appeared in my mind's eye. And I wondered: Neither the red and black of the previous week nor the yellow, white and blue of more recent days. Instead, I felt two colours before I could see them. A powerful orange and a sunny green. Together giving an impression of the rice fields on that morning. I felt a pleasant joy and peace inside me, enjoying the mood I was in.

After a while, the colours were transformed into shapes and I felt that my next picture was developing.

Remaining in my inner concentration, I fetched my watercolours, placed a warm yellow and a delicate, light green from the paint box near me, together with a paintbrush and water, closed my eyes and gave the motive time to develop. *I saw the sun as a ball in shades of transparent white, powerful yellow-orange and yellow the colour of light. I painted this large shape on the top third of the sheet of paper. Beneath an open hand, larger than the ball of the sun, was being formed in light and medium shades of green. It was holding the ball of the sun. The two main colours became transparent and covered the whole background. Held by God's hand, the light brightening my path*, I wrote on the back of the paper when the watercolour was finished.

For quite a while I sat contemplating my new creation, feeling the light and the peace expressed in the colours. I shook my head slightly. "The change in the colours is most interesting. No black, no dark blue, no blood red any more, instead *my colours, the yellow and the green*. They have come back to me!"

I was aware that the morning hike with Paola and her joy across the rice fields flooded with light had given wings to my soul.

Smiling inwardly, I sat in the light, surrounded by the darkness of night, yet feeling sun and warmth in my heart.

After the days of retreat in which I had gone through all my unhappiness and pain, I was now looking forward to further encounters with other people.

Open for wonderful encounters!

Bali's mysticism and spirituality

I was relaxed and happy when I woke up the next morning. On the previous evening, as on every other evening, I had been to Sterling's place to send e-mails to Noe and my sister. Sometimes we spoke to each other on skype. Every time I was with her, I hugged Sterling out of pure thankfulness. Since our ways had crossed, happiness and joy were following me. I had my contacts again and, with them, the feeling of belonging somewhere.

Of course, I started this day too with a morning hike. Courageously, I decided for the walk over the hilltops with the incredible panoramic view on which I had had my terrible fall the last time. This time I concentrated on the intoxicating view over the vast distance. Over fertile rice fields, vast areas of grassland and a radiant blue sky. Again and again, I stopped to take a deep breath, amazed at it all. I opened my arms up to heaven and thanked God for this wonderful morning. Again I walked to the small shop, the *Warung* with the fresh coconuts, sat down on the wooden bench, gave the proprietress a friendly greeting and pointed at the coconuts on the ground. She made an opening in the outer crust with a sharp knife that looked like an axe, gave me the natural drink which I slowly enjoyed with a drinking straw.

"Enak." Full of anticipation I pointed to the coconut. She really tasted delicious! The proprietress smiled at me, when I gave her a tip in addition to the payment. Strengthened by the short rest, I set off back on the hilltop way. With springy steps, I was walking down the narrow path, absorbing the warm shades of green, the light, warming breeze and the soft rays of the morning sun, when a young woman with long, black hair in a tightly fitting sports outfit came from the opposite direction. Giving her a friendly smile when she passed me, she looked at me and said: "You look so peaceful!" I was quite taken aback and said "Thank you" as an answer. After a few more metres, I stopped, turned round and shook my head.

"Was that an angel?" I murmured to myself. At that moment, I could not think of any other explanation. Chuckling to myself, I managed the way back easily.

Right behind the entrance gate to Wayan's apartments sat a Ganesha statue, the elephant-headed Hindu god of beginnings, decorated with a flower chain. I glanced at the breakfast table, wondering who I was going to meet there. Emma and Claire were having their breakfast. It seemed, that Paola was already on her way to the airport. I walked by.

"Hello, Chris, how are you?" Claire smiled at me.

"Thank you, I'm well!" I answered from the bottom of my heart. I really was feeling fresh and strengthened after that morning hike. I joined them by sitting down at the table. Ketut came out of her kitchen and asked me with a relaxed voice what I wanted for breakfast. I ordered fried rice with vegetables and ginger tea.

We started an interesting conversation. Claire told us, how she had got to know Wayan some years before. They met at an art exhibition in Basel, in which he were presenting some of his paintings. She was fascinated by some of his works and got the chance to talk to him. She told him about her own artistic work and the annual presentation of a group of artists that she belonged to. On the spur of the moment, she invited the Balinese painter to the next exhibition in her village. He gladly accepted this offer to show his artwork with the group.

"From then on, we have been friends and talk about art together," Claire concluded with a firm voice, as though she were speaking to my heart.

"We have something in common here, Claire," I began, telling her how we had got to know him.

"More than fifteen years ago when Bali was already our dream island, we were hiking through the villages and fields round Ubud. Countless artists lived here, whose studios we mostly visited spontaneously, to watch them at work. At that time, the Balinese used to work in groups on one picture. Each one painted his speciality, a traditional motive, so it didn't matter who would continue painting on which picture. We found this collective work interesting, just the opposite to our western idea of individual works of art. On our hikes, I became interested in the work of one artist, who was treating the traditional motives in an abstract way and producing something individual, personal. And, in addition, he was frequently using yellow and green, my favourite colours. I told my husband that I would like to get to know this artist. We enquired as to the artist's name and place of residence, found this paradise-like place here and got to know the artist Wayan. We soon felt we were on the same wavelength, visited him again on our next trip, getting to know his family at the same time. And, like you, Claire, we got round and invited him to live with us for a while, to paint and exhibit his art in our town. He was amazed and incredibly happy about our invitation. Really, the weeks with him were an enrichment for us. Yes, and from then on we have been renting an apartment here. I'm specially pleased that when I get in touch about my next visit, they ask us if they can reserve 'my' apartment for me. That makes me feel at home."

Smiling dreamily, we talked about our memories and the various artists on Bali who expressed themselves creatively and in bright colours - whether it was in the medium of painting, wood or stone carving or gold and silver jewellery. We forgot about the time through our stories, which was already getting towards midday.

Claire concluded our conversation. "Unfortunately I have to go on. You know that I'm leaving tomorrow afternoon and I still need some souvenirs. Would anybody like to come with me to a walk round the town?"

Emma shook her head: "I don't want to smell the stinking motors."

But I found the spontaneous invitation enticing. "Oh, that's a good idea. Then I'll be among the people. I'll join you."

Only some minutes afterwards, we set off on the way to Ubud. Right at the start, we climbed down fifty steep steps. At the bottom, a line of stinking traffic, consisting of tourist buses, cars and motor bikes, was making its way into the town centre.

"This is the unpleasant side of Bali! Sometimes I'm overcome with fear that I might be run over on the pavement!"

I looked at the motorbikes that were making use of every opportunity of overtaking any vehicle on four wheels.

"Most of the motorbike drivers haven't got a licence, or they get one presented to them after only a very short training course. And so they drive according to their own rules entirely and take hardly any notice of road signs."

"Yes, that's right," Claire confirmed. "I recently spoke to a taxi driver. He told me that he got his licence after he had taught himself to drive. He simply drove to the police station and collected it."

We laughed at this story, shaking our heads emphatically, and turned into the short cut which took us away from the main road, because the main road went through a narrow ravine, which made the traffic extra loud.

"Your local knowledge is a great help to us now," I said to her, smiling with relief, as we were climbing up the steep hill.

"Just look at these exceptionally beautiful flowers," she called enthusiastically, pointing at a display of bright red blossoms amid filigree leaves, and picked one of them.

"Fantastic! The flowers are like mimosa, but they make a much stronger impression."To satisfy my curiosity, I walked up to the tree and noticed that we were looking down into the top of it. I looked for the trunk and discovered it was right down in the ravine where the street was, at the side of the main road. "Look at that! The tree is living under extremely difficult conditions and produces such splendid blossoms in its crown," I admired its capacity for survival and was thinking about my own situation in life as we walked on slowly.

"Here is the herbal shop I was looking for. Come in with me, we'll be sure to find a nice present here," she interrupted my thoughts.

The handmade cakes of soap and shower gels gave the shop an unbelievably sweet perfume that reminded me of the smells I experienced during my hikes.

"Now I have the feeling that the whole of Bali is one enchanting cloud of perfume."

Claire smiled in agreement, as she was looking for a suitable present: "Yes, everywhere there is an intensive, enticing perfume from the joss sticks or from flowers going through the air." In the meantime, she had chosen a few cakes of soap and was asking about the price, which usually led to bargaining on Bali. But the saleswoman replied curtly. "Fixprice." Rather reluctantly, she paid the fixed price and remarked when we were out of the shop: "What a pity! More and more shops on Bali belong to Australians, Europeans, or Americans, who demand fixed prices you can't argue about. I prefer the culture of bargaining that is the tradition here."

Our short cut was bringing us back onto the main road, where there was a row of small shops, like the beads on a necklace.

"Look, what they have on offer is intended to attract tourists and it's getting more and more one-sided. Clothes, works of art, a restaurant, massage or spa. Do you remember what it used to be like, when the Balinese had things they had harvested or made themselves for sale? That was a larger selection. Now everything looks so similar."

I agreed with Claire that there was far less variety. In the tourist centres, they only offered what could be sold easily just then. As we had both known Bali for more than twenty years, and in the time when there was more variety in the shops, we were yearning to have this time back.

"Over there, at the front, in the bazaar, you can find the traditional Bali," I comforted Claire. Of course, the bazaar had changed, too and adjusted to the needs of the tourists who passed along between the stalls from the morning to the evening.

"Well, let's go right into the crowd. Here you can bargain!" I could see Claire's love of bargaining written on her face. "I'd like to buy a few *sarongs*. I like giving them away as presents."

The brightly printed cloths had, indeed, plenty of uses: as a bath towel, a skirt or even a dress, if you wrapped it round your body tightly enough. Claire drew me with her into the crowd and was already hurrying up to a stall, which had countless *sarongs* in subdued colours with large motives on them. Only a few minutes later, she was radiant because she had negotiated and got these three cloths for below half price.

"You look so happy, Claire."

We had already gone in the direction of the stalls selling fruit, because I wanted some fresh mangos. It was quite clear to both of us that the saleswoman would have put her prices up in advance, and would then be willing to reduce them. Well, it was certainly fun, more than simply paying a fixed price. At the stall with the mangos, I tried my luck at bargaining a price. The saleswoman first of all shouted *"bankrut"* at me, before reluctantly agreeing.

"Mmhh!" I sniffed at the thin skin of a ripe mango and started looking forward to the sweet, soft flesh of the fruit inside, which I would enjoy at home.

Continuing to stroll through the crowd, we were amazed at the stalls selling handmade cakes of soap, brightly painted toys, bamboo windmills, t-shirts printed with "I love Bali" and much more. I soon became tired from the wide selection and looked for a place where I could sit down. I caught sight of a small restaurant with young coconuts on the ground in front of it.

"Let's go inside Claire, to drink some fresh coconut milk. It tastes delicious and it's very healthy, too."

"That's for sure!" she chimed in while we were going up to the restaurant. "In addition to various vitamins, it contains potassium, calcium, magnesium, zinc, selenium and iron."

"Did you learn that by heart?" was my spontaneous response.

"Well, yes, because I find the milk from young coconuts so tasty. And so I took note of what it contained."

Our rest was only short, just long enough to drink all the fresh coconut milk. Strengthened by it, we set off on the way home, exchanging our memories of Bali as it had been twenty years previously.

"Can you remember the dogs thinking the street was part of their territory, therefore using it for sleeping, walking, fighting each other and having sex, without taking any notice of the traffic? The cars all drove round the dogs or waited for them to clear the road for them."

"Yes," she laughed loudly, "at this time I was sometimes driving past on my motorbike and knew quite well that dogs had priority. It was particularly dangerous at night, because they used to bark at you as you drove past, showing their sharp teeth, running after you, and often a pack of them followed you. Sometimes that was very dangerous."

"That's right. Bali's packs of dogs used to dominate the street," I snorted, remembering certain situations when I had been happy that they had not done anything to me on my motorbike. Yet, it was a necessity: Realising that I had to drive round them if I wanted to pass them unscathed. I had seen the Balinese doing that, too: peacefully walking or driving past the dogs. I guess they had accepted the dogs' power. In exchange, they protected their houses and territories from trespassers. The Balinese have never heard of leads, so the dogs are free in every respect.

Claire had already come to another area in her thoughts. "Do you remember the time when older women used to walk around with no clothes on the upper part of their bodies, according to the tradition?"

"Yes, and the young men who met by the river before sunset to have their *'mandi'*, their bath together. They were naked, laughed loudly, told each other what they had experienced and sang songs."

"Indeed, they were loud! But it seemed to be having fun bathing together. They were not at all bothered by being naked all together."

"Sometimes I found that embarrassing when I was riding past on my motorbike. They also bathed in deeper streams, directly beside small village roads," I laughed. We were so absorbed in our memories that we hardly noticed that we had arrived at the steep steps leading to our apartments. Claire seemed to want sit down anywhere again.

"Chris, would you like to go to a little outdoor restaurant?"

"That's a good idea! You are leaving tomorrow and I'm really enjoying spending some time with you. We have a lot in common. Let's go to *Lalalili*, the small restaurant next to our place. The proprietress cooks herself and makes an excellent job of it."

"A garden salad, please and a fresh pineapple juice with just a little sugar," I was placing my order a few minutes later and turning to Claire, who also decided for a salad.

"It's fantastic that we can order a salad here without any fear of bacterial impurities. We can trust the proprietress. I think she opened the restaurant twenty years ago and knows what the people who frequent it need. Even now, when I'm here alone after my husband's death. Here I don't feel lonely as I do in some other restaurants. I know the proprietress, the waiters and waitresses, their cats and their goldfish."

I chuckled at my last statement, although I was already feeling a lump in my throat after broaching the subject of Ray's death. To my great surprise, I was starting to talk about my own situation.

"Claire, my husband's death brought me right off track. I'm suffering badly."

She looked at me in sympathy and was silent for a while. Our looks went in the direction of the small pond with the lotuses.

"I can imagine that," she said, looking at me. "Losing the partner you love must be an event with far-reaching consequences."

I had difficulty in holding my tears back, and was feeling my deep wound that was suddenly lying open

331

again. "It felt as though someone had cut the heart out of my body."

Claire raised her head, looked at me with wide eyes, then looked down again and seemed to be reflecting. "Hm," she took a deep breath, "for someone who has not experienced that, it is unimaginable."

"Yes. You won't believe it, but it was also unbelievable for me in the phase when the loss was giving me great pain. I would have much preferred to take the dress of pain off. But there turned out to be another way: my inner voice whispered to me that I should fly away from it all." I laughed at the last words. "Flying away. Yes, my soul was given wings. I landed here on my dream island and feel I'm being well looked after here."

Claire seemed to be deep in thought. "The Balinese treat death quite differently from the way we do. Perhaps you were unconsciously looking for this. Death is integrated into everyday life here, it is celebrated publicly. From young to old, everyone is present. I always have the impression that they are celebrating the burning ceremony."

I smiled and nodded, as that was my impression, too. The burning ceremonies I had been to reminded me of a village festival. It started in the house of the deceased, where the dead body was washed in the presence of all the relatives' guests, while the priest and his helpers were devoting themselves to the rituals. Hours later, when the body, covered with just a single cloth, was being carried to the cemetery, in a procession accompanied by the gamelan orchestra with its wild rhythms. The people seemed relaxed as they were walking along. And when the priest was fanning up the flame and the corpse was burning, I did not observe any emotional reactions.

"The Balinese don't cry, and, at least in public, they shed no tears. That has its effect on the atmosphere. Here, death does not seem to bring anyone out of balance," I said with conviction.

"On the other hand, I felt sad and empty at Ray's funeral service. And afterwards, over coffee, which, at Ray's wish, was meant to be a celebration of life, I was preoccupied with organisation and conversations. And there I felt that I wasn't at my husband's funeral. It was not until some days later, when I had calmed down, that I was overwhelmed with a feeling of having been left behind. I really felt totally down. Some weeks later, I became worried about my labile condition. That was the moment when my inner voice told me what to do. I think it was the right thing to come to terms with my grief here on Bali. At home, I would not have managed it, as I didn't. I needed time just for myself, on the other hand I trusted in Suryanis Hypnotherapy. It worked. Actually, I feel I've regained my sense of balance. You certainly notice that I'm still reacting emotionally and need to have someone to talk to, but that is all right." I leaned back, took a deep breath, and had a good look at Claire. "Thank you for your spiritual support Claire. It is building me up."

"I'm glad about that. Our honest conversation has also been a great help to me." She reflected for a while. "As far as I know, the Balinese hardly tell each other about their inner feelings. They continue with their everyday."

"Right! My friend Suryani has told me about that. People suffering from a trauma, sometimes come into her surgery because they hardly come to terms with their problems."

I stopped talking because memories came over me. Our last days together were beginning to come clearly in the form of pictures. In these he barely spoke. Nevertheless, we experienced an extraordinary depth of our feelings. This days were especially significant for us all, for Noe, for Ray's sister and my sister; also for his close friends. This time of farewell is fixed in my memory for ever.

"In spite of all the good things happening to me, I cannot understand, Claire, why I suffered so terribly after his death. Has it something to do with our culture of mourning?"

Claire repeated one aspect: "The Hindu religion gives them the joy of looking forward to reincarnation."

I replied: "We Christians don't believe in reincarnation nor in the possibility of coming back to the world in one of their descendants, as the Balinese do. Yet because of Jesus' death and resurrection, we have no fear of death, as it has no power over us. Like Jesus, we overcome death and expect eternal life with God. We say that is Paradise, don't we?" Claire seemed very focused. I continued: "If I'm honest, the fact is that our culture we like to concentrate on the loss of the beloved. We miss them and complain about that. I was very disappointed because Ray had to die so early, which was also against his will. At that time I failed to feel joy!"

"I can imagine that, Chris", she said, nodding at me in understanding.

"I hardly experience at funerals the joy that the deceased is now with God. What's about you?"

"You may be right in that point. That is something we Christians could possibly think about. That would bring us closer to the Balinese, for whom death is indeed a source of joy. They also see death as a part of life and therefore don't react so emotionally." Claire smiled faintly.

"I admit that the thought, that Ray is with God now, didn't occur to me until some weeks after his death." I stopped speaking. My thoughts were drifting back to that time after his death.

"Thank you, God," I prayed silently, "for being with me all the time. Now I'm feeling better. *I am feeling something like balanced.*"

As though Claire had read my thoughts, she cleared her throat and latched on to my last thoughts. "The Balinese are concerned with balance in all areas of their life. In order to achieve this, they look at both sides of the coin. Not only human beings and nature, but also the universe surrounding them. Also there is light and shadow everywhere, good and bad."

"Oh!" I took a deep breath. Claire's words really touched me. They expressed my conviction exactly, that there is more than we see, know or believe.

"What do you think?" I asked to give her food for thought. "Do we in our Christian culture still have a chance of living out our faith holistically? Our emotions, our spirituality, our creativity? Or are we already too far away from it? Our lives are strongly orientated on the material and on reason. Our faith is administered by means of rules and ordinances." I was purposely formulating my question as a challenge. But Claire was not put off. She continued concentrating on the Balinese culture.

"The Balinese manage that quite well. Perhaps because Hinduism is networked with every temple congregation, village community and right into the families. Everything on Bali runs in the community. For better or worse, they participate in the countless temple festivals, in the singing, dancing, theatrical performances, puppet shows, orchestral music, trances, and processions. In all these things, they live out their emotions. Anyone experiencing the temple festivals here feels it in their bones, it simply vibrates. Yet, like everywhere else, the West has long since been here with its individualistic culture in life. The media, the internet and, above all, the tourists are changing their tradition of collectivism. The Balinese are clever. They make rules to counteract this. Anyone who does not participate has to pay a fine. Anyone leaving the community can hardly find another home, because every village lives with the same structures."

Claire stopped and reflected briefly. "You ask whether we western Christians could succeed in having a communal and enthusiastic faith?" She closed her eyes, as if she were wanting to collect her thoughts.

"Maybe, if we were to structure our days again with spiritual rituals, if we were to live out our spirituality confidently and publicly, if we were to integrate dying and death into our everyday lives. Then I could see that happening. Our need for it still exists. There are certainly reasons why a trip to Bali is a hit. The tourists like to become involved and feel enchanted at the temple festivals. They are enthusiastic about the spirituality here. But I have my doubts as to whether we could do something similar at home. It would be hard to get away from the duties of everyday life: work, family, social engagement and our addiction to pleasure would work against it. We are busy striving after money, often without taking any notice of our true needs or of our environment."

I added: "Can we do without our luxury and rather give our attention to the simple, spiritual life? Can we succeed in seeing both sides of the coin? The visible, material world and the invisible, spiritual world? Can we succeed in treating God's creation with respect and being thankful for it? Oh, Claire, I think we have opened Pandora's box!"

I was well aware that we would not be able to exhaust this subject on that afternoon and was pleased when the food we had ordered was brought to us. The freshly pressed fruit juices not only looked delicious, they tasted exquisite. I had decided for a pineapple juice. Claire for a mango juice. Our salad was decorated with fresh avocado strips, pieces of tomato, cucumber, with soy sproats and fried tempeh.

"Enjoy your meal!"

"You, too." We started eating in silence.

"It's a good thing that the small restaurants belonging to the native inhabitants still exist," I reflected after a while.

"You are right. It's something I am always looking for. I also like to stay with Balinese families. I love to get to know other cultures. I am interested in their everyday life. I like conversations with them, join them to their festivals, if I get invited. In this way I learn a great deal about their lives and their faith. And, most of all I like eating their meals."

"That's something else we have in common," I laughed.

Claire suddenly looked in the direction of our apartment and said: "Chris, let us pay straight away. I just remembered that I still have to pack my suitcases, as I'm going back to Switzerland tomorrow."

On the way to our home, we walked past a rice field that the rays of the sun had lit up to appear in a yellowish green colour. I smiled to myself, saw the cheerful scenes I had experienced with Paola and knew: *"My soul and spirit are seeing the light in the darkness again."*

"Chris," Claire turned to me, "I have been able to get to know you a bit here and have the impression that you're actively going on your way that will take you out of your grief. I'd like to encourage you. *Bali has an intensive power to heal in it.* That will help you. And, you will continue to meet wonderful people to support you. God be with you."

338

I looked gratefully at Claire. "I am so thankful meeting you." We hugged each other and waved goodbye.

Upstairs on my balcony, lying on my favourite sofa enjoying the view into the splendid, tropical nature. It seemed to me much fresher. I asked myself why? Because of the rain on the last few days? Because of my inner light, that brightened up? The wind played gently in fine leaves of the coconut palm trees in front of me. Just behind, the fat shiny dark green leaves of an old mango tree. And between, I discovered the bright red flowers of the tall hibiscus that were stretching out towards the rays of the sun, wide open. Inspired by this wonderful little corner of Paradise, my thoughts turned to my situation in life:

> *"Look! The flowers are showing you what to do. They are making their way through the darkness into the light and displaying their individual beauty there."*

My thoughts were interrupted by a high-pitched voice: "Hey, Chris! Where are you?" Sterling hurried up the stairs and ran right up to me. "How are you?" she asked enthusiastically, kissing me on both cheeks. Giving me no time to answer she continued:. "Come on, you've got a message."

That sentence meant a lot to me. It was like an burst of energy! I really wanted to tell my loved ones all that was happening around me. And I loved to read their letters. Beaming with joy, I jumped up high, took

Sterlings hands and danced through the room with her. Quite unexpected I felt, that Ray was dancing with me.

Oh, how much I enjoyed to dance with him!

I enjoyed the situation, the place, the tropical landscape, the warmth and the wonderful friend. I felt thankful for all what was happening the last couple of days.

"Did thankfulness contribute to my healing? I am convinced it did." I felt like my life was getting back to normal. I was happy I took the time to proper mourn and heal. I felt rejuvenated.

Full of gratitude I opened my arms and *thanked God.*

Acknowledgements

With this book I would like to present you a special story, a very intense experienced phase of my life. I am grateful and thankful for all the support I received while writing and publishing my book.

I first thank God for helping and guiding me. I would like to thank my family and friends who have accompanied me with their love and loyalty. In writing, especially to Andrea, whose clever ideas and enthusiasm shaped my book. Thank you for your inspiration, gentle critique and suggestions to Nora, Eva, Erdmuth, Gitta, Christiane. My appreciation and gratitude go to Peter for his wise remarks.

I extend my heartfelt appreciation to my Balinese sister and friend, Prof. Dr. Dr. Luh Ketut Suryani, Denpasar, her husband Prof. Dr. Cok Alit, their sons Yaya and Wawan, and their families. To Wayan Karja and his family for providing "my apartment" in Penestanan. It would not have been conceivable to come to terms with my grief without it.

My gratitude goes to everybody who finds this book helpful in their own journey, searching for their light, to find healing during difficult times.

With much love,

Christiane

About the Author

Christiane P. Simon is a german Author. She studied Art, German language and Sports in Erlangen and Ludwigsburg, working as a teacher for many years and delegated in between to the Baden-Wuerttemberg Ministry of Education. During her master's  degree at the University of Tuebingen she focused on the questions: What strengthens people? What keeps their health? How does someone successfully cope with life crises? What makes people resilient? She is convinced of holistic health. Body, mind and spirit form a unit. Healing someone could be more successful, when the person concerned is involved in a treatment plan. The patient's view of life, their experience and their knowledge about their own body are significant.

For her master's thesis she traveled to Bali and interviewed young Balinese about their behavior in stressful situations in order to compare it with the behavior of young Germans. While this research she met Professor Dr. Dr. L.K. Suryani who researched a similar question. Since then, a deep friendship has developed between the women that continues. The Author felt also closely connected to the island of Bali ever since. She shows that in her book, which contains detailed knowledge about the Balinese people, their culture and spirituality.

Christiane P.Simon runs a practice for holistic health, relaxation and meditation. Sie is a trained systemic coach and meditation teacher.

With this account of a part of her impressive life story, the authoress wants to give anyone, going through a difficult phase in life, encouragement and hope. She gives confidence when she says:

In every darkness you will find light-flooded paths.

If you would like to contact the author please

E-mail: praxis-dein-weg@gmx.de

Website: lichtdurchflutet.org

Thank you for your positive review, comments and recommending my book to others!